Palgrave Studies in Prisons and Penology

This is a unique and innovative series, the first of its kind dedicated entirely to prison scholarship. At a historical point in which the prison population has reached an all-time high, the series seeks to analyse the form, nature and consequences of incarceration and related forms of punishment. Palgrave Studies in Prisons and Penology provides an important forum for burgeoning prison research across the world.

Tom Daems
Editor

Body Searches and Imprisonment

palgrave
macmillan

Editor
Tom Daems
Faculty of Law and Criminology
KU Leuven
Leuven, Belgium

ISSN 2753-0604 ISSN 2753-0612 (electronic)
Palgrave Studies in Prisons and Penology
ISBN 978-3-031-20450-0 ISBN 978-3-031-20451-7 (eBook)
https://doi.org/10.1007/978-3-031-20451-7

Cover illustration: SEAN GLADWELL

This Palgrave Macmillan imprint is published by the registered company Springer Nature Switzerland AG
The registered company address is: Gewerbestrasse 11, 6330 Cham, Switzerland

Preface

The chapters in this book were first presented and discussed at the international workshop "Body searches and imprisonment" which was organized on 21 April 2022 at the Leuven Institute of Criminology (LINC), KU Leuven, Belgium. In that workshop we aimed to explore body search practices in prisons from different angles (criminology, sociology, philosophy and law) and study such practices comparatively in different national contexts within Europe. What exactly makes such control measures problematic in a prison context? How do such practices come to be regulated in an international and European context? How are such rules translated into national law? To what extent are laws and rules respected, bended, circumvented, denied? And what does the future hold for body searches?

I am very grateful to all the speakers and participants in the workshop for excellent papers and lively discussions. The authors did a great job in meeting deadlines when turning the draft papers into chapters and answering my queries when producing this volume. I am grateful to the editors of the wonderful *Palgrave Studies in Prisons and Penology* series for welcoming this volume to the Series and to Josie Taylor and her team at Palgrave Macmillan for their help and assistance in producing this volume in a timely manner.

The workshop was organized during a 6 month period of sabbatical research leave (February–July 2022). Most of the editing and writing for this volume was done during this period. I am grateful to the Faculty of Law & Criminology at KU Leuven for approving my research leave and the Research Foundation Flanders (FWO) for awarding me a generous research grant which allowed me to travel, read and write. My sabbatical leave was only possible with the support of Diego Zysman, Máximo Sozzo, Malcolm Feeley and Jonathan Simon who made it possible for me to travel to—and spend valuable time in—Buenos Aires, Santa Fe and Berkeley.

Last but not least, thanks a million to my family and—especially—*mi mariposa* Eva, for all their patience and support.

Leuven, Belgium Tom Daems
September 2022

Contents

Contributors

Jamie Bennett University of Oxford, Oxford, UK; Youth Justice Board, London, UK

Barbara Bernath Association for the Prevention of Torture, Geneva, Switzerland

Conor Byrne Ulster University, Belfast, UK

Tom Daems Faculty of Law and Criminology, KU Leuven, Leuven, Belgium

Joana Falxa Université de Pau et des Pays de L'Adour, Pau, France

Cristina Güerri Instituto Andaluz Interuniversitario de Criminología, Universidad de Málaga, Málaga, Spain

Natasa Mavronicola University of Birmingham, Birmingham, UK

Linda Moore Ulster University, Belfast, UK

Anaïs Tschanz National Correctional Administration Academy (ENAP), Agen, France

Aurore Vanliefde KU Leuven, Leuven, Belgium

Jason Warr School of Sociology and Social Policy, University of Nottingham, Nottingham, UK

Elaine Webster University of Strathclyde, Glasgow, UK

List of Tables

Body Searches as Contested Control Measures

Tom Daems

1 Introduction

In his book *Asylums* Erving Goffman (1961: 76) famously wrote about a '…constant conflict between human standards on one hand and institutional efficiency on the other'. Such a conflict is typical for total institutions, so he argued, that is, '… a place of residence and work where a large number of like-situated individuals, cut off from the wider society for an appreciable period of time, together lead an enclosed, formally administered round of life' (Goffman 1961: 11). This applies to the kinds of institutions that Goffman was studying (his fieldwork was in St. Elizabeth's Hospital, Washington, D.C.) but also, and in particular, to other total institutions, such as prisons. Indeed, this constant conflict is omnipresent in penal institutions where striking a balance between

T. Daems (✉)
Faculty of Law and Criminology, KU Leuven, Leuven, Belgium
e-mail: tom.daems@kuleuven.be

T. Daems (ed.), *Body Searches and Imprisonment*,
Palgrave Studies in Prisons and Penology,
https://doi.org/10.1007/978-3-031-20451-7_1

safety, order, and control (Goffman's 'institutional efficiency') on the one hand, and dignity and respect (the Goffmanesque 'human standards') on the other hand, is (or should be) a never-ending pre-occupation.

This tension is perhaps most tangible when prisoners are being subjected to body searches, that is, when they have their bodies exposed to the eyes of—or touched by the hands of—strangers, in an overarching context of punishment and control. Body searches are invasive, potentially degrading, and therefore deeply controversial control measures. But at the same time they are widely used in prison systems across the globe. Indeed, body searches are perceived as indispensable to prevent forbidden substances, weapons, or communication devices from entering into the prison (Daems 2014).

It is somewhat surprising, then, that, despite their controversial nature, body searches have, as far as we know, seldomly been at the center of book-length studies or collections of essays. In the academic literature there is quite some reflection on body searches but this happens mostly at the margins of other discussions, on prison security, human rights and dignity, penal power, or the sociology of the body and sexuality. With this book we aim to move body searches from the margins to the center of scholarly study and policy debate. Throughout this book we aim to demonstrate how body searches can be explored and studied from different angles and perspectives, including prison sociology, security studies, law and human rights, criminology, and philosophy. In doing so, we want to invite readers, scholars, and policy makers to engage in a dialogue on the future of body searches in prisons across the globe.

2 Scope of This Book

The term 'body search' can refer to different types of control measures (see e.g. APT and PRI 2015). First, a frisk, rub-down, or pat-down search involves the touching of the outer clothing of a person. In such cases prisoners keep their clothes on and a prison officer usually checks if the prisoner has any forbidden substances on him by touching the outer clothes of the prisoner. This type of search is often perceived to be the least intrusive and can therefore be executed in a routine way; it is considered to be a normal part of everyday prison life that does not require any specific risk assessment on behalf of the prison authorities. Second, a strip search or full body search includes the removal of parts or all of the clothes of a prisoner. In such cases prison officers can do a visual inspection of the naked body of the prisoner, including the genitals and the openings and cavities of the human body. However, a strip search should not involve any physical contact between the prison officer and the prisoner. Third, body cavity searches allow for physical contact and inspection of genital or anal regions of the body. Such procedures usually can only be executed by a medical practitioner and are, given their very invasive nature, not a regular part of prison life.

Most chapters in this book deal with strip searches and, to a lesser extent, with frisk or rub-down searches. Body cavity searches are exceptional control measures which are not extensively discussed in this book. Moreover, the chapters in this book only touch upon body searches in a prison context, that is, prisoners being subjected to body searches. This implies that search practices by, for example, police officers are not being discussed in this volume. This does not imply that police scholars cannot find anything interesting in this book. On the contrary, many of the controversies with respect to police searching practices, such as questions related to the effectiveness, intrusiveness, and selectivity of search procedures, also return in a prison context (see e.g. Grewcock and Sentas 2019). It would be good to see more research and debate in the future on comparing the uses and abuses of body search practices in different areas of the criminal justice system, from prisons to police, from migration to youth detention.

3 A Brief Overview

In the next chapter Jason Warr explores body searches from a 'sensory criminology' perspective. Warr focuses in particular on the first type of body search, that is, tap-down or frisk searches, where the experience of touch is so important. Indeed, unlike most other chapters in this book, which tend to focus on the visual aspects of searching (seeing and watching the naked body of a prisoner), Warr draws attention to the role of enforced, imposed touch of powerful others. How does it feel like to feel the hands of strangers so many times on your body? What does that communicate?

In chapter three Jamie Bennett discusses body searches within a wider context of prison security. Search practices are part of modern prison systems and such measures are necessary and essential. Indeed, as Bennett suggests, where prison escapes used to be a major concern in the past, now criminal activity within prisons is an important challenge for prison management. Bennett outlines a model for prison security and, in line with Loader and Walker's work (2007) on 'civilizing security', calls for 'civilizing' prison security: security in prisons is not an end in itself but as a social good, it can '…create the conditions in which people experience increased safety, confidence and can participate more fully in the prison community'.

The next three chapters all deal with the international and European regulation of body searches. In chapter four Barbara Bernath explains the key role prison monitoring bodies, such as the National Preventive Mechanisms (NPMs), can play. Monitoring bodies can visit places of detention and talk in private with prisoners. According to Bernath such monitoring bodies offer indispensable oversight: indeed, they can analyze how international human rights standards are being applied in practice. In chapter five Natasa Mavronicola and Elaine Webster discuss strip searches through the lens of the prohibition of inhuman and degrading treatment. Their chapter is complementary to the previous one: whereas Bernath's focus is on the preventive role of monitoring bodies, there Mavronicola and Webster zoom in on the reactive, judicial approach, in particular the role of the European Court of Human Rights: under what conditions does the Court consider body searches incompatible with respect for human dignity? In chapter six Aurore Vanliefde draws attention to the impact of body searches on vulnerable groups: indeed, some groups in prison (such as women and LGBTQI+ people) can experience body searches as significantly more degrading or humiliating. What are their experiences and how are their specific needs and sensibilities being addressed within the international and European human rights framework?

In chapters seven till ten the reader can find various explorations of body search practices in four European countries: Belgium, France, Spain, and Northern Ireland. In chapter seven Tom Daems examines the history of the regulation of strip searches in Belgium. Daems demonstrates how the rules on body searches, as set out in the Prison Act of 2005, have often come to be violated in practice. Daems also discusses the findings of a large-scale research project, conducted by the federal Ombudsman, and explores how the new Complaint Commissions, which were introduced in Belgian prisons in October 2020, have dealt with complaints related to strip searches. In chapter eight Joana Falxa discusses the evolution of strip searches in France. Falxa describes how Article 57 of the Prison Act of 2009 was originally adopted to prevent abuse in the use of body searches in prison. However, like in the Belgian case, we can see how also in France legal rules aimed at restricting and regulating body searches came to be challenged. Indeed, the law was being adapted in order to give the prison administration more flexibility in the use of body searches. In chapter nine Cristina Güerri explores the practice of strip searches in Spanish prisons. Interestingly, Güerri is able to document the extensive use and limited effectiveness of strip searches with empirical data from the Catalan prison system. She also demonstrates how certain standards (e.g. avoiding that a person is completely naked during a strip search) are often violated. In chapter ten Conor Byrne and Linda Moore paint a disturbing picture of the uses and abuses of strip search practices in Northern Ireland. They focus on the searching of republican prisoners and document how in a context of political conflict strip searching can become a technique of oppression and degradation.

Most chapters in this book examine the invasive character of body searches and discuss attempts at regulating and restricting such practices. The problematic character of body search practices raises the question whether modern prison systems really need body searches: are there any alternative methods available? In the penultimate chapter, Anaïs Tschanz explores whether technological devices, such as the Body Orifice Security Scanner (BOSS), could offer such an alternative. In the concluding chapter of the book we also return to this important question: what future for body searches in prisons?

References

APT and PRI. 2015. *Balancing Security and Dignity in Prisons: A Framework for Preventive Monitoring*. London: PRI. https://cdn.penalreform.org/wp-content/uploads/2016/01/security-dignity-2nd-ed-v6.pdf.

Daems, T. 2014. 'Ceci n'est pas une fouille à corps': The Denial of Strip Searches in Belgian Prisons. In *Punishment and Incarceration: A Global Perspective*, ed. M. Deflem, 75–94. Bingley: Emerald Group Publishing.

Goffman, E. 1961. *Asylums: Essays on the Social Situation of Mental Patients and Other Inmates*. London: Penguin.

Grewcock, M., and V. Sentas. 2019. *Rethinking Strip Searches by NSW Police*. Sydney: UNSW.

Loader, I., and N. Walker. 2007. *Civilizing Security*. Cambridge: Cambridge University Press.

The Imposition of Power Through Touch: A Sensory Criminology Approach to Understanding Body Searches

Jason Warr

1 Introduction

> They kept touching me. I told them I didn't want them to but …but … they just held me down. Their hands were all over me. I hated it. Hated it. I was so scared …
>
> (15 yr old, male, in Angmar Secure Training Centre)

Touch. Being touched. The placing of hands upon you. How much do we think about "touch" in criminology? In most criminological contexts if we were to discuss the placing of unwanted, powerful, hands upon the bodies of vulnerable people we would be in the realms of sexual

J. Warr (✉)
School of Sociology and Social Policy, University of Nottingham, Nottingham, UK
e-mail: jason.warr@nottingham.ac.uk

T. Daems (ed.), *Body Searches and Imprisonment*, Palgrave Studies in Prisons and Penology, https://doi.org/10.1007/978-3-031-20451-7_2

offending. Yet … yet this is a reality that people face in places of detention and incarceration on a daily basis and it is accepted as the norm. Just a part of the Good Order and Discipline of the institution. A necessary component of the environment. A practice with security implications, something that is done to ensure safety. Something preventative. Something necessary. Something almost good, moral. However, as the quote above indicates that touch, the hands of the powerful, are not experienced so benignly. The 15-year-old in question was interviewed as part of a project into complaints procedures within the youth detention estate here in England and Wales. Angmar STC (a pseudonym for the purposes of this chapter) is a youth prison that holds children between the ages of 12–17. This experience, being held down to be searched after having initially resisted, was their first experience of the prison as it happened in the reception area. A scared and vulnerable child, in their first moments of incarceration, being held down and forcibly searched by adult men. This may seem extreme, but it is not (see Willow 2015, Chapter 4 "I Think Its Quite Like Rape"). This is the very stuff of everyday life in our places of confinement and punishment.

This chapter explores the reality of searching practices through the lens of sensory criminology, and sensory penalities more specifically. In particular this chapter will focus not only on how concepts of penal power are communicated through securitised touch, but also how negative, moralised conceptions of those "inside", the civic dead, are simultaneously communicated via that same touch. This goes to the heart of what, and how, Herrity et al. (2021) define *Sensory Penalities*. Sensory Penalities, the study of how varying forms of penality are communicated via sensorial means, has three fundamentally interlocking themes: These include: Firstly, the manner in which "…the political, symbolic, and ideological are not only inherent to places and processes of punishment and social control but are encoded in the sensorial outputs and transmissions occurring within those places and processes" (Herrity et al. 2021: xxiii). What we mean by this is that the very penal ethea (those disciplinary and constraining ideations that govern, define, and characterise penal practices/spaces) are intrinsic to the sensory experiences evoked by such places of confinement and control. Secondly,

"...that places and processes of punishment and social control are experienced sensorially by those subject to them, those who work within them, and those who are researching them" (Herrity et al. 2021: xxiii). Fundamentally, those within the carceral walls, regardless of role or purpose, cannot escape these sensorially communicated ethea, as they are inherent to the very space in which these individuals find themselves and in which their senses are evinced. Thirdly, that we cannot, in all honesty, say that we fully understand, or have fully captured theoretically, how these spaces of confinement and control work or are experienced until we are able to fully explicate these sensorial realities, and explain their implications.

As Vannini et al. (2012) point out, as humans who are corporeal entities who live in material environments, we are constantly engaged in sensory work (see also Cox et al. 2016). We hear, we make sounds and noises, we smell (and we smell), we see, we are seen, we touch and are touched, and in this we cannot divorce ourselves from the sensory existence we have (see Butler 2015). Serres (2008) takes this a step further and argues that we are inherently sensorial creatures, who inhabit a sensory rich world, and derive our fundamental knowledge from our sensory experiences. This means that, as individuals with an internal, operant, sensorium (Pink 2011), we are not only constantly inundated with sensory data, but that this sensory data explicitly shapes how and in what way we draw distinct meaning and understanding from the contexts/environments in which we find ourselves. This is because the sensory explicitly involves the communication of packages of information that we then interpret. Think about the meanings communicated by an alarm, or the smell of gas (or the mercaptan that is added to it so we can smell it), or the foul taste of something turning rotten. Each tells us something about what we are experiencing. As such, our sensory knowledge and understanding is inherently symbolic in nature (Vannini et al. 2012). Yet, throughout the modern history of the social sciences, and in particular socio-legal, psychological, and criminological fields, this facet of our lived realities has either been overlooked or actively ignored. Part of the problem here is that a focus on the sensory seems to push us towards phenomenological accounts of social life with all their attendant issues (Noë 2007). However, as we have argued elsewhere (Herrity et al. 2021: xxviii), attending to the sensory and focusing on the symbolic communication that occurs with it, "…can allow us to avoid some of the more pernicious ontological traps associated with phenomenological approaches". It does this because, by focusing on the communicative nature of the sensory, it enables us to move beyond the thorny, subjective problems of qualia to the more knowable elements of shared symbolic interactions (Mead 1934).

However, there is a further problem evident in our epistemological history that has, in many ways, obfuscated the knowledge that we can derive from a sensory focus. This relates to a scientific idealism that has not only privileged the visual in our investigatory methods but has dismissed anything that deviates from this ocular-centric, Enlightenment-originated, orthodoxy (Classen 1997a). As Howes and Classen (2014) point out, the pre-eminence of the visual in our traditional, positivist, observational methodologies, has inculcated a distorted hierarchy of importance when it comes to methods of research. As social scientists, in particular, we are taught to think in the fetishized observational terms of the natural sciences; something that has dogged our social scientific evolution (see Mills 1959). In many ways this revenant of our positivist past (Cox 2018) still haunts our contemporary practice and has, for too long, prevented us from realising the potential of using the sensory to expand how we make sense of our social world. This has, however, begun to change in the social sciences in recent years as critiques of this Western ocular positivism have gained ground (see Classen 1997a; Howes and Classen 2014; Mbembe 2017; Pink 2009). Once more we seem to be on the verge of becoming more cognisant of our empiricist legacies upon which our contemporary social science is based (see Simmel 1912). Criminology and socio-legal studies are, inevitably, somewhat late to the game but even here we are seeing progress in terms of formal challenges to this historically established *ratio cognoscendi* (Herrity et al. 2021). We are now developing a sensorial imagination, and accompanying methodologies with which to investigate the criminological anew (see Herrity et al. 2022).

2 Research Context

The information contained in this chapter comes from a range of research projects, ethnographic observations, and discussions, as well as my own experiences as someone who has been subject to over 8,000 rub-down searches and more than 1,000 strip searches within the criminal justice system (this excludes searches conducted by the police in various stop and search scenarios that I endured as a young child). Though never having been the direct subject of any of the projects from which information has been extracted, the topic of searching has arisen frequently. For instance, the quote at the start of this chapter occurred in a focus group conducted in Angmar STC that focused on complaint procedures in the institution. I worked on that project as an employee of a criminal justice-based 3rd sector organisation. The quotes by the forensic psychologists were drawn from my doctoral research on the experiences of those practitioners in the contemporary prison. Other details and examples are drawn from two projects that ran in two distinct prisons for the same 3rd sector organisation. My work in these institutions (HMP Lazaretto House and HMYOI Neverland) as a prison council facilitator, involved in depth, quasi-ethnographic, fieldwork, accompanied by meetings with various groups of prisoners and staff, in order to uncover deep rooted issues and contentions within the institutions so that these could be discussed and overcome. This allowed me a great deal of access to these sites and to witness the quotidian life within them. In this sense I saw prisoners and staff of all types be subjected to, experience, and endure the searching practices of the prison. With regard to some of the staff I even had some direct conversations with them about searching after having sat in a reception area and a workshop and seeing them conduct dozens of searches in a short period of time (discussed below). These collective research experiences have given me a great deal of material to think about in terms of the topic of this chapter.

It must be noted that my positionality in terms of these disparate research projects is somewhat complex. In each separately, and now collectively, I have straddled multiple positionalities, acting as a male, independent (external) project facilitator, a quasi-ethnographic researcher, a focus groups facilitator, a doctoral researcher, a released lifer, a criminologist, and even perhaps a person of jumbled ethnicity, of a working-class background all of which creates a complex stew that must be disentangled. In this sense it is important to understand the impact of this complex web of positionalities as this affected, not only the relationship between myself and the participants, but also impacted on the results (Hopkins 2007; see also Soni-Sinha 2008). One key component of this reflexive examination is to ensure that these laminated positionalities do not negatively impact research, nor data analyses (Kochan 2013; Marshall and Rossman 2006). I have discussed the complexities of the former extensively in numerous publications elsewhere, and to replicate that material here, would be to detract from the main discussion. However, the latter does warrant a brief answer. As Kohler Reissman (2015) notes, it is important to identify and account for those relevant biographic factors that shape the individual as a knowledge producer and the knowledge produced. With distance, both temporal and emotional, from the data and the processes by which it was produced allowed me to clearly distinguish between my understanding of my own experiences of being searched, and those of others. It was clear revisiting the varying material for this chapter that there were both supporting and counter narratives in operation here. As such, I attempt here to capture both of those existing understandings of being searched and what the contradictions between them mean for how we can understand the sensory penalities of body searches.

3 Background

In sensory terms "touch" has quite a unique place. As Le Breton (2017) notes, it has a primacy in our sensory pantheon as without the sense of touch, an individual is cast adrift in a material world. As he argues, unlike with the loss of other senses wherein an individual can still operate in society, the loss of the sense of touch "… is to be robbed of any possibility of autonomous action" (Le Breton 2017: 96). Without touch it becomes impossible to stand, to lie, to move, to eat, to drink, without the ability to detect the corporeal around us. However, he goes on to argue that our skin, as the medium of touch, is not only essential to our material existence it also becomes central to our symbolic communication with our physical world. In this regard it becomes a semi-permeable barrier in which it acts as both boundary to the intrusions of the outside world but also a communicator of it. Touch, then, has a double functionality in our lives. Something true of any sense and sensation (Serres 2008). Much of the literature on touch and power (do a Google Scholar search for "touch" and "power" and you will see what I mean) comes from a therapeutic or nurturing focus and concentrates on the healing and positive communicative function of touch in varying settings. However, there is a peculiarity to the socio-cultural contexts in which we touch and can be touched, that places this double functionality firmly in the realm of the political (Manning 2007). As Classen (2020: 1) notes, "Touch is not just a private act. It is a fundamental medium for the expression, experience, and contestation of social values and hierarchies". Who can touch, who has the power to touch, who can resist a touch, and who cannot become fundamental to our understanding of power, who wields it, how they wield it, how it is imposed upon those subject to it, and how it is experienced.

In the prisons of England and Wales the rules and regulations that determine the official practices of body searches (or searches of the person) are set out in the National Security Framework 3.1: Prison Service Instructions 07/2016 (HMPPS 2016). This document sets out the processes of different types of rub-down-search or for, what are euphemistically called, full searches which are, fundamentally, strip searches. The rub-down-searches, which are based upon levels of intensity of the search (Levels A and B for men; Levels A and B for women), can be either routine or targeted searches, and are to be conducted open hand whilst the person is clothed. These can be carried out on anyone in the prison by a single officer (though should be noted that female identifying prisoners can only be searched by female staff). The strip searches have slightly different rules for men and for women (predicated on sex, health, and clothing). For instance, Level 1 searches for females will not require the removal of underwear, but Level 2 (intelligence led) searches will. Full, or strip, searches must be conducted with two officers of the same sex as the person being searched present and no contact is allowed, nor should the prisoner (who are most frequently the subject of such searches, though staff and visitors can also be requested to undergo such a search but cannot be coerced into complying) be fully nude at any point in the search. Unlike in other jurisdictions (for instance see Maculan et al. 2013; Davis 2011), intimate searches are not allowed to be conducted by any officer and can only be conducted by designated healthcare staff, if the prisoner consents to the intrusion. In this regard the regulations are, seemingly, in accordance with the Mandela Rules (see Coyle and Fair 2018).

The regulations above also set out the procedures for the use of scanning technologies as they relate to the searching of the person. However, these lie beyond the scope of this chapter and as such shall not be considered here. What is of more importance is that the regulations highlight that rub-down-searches should not be considered as intimate as they "… should be conducted thoroughly within the parameters of the national policy/procedures, they are not intended to be intrusive searches" (HMPPS 2016: 28). However, this is something of an obfuscation, if not an outright denial with regard to both the nature of searches and how they are experienced. I think it is important here, at the outset, to recognise that searches of this nature are necessarily experienced differently by different populations within the prison. The nature of that experience is necessarily shaped by the position to power that the individual has. Those with the least amount of power (even those made to feel that way—see below) have a very different relationship with being searched than those who ordinarily wield some modicum of power within the institution.

4 Discussion

I stand there, powerless.

I feel the hands on me, rubbing along my arms, my collar, my chest. Moving down my body. I grit my teeth.

The unwelcome hands continue their slow journey around my body, assured, strong, practised, down over my stomach, around the waist of my

scratchy, well worn, aged and threadbare jeans, down my outer thighs, halting, returning, towards my groin.
I brace myself.
I feel vulnerable. Small.
I want to punch them in their face, to fight them, to take back some power ... but I don't. I acquiesce.
I let it happen.
Anger.
Shame.
The hands stop.
He says: "Next".
I amble on, hating myself.
(Warr 2020b)

This was how I introduced my subjective experience of being searched in a blog post on this issue for *Sensory Criminology*. This particular description could have related to any of the 1000s of times that I was forced to endure the powered touch of another as I exited or entered some portal within any of the numerous prisons I experienced. However, I can remember this exact feeling and thoughts one day when leaving a workshop to return to the wing. The prisoners were all lined up silently awaiting the rather bored officer to pick us off one-by-one as we left. I remember the group of men who had been loudly and boisterously bantering only a few minutes before falling silent as they waited dully for their turn. I can remember the resentment in me building as I shuffled closer to my inevitable ordeal. I always found it an ordeal. I remember seeing the lad in front of me tense as the hands started pawing at him. I remember him relaxing as it finished and his exiting the workshop and immediately, once more, beginning to banter with his mate who was waiting outside. Like nothing had happened. I remember stepping forward and gritting my teeth in preparation to being touched by this uniformed man. It was always the same. I never got used to it really, just "... inured and conditioned into the routine. Arms up, legs slightly apart, passive, waiting for the touching to commence. To cease" (Warr 2020b). I would always acquiesce, so as not to invite a more brutal touch. What else were you going to do but to grit your teeth and think of something else. To try to close your mind to the feeling of unwanted hands on you. It always made me resent those officers. Why?

Power. Their monopoly of it. My absence of it. In every touch, in every laying on of hands, in every instance of being made to stand there and endure the experience, in every knowing that resistance was futile and would only bring more hands, more touching, this time accompanied by pain, in every swallowed resentment the power imbalance between you and them is made evident. Your place, who you are now, what you represent, everything you have lost, everything that has been taken from you, everything that you will never have is represented by, and communicated through, those touches. Those touches shout at you that you are now a prisoner, nothing but a prisoner. A prisoner deprived of autonomy (Sykes 1958). The communication is as inescapable as the unwanted hands. As Herrity et al. (2021) note, when it comes to the varying penalities which underpin penal (and social control) practices, they are inherently communicated through and by the sensory experiences evinced by and within the institution itself. From the cluncking locks and jangling keys, bells, alarms, and screaming violence, to the forced proximity to the stench of another's secretions and excretions, each sound and smell is a powerful communicator of the prison's power and intent. There are a panoply of sensory penal intrusions that imposed the materiality of the prison on the body, and thus the mind, of those incarcerated. This is, perhaps, more explicitly true with touch, and the routinised power of searching is the most evident form therein. The touch, the search, sends a message to you about who and what you are and it reinforces the power of the prison with every instance.

These experiences are not just personal to me. We have already seen that the child in Angmar STC had a similarly visceral response to being searched which led to further restraint. These issues arise from the routinised use of searching that all within the prison can and are subjected to. These speak to the sensorial experience of power in the everyday. However, that power and the expressive functions of touch in this regard, can also be used in more directed ways that take us beyond issues of routine control. Another young person in the same STC, engaged with the same project regarding complaint procedures, asked if it was possible (many were unclear about how and for what reason they could use such procedures) to make a complaint about a staff member who they felt was picking on them for racialised reasons. They explained that this member of staff always singled them and some other Black children out for a search, was always a little rougher and more explicitly thorough in the search with them than with the white kids, and would make comments about "kids like him" (Black, and from South London) whilst conducting the search. This child made it clear in the discussion with us that this member of staff was well known amongst the Black population in Angmar for this type of behaviour.[1] After this, a number of the other children of colour to whom we spoke also identified this racialised element of searching. What was apparent was that, like in other contexts where racism is expressed through touch (see Kamaloni 2019), these children felt that the routine practice of searching, and the power inherent to that, was being subverted here to express the deeply held view and beliefs of the individuals wielding that power. This changed the way that they experienced not only the touch of staff members but the very nature of searching in and of itself.[2]

I found a similar issue in the accounts of some of the women who I interviewed in relation to their experiences as forensic psychologists within contemporary prisons. The experiences of these women within the prison were often shaped and coloured by varying forms of overt and covert sexism (Warr 2020a). This sexism, and in some cases overt misogyny, were often expressed in either directly impositional or isolational ways. Something left out of the book as it was only directly referred to by two of the women, related to how searching could be used a form of impositional dominance (whereby uniformed staff would demonstrate their power over others via various impositions of that power). One woman described how there was a security officer who seemed to have a personal vendetta against the psychologists (and indeed women) within

---

[1] Subsequent HMIP Inspections found distinct problems with racism and institutional racism within Angmar and a number of staff were removed/sacked from the institution after an investigation into a number of incidents of staff violence.

[2] For an example of how racialised prejudice can be expressed through searching practices see the case of Child Q, a 15-year-old girl who was strip searched in a school in London which led to a serious safeguarding review: https://chscp.org.uk/wp-content/uploads/2022/03/Child-Q-PUBLISHED-14-March-22.pdf.

the prison. She explained that if this officer was on duty or in the gatehouse then she would become subject to the "random" searches that staff would sometimes be subjected to. However, she noted that after this had happened a few times she had raised the issue with her line manager, in case there had been a security incident report put in against her that was leading to these searches. Upon finding out that this was not the case, and that this had been happening to others in the psychology department, she had realised that it was this officer using those procedures to reinforce their power over them as women and psychologists.

> He clearly had a problem with us [women] working in 'his' prison. Doing the randoms [searches] on us was his way of telling us …

Another highlighted a similar, but more disturbing, facet of this impositional dominance which related to another male security officer, who this person often encountered in the gatehouse on their way into the prison. This woman noted that they had first met this particular officer at their initial security briefing. She noted that the officer had asked her out during the briefing by whispering in her ear whilst his colleague explained some detail or concern. She said that she was immediately uncomfortable and had politely declined. After that she said that "… he just would not leave me alone. He asked me out a number of times. I always said no but … but he would laugh in a really creepy way and ignore my answer". She went on to explain that eventually he stopped asking her out but then took a more hostile approach asking her if she was "gay" and "didn't like men". Things escalated quickly but she, like many others in the same context, felt that she could not complain about it as she was made to feel as if it was all in her head (Warr 2020a; see also Britton 2003). One aspect of this officer's behaviour involved getting a female member of staff to search her when she entered the prison. Again, at first, she thought this was just part of the normal security routines. However, she soon realised that he would be watching intently, pruriently, as she was being searched and that this was part of his "thing". She noted

> When [I] realised ... I was just, just so uncomfortable you know? He would be standing there just staring at us. Every time. Staring with this really creepy look on his face as I was patted down ... it [was] horrible. The [female] officer was completely oblivious to what was going on but ... that just made it worse, you know? I felt like I was being assaulted... by proxy. He was using this poor woman to assault me. He was doing that to me, and wanted me to know that.

She went on to explain that she started applying for new jobs immediately after this realisation and soon left to work in another psychology department in another prison much further away. Though this was a somewhat extreme example the impositional dominance evident here was not dissimilar to that women psychologists were commonly exposed to in the prisons of England and Wales (Warr 2020a). As Hutchison (2020) notes, not only are searching practices inherent manifestations of terrible penal power, they are also contexts where that terrible power can be subverted for more nefarious means/ends. Part of the problem here is the routine nature of searches. Where impositions of power become entirely routinised the effects and experiences of that power become effectively obscured and unconsidered; in such situations abuse and abuses of power often go undetected (Williams and Keating 1999; see also Cohen (2001) on Normalisation and Denial at Work).

What we see in all the accounts here is different forms in which the searching practices, and the laying on of hands, could be experienced as assaultive—whether that be in terms of prisoner status, racially, or even misogynistically. Touch can be experienced as assaultive in this way, despite what the regulations say, because it is both necessarily intrusive and communicative of power (Willow 2015). However, this is a power and an experience that is not always either recognised nor even considered by those officers who conduct these very searches on a daily basis. During a period of initial quasi-ethnographic immersion into HMYOI Neverland, I was in a workshop observing officers as they searched the prisoners before they returned to their wings. In that instance, I recalled my own experiences and wondered how the staff feel about it. So I asked. The two officers basically laughed and said that they didn't really think about it, it was just one of those duties they had to perform.

> It's just something that you have to do innit. You gotta make sure they ain't carrying any'fing back that they shouldn't, innit? No biggie ...

I asked them if they ever felt uncomfortable doing the searches. One looked at me as if they did not quite get what I was speaking about, but the other noted that they had when they first started but not anymore, they had gotten used to it. I asked them if they had ever been searched. Both said "of course" but dismissed this as anything to be troubled by as, one of them said, "... it's expected, right? If you got nothing to hide it ain't anything that should bother you". This last point is something that comes up time and again when the issue of searching or surveillance by authorities is discussed (Gilliom 2001). The argument itself is a dismissal of the power imbalance at the heart of the relationship between those doing the searching and those being searched and the potential for any suffering to arise from it. In effect, it is a form of implicatory denial inherent to those found in various workplaces (Cohen 2001). At a later point at HMP Lazaretto House, I spent the morning observing the reception area as a number of new foreign national prisoners were brought in from other prisons. I watched as the three white officers searched a succession of young men of colour. I asked them if it ever felt weird to search people and they all laughed it off in the same way that those at Neverland had. One finally said it could be uncomfortable, especially if the prisoner "... stank like some of them do". The others nodded to this accepting that this was one of the more unpleasant aspects of prison work but said it was, and I paraphrase here, *just one of those things you get used to doing*.

5 Conclusion

> *You get used to doing ...*

There is something fundamental to the nature and exercise of power in that statement. Those who wield power rarely recognise the power that they wield. Why? Because it has become so routine to them, part of their everyday practice that they rarely if ever consider the implications of their actions. More importantly, they would often not recognise either the power inherent to their practice, nor accept the consequential experiences of those others who are forced to endure it (Cohen 2001). This is not an abnormality, nor something that is peculiar to the prison. It is just that the prison is where it is most stark, for there are few such places in our social worlds where the power imbalance is so intentionally marked. Yet if we are to understand the nature of power, and especially penal power, we cannot ignore the manner in which it is experienced and/or denied. Considering the sensory in this regard helps us to gain further understanding of these most vexatious issues (for other work related issues see Hockey and Allen-Collinson 2009).

A consideration of sensorial penality (Herrity et al. 2021) allows us to consider how a child finds being searched a traumatic experience whilst the person doing the search may have no cognisance of that fact. It allows us to explore why they may not recognise the rejection as coming from a place of bodily discomfort, but rather interpret is a rejection of their authority—and thus just impose the power at their hands more forcefully. This is something that might be worth much more consideration given what we are beginning to understand about neuro-diversity amongst prison populations (see HMIP 2020) and the prevalence of sensory sensitivities, especially "tactile defensiveness" (Belek 2019), in such populations. Where we have potentially high numbers of people with such issues we need to consider the impact on them of imposing routinised physical touch, that not only will they inherently experience as assaultive but which will result in serious psychical distress.

A similar point could be made with regard to the number of people in prison who have experience of physical and sexual abuse. I have been lucky in my life to never have been physically or sexually abused as we commonly define those offences. However, nearly a third of those who come into contact with our criminal justice system, from police to prison, have (see PRT 2021). So many have had lives blighted by prolonged and continual abuse of every physical description. How do they experience the coerced intrusion, the unwanted touch, the imposition of powerful hands? As Hutchison (2020) notes, searches, which you do not have the power to say no to, can on the one hand be experienced as akin to other forms of sexual assault, and, on the other, can evince historical experiences of such assaults. What then are the consequences of routinely inflicting this breach of bodily autonomy? What are the long-term effects on psyche and self for victim survivors? What does it tell us about the prison that they don't currently consider this?

Lastly, one of the elements revealed here is how routine searching in the prison and places of confinement can be subverted for more nefarious or malicious ends. As Barter (1999) argues, in all institutions where abuse does take place, it does so because the abuser is able to subvert the power and authority of the institution in order to exercise their subjective intentions. They are often able to hide their abuses in plain sight of the institution because the imposition of authority is an inherent and routinised aspect of that institution, and it is that authority and its routines that is being deployed in order to abuse. Given the institutional blindness here, and the more general forms of denial (Cohen 2001) inherent to such places, it is only through explorations of the experiences of being searched will we begin to understand these issues and the manner in which they need to be investigated.

This also has implications for the way we consider human rights and its breaches in places of confinement. When it comes to impositions of power in coercive places of detention, and how these may relate to breeches of human rights, we tend to focus on the visual. We tend to view the issues around breaches of dignity and other enshrined rights through the lens of the surveillance state and how this can render the imprisoned naked, vulnerable. This panoptic focus is understandable in fields of social enquiry significantly grounded in gendered and colonial histories that privileged an ocular-centric positivism (Classen 1997a). However, opening up these forms of enquiry to include a broader sensorial inquiry, to include touch, smell, sound/noise, temperature, time, taste, etc. can extend our understanding of these issues (for instance see Webster and Mavronicola 2022). This is the benefit of not just sensory penalities, but more specifically, a sensory criminology and its attendant imagination.

References

Barter, C. 1999. Independent Investigations into Institutional Child Abuse: Developing Theory and Practice. In *Institutional Abuse: Perspectives Across the Life Course*, ed. N. Stanley, J. Manthorpe, and B. Penhale, 66–88. New York: Routledge.

Belek, B. 2019. Articulating Sensory Sensitivity: From Bodies with Autism to Autistic Bodies. *Medical Anthropology* 38 (1): 30–43.

Britton, D.M. 2003. *At Work in the Iron Cage: The Prison as Gendered Organisation*. New York: New York University Press.

Butler, J. 2015. *Senses of the Subject*. New York: Fordham University Press.

Classen, C. 1997. Engendering Perceptions: Gender Ideologies and Sensory Hierarchies in Western History. *Body and Society* 3 (2): 1–19.

Cohen, S. 2001. *States of Denial: Knowing about Atrocities and Suffering*. Cambridge: Polity Press.

Coyle, A., and H. Fair. 2018. *A Human Rights Approach to Prison Management: Handbook for Prison Staff*, 3rd ed. London: University of Birkbeck, Institute of Criminal Policy Research.

Cox, A.M. 2018. Embodied Knowledge and Sensory Information: Theoretical Roots and Inspirations. *Library Trends* 66 (3): 223–238.

Cox, R., A. Irving, and C. Wright. 2016. Introduction: The Sense of the Senses. In *Beyond Text? Critical Practices and Sensory Anthropology*, ed. R. Cox, A. Irving, and C. Wright, 1–19. Manchester: Manchester University Press.

Classen, C. 2020. Fingertips: Writing about Touch. In *The Book of Touch*, ed. C. Classen, 1–12. London: Routledge.

Davis, A. 2011. *Are Prisons Obsolete?* New York: Seven Stories Press.

Gilliom, J. 2001. *Overseers of the Poor: Surveillance, Resistance, and the Limits of Privacy*. Chicago: The University of Chicago Press.

Herrity, K, B.E. Schmidt, and J. Warr. 2021. Introduction: Welcome to the Sensorium. In *Sensory Penalities: Exploring the Senses in Spaces of Punishment and Social Control*, ed. K. Herrity, B. Schmidt, and J. Warr, xxi–xxxiv. Bingley: Emerald Publishing.

Herrity, K., B.E. Schmidt, and J. Warr. 2022. Sensory "Heteroglossia" and Social Control: Sensory Methodology and Method. In *Qualitative Research in Criminology: Cutting Edge Methods*, ed. M. Dodge and R. Faria. New York: Springer.

HMIP. 2020. *Neurodiversity in the Criminal Justice System: A Review of Evidence*. London: Ministry of Justice, Her Majesty's Inspector of Prisons.

HMPPS. 2016. *Prison Service Instructions 07/2016—Searches of the Person.* National Security Framework 3.1. London: Ministry of Justice, Her Majesty's Prison & Probation Service.
Hockey, J., and J. Allen-Collinson. 2009. The Sensorium at Work: The Sensory Phenomenology of the Working Body. *The Sociological Review* 57 (2): 217–239.
Hopkins, P.E. 2007. Positionalities and Knowledge: Negotiating Ethics in Practice. *An International E-Journal for Critical Geographies* 6 (3): 386–394.
Howes, D., and C. Classen. 2014. *Ways of Sensing: Understanding the Senses in Society*. London: Routledge.
Hutchison, J. 2020. "It's Sexual Assault. It's Barbaric": Strip Searching in Women's Prisons as State-Inflicted Sexual Assault. *Affilia* 35 (2): 160–176.
Kamaloni, S. 2019. Can I Touch You? Everyday Racism. In *Understanding Racism in a Post-Racial World: Visible Invisibilities*, ed. S. Kamaloni, 65–98. London: Palgrave Macmillan.
Kochan, J. 2013. Subjectivity and Emotion in Scientific Research. *Studies in History and Philosophy of Science* 44 (3): 354–362.
Kohler Reissman, C. 2015. Entering the Hall of Mirrors: Reflexivity and Narrative Research. In *The Handbook of Narrative Analysis*, ed. A. de Fina and A. Georgkopoulou, 219–238. Chichester: Wiley.
Le Breton, D. 2017. *Sensing the World: An Anthropology of the Senses*. London: Bloomsbury Academic.
Maculan, A., D. Ronco, and F. Vianello. 2013. *Prisons in Europe: Overview and Trends.* Rome: European Prison Observatory—Detention conditions in the European Union.
Manning, E. 2007. *Politics of Touch: Sense, Movement, Sovereignty*. Minneapolis: University of Minnesota Press.
Marshall, C., and G.B. Rossman. 2006. *Designing Qualitative Research*, 4th ed. London: Sage.
Mbembe, A. 2017. *Critique of Black Reason.* Johannesburg: Wits University Press.
Mead, G.H. 1934. *Mind, Self, and Society*. Chicago: University of Chicago Press.
Mills, C.W. 1959. *The Sociological Imagination*. New York: Oxford University Press.
Noë, A. 2007. The Critique of Pure Phenomenology. *Phenomenology and the Cognitive Sciences* 6 (1–2): 231–245.
Pink, S. 2009. *Doing Sensory Ethnography*. London: Sage.

Pink, S. 2011. Multimodality, Multisensoriality and Ethnographic Knowing: Social Semiotics and the Phenomenology of Perception. *Qualitative Research* 11 (3): 261–276.

PRT. 2021. *Bromley Briefings Prisons Fact File: Winter 2021*. London: Prison Reform Trust.

Serres, M. 2008. *The Five Senses: A Philosophy of Mingled Bodies*. London: Continuum International Publishing Group.

Simmel, G. 1912. Essai sur la sociologie des sens. In *Sociologie et épistémologie*, ed. G. Simmel, 223–238. Paris: Presses Universitaires de France.

Soni-Sinha, U. 2008. Dynamics of the Field: Multiple Standpoints, Narrative and Shifting Positionality in Multisited Research. *Qualitative Research* 8 (4): 515–537.

Sykes, G.M. 1958. *The Society of Captives: A Study of a Maximum Security Prison*. Princeton, NJ: Princeton University Press.

Vannini, P., D. Waskul, and S. Gottschalk. 2012. *The Senses in Self, Society, and Culture: A Sociology of the Senses*. New York: Routledge.

Warr, J. 2020a. *Forensic Psychologists: Prisons, Power, and Vulnerability*. Bingley: Emerald Publishing Limited.

Warr, J. 2020b. The Power of Touch. *Sensory Criminology*, https://sensorycriminology.com/2020b/06/.

Webster, E., and N. Mavronicola. 2022. A Human Rights Law Perspective on Sensory Experience and Dignity in Detention. *Sensory Criminology*. https://sensorycriminology.com/2022/06/27/a-human-rights-law-perspective-on-sensory-experience-and-dignity-in-detention/.

Williams, J., and F. Keating. 1999. The Abuse of Adults in Mental Health Settings. In *Institutional Abuse: Perspectives Across the Life Course*, ed. N. Stanley, J. Manthorpe, and B. Penhale, 130–151. New York: Routledge.

Willow, C. 2015. *Children Behind Bars: Why the Abuse of Child Imprisonment Must End*. Bristol: Policy Press.

Searching, 'State of Security' and the Structuration of Prison Security

Jamie Bennett

1 Introduction

Everyday in prisons across England and Wales, thousands of searches are conducted—people, places and property and all subjected to regular physical scrutiny in order to detect drugs, weapons, mobile phones and other contraband. People entering prisons or moving about them will be subject to searching, whether that is rub-down searching or full searching, which involves the removal of clothing (sometimes referred to as strip searching). Cells and other areas are regularly searched, while vehicles, property and other items that enter the prison are also searched. Searching may be carried out by people using touch and sight to detect

J. Bennett (✉)
University of Oxford, Oxford, UK
e-mail: Jamie.Bennett@yjb.gov.uk

Youth Justice Board, London, UK

T. Daems (ed.), *Body Searches and Imprisonment*, Palgrave Studies in Prisons and Penology, https://doi.org/10.1007/978-3-031-20451-7_3

illicit items and may also be conducted using specially trained dogs and technical aids such as x-ray scanners, metal detectors and drug trace detection equipment. The practices of searching are deeply embedded in contemporary imprisonment and are fundamental to how security is managed in many other settings, such as airports, and yet there is an absence of sustained and in-depth sociological examination. This chapter will pay particular attention to searching as a significant element of security practice and one that illustrates the tensions, limitations and potential of reforming prison security.

A descriptive and reflective approach will be taken in this chapter, exploring emerging discourses in the security policy of HM Prison and Probation Service (HMPPS) in England and Wales. During my tenure as Head of Operational Security for HMPPS (2019–2022), there has been a conscious effort to draw upon security theory and refashion the approach to security practices to make them more legitimate. The methodology in this chapter is a form of reflective practice, which "facilitates the ability to apply theory to practice and to learn from experience" (Bruster and Peterson 2013: 171). The chapter will pay attention to both 'reflection-in-action' (Schon 1983), that is the theory and ideas used to inform the development of security practice at a particular time, and 'reflection-on-action', looking back and critically questioning the approaches taken. The use of reflective practice by practitioners is encouraged as part of the professionalisation of security (Hasenstab 2018; Button 2021). The chapter will set out the key theoretical and empirical work that has informed developments and describe how it has been operationalised, before looking in more detail at what this new approach means for the specific practice of searching. The chapter concludes with some reflections on the next steps including further research and developments in practice.

2 Understanding Prison Security

The fundamental nature of prison security means that it is often taken for granted; assumptions are made about the underpinning concepts, beliefs and values, but these are often obscured or simply not articulated. As a necessary precursor, I want to excavate some of those assumptions by asking what is prison security? What are the primary practices? And what are the key values and strategies in security leadership? This discussion is based upon the research that has informed the new, emerging approach to prison security, as well as providing a more considered and critical perspective on prison security, revealing some of the tensions that shape the terrain.

First, what is 'security' and how should it be defined? Security is a contested term that has been widely discussed and debated in theory and practice. Lucia Zedner (2009) summarised the four key ways in which 'security' has been defined: as an "objective state" in which people are protected from material threats (p. 14); a "subjective state", in which people have their fears allayed and feel sufficiently safe (p. 16); a "pursuit" in which threats evolve and change so that security has to be continuously revised in an ever-changing context (p. 19); and a "symbol", which has a function in persuading and reassuring people, whether or not it has a material benefit (p. 21). Critics of prison security have focused on the symbolic role. For example, in her ethnography of a high security prison, Deborah Drake (2012) argues that the extensive practices of security such as CCTV monitoring, routine searching of prisoners' cells, dog patrols, surveillance and intelligence information gathering do not offer material or subjective security but are instead a chimera deployed to justify a form of authoritarian control.

Any defence, justification or response to the critical argument that security is merely a symbolic practice that enables the exercise of power, must start by outlining the material threats that prison security is addressing. Prison security is often assumed to be concerned with preventing escapes and managing the smuggling of contraband into prisons (e.g. Drake 2012). The purposes, however, are broader and critical accounts sometimes underplay the significance of ongoing criminality and organised crime in prisons (Button 2021). Organised criminals can and do continue to operate from within prisons, often using illicit mobile phones, and prisons themselves are increasingly becoming a lucrative marketplace for organised criminals trading illegal drugs (National Crime Agency 2018; Gooch and Treadwell 2020). The illicit economy is a key driver of prison violence, including exploitation of the vulnerable, and so organised crime is not only a risk in itself, but has implications for the wider prison community (Gooch and Treadwell 2019; Sturt and Gooch 2021). With over 25,000 assaults committed in the 12 months to March 2021 (HMPPS 2021a) and with almost 15% of random drug tests resulting in a positive result from illicit drugs or psychoactive substances (HMPPS 2020a), there is clearly a material basis for concern about the threat to prison security. Within prisons, over 6,500 prisoners are identified as being members of organised crime groups (HMPPS 2019) and it has been argued that organised crime groups have exploited the opportunity of reduced prison staffing and the demand for psychoactive substances to take a significant grip on the prisoner society (Gooch and Treadwell 2019).

Former Director of Security, Order and Counter Terrorism in HMPPS, Claudia Sturt, articulated the purpose of prison security, which she defined as "the protection of an organisation, its mission and objectives against hostile activity" (Sturt and Gooch 2021: 9). She described how following a series of high-profile escapes in the 1990s (Woodcock 1994; Learmont 1995) prison security was concentrated upon escape prevention, which remains relevant, but there is now an increasing focus on criminal activity within prisons, often enabled by developments in technology, such as mobile phones: "prison security now is as much about tackling the illicit economy and ongoing criminality as it is about preventing escape" (Sturt and Gooch 2021: 9). This account emphasises both security as an objective state, addressing material threats, and security as a pursuit, with the threats evolving and changing over time. Sturt also articulated that prison security is not an end in itself, but contributes towards a more ordered and safe prison community: "creating the bedrock for rehabilitative cultures and opportunities" (Sturt and Gooch 2021: 9). From this perspective, security offers a subjective state in which people can move from fear and survival to participating in community life and making use of opportunities for personal growth. The role of prison security, as articulated by Sturt, is of security as a 'public good' (Loader and Walker 2007; Zedner 2009), in which the absence of security contributes towards violence, disorder and weakened civic engagement, while effective security can create the conditions in which people experience increased safety, confidence and can participate more fully in the prison community. This approach reflects a broader trend in security, with the growing importance of the concept of 'human security' with its people-centred emphasis and concern with creating protection for individuals and communities so as to foster conditions for human fulfilment (e.g. Alkire 2002). The approach set out by Sturt is significant as it offers an account of prison security that is concerned with tackling and reducing material threats that undermine the purpose of HMPPS, such as escape and criminality, but she also situates security within the wider strategic aims of the organisation, particularly creating a safer and more rehabilitative milieu, in which individuals feel safe and can productively engage with the opportunities available.

Having set out the purposes of prison security, I now turn to the second question concerning the practices of security. Again, this section discusses specific empirical and theoretical work that has informed HMPPS strategy and policy development in recent years. As has been described by Sturt above, there has been an ambition to integrate security and the rehabilitative aims of prisons. This is an echo of the seminal study by Sparks et al. (1996) analysing the strategies for maintaining order in two high security prisons. Sparks et al. identified two predominant strategies that were discernible in practice. The first was 'situational' approaches, which are based upon the assumption that people have a disposition to offend, but the use of targeted measures can alter the degree of risk and opportunity, so reducing offending. Such approaches assume a degree of rational calculation by potential offenders. Examples of such measures in prisons include electronic surveillance such as CCTV, control of movements, restrictions on property, segregation of specific individuals and the use of searching. In contrast, 'social' approaches attempt to strengthen social relations as a means to reduce crime, being based upon the assumption that the disposition to offend varies in relation to social conditions. Examples of such approaches in prisons include legitimising rules through explanation, participation and education; involving peers or representatives in community life; having credible grievance processes; recognising and rewarding compliance; and sanctioning breaches. Sparks et al. argued that these approaches reflect a respective emphasis upon structure (situational) and agency (social), and that in practice, prisons would blend the different approaches, which they described as "the structuration of prison life", in a search for "practical viability and moral defensibility" (Sparks et al. 1996: 325). Ultimately, creating an appropriate balance, they suggested, is a means to generate a stronger sense of legitimacy with prisoners, which provides a more stable social foundation. This work has been central to recent developments in security policy and strategy, informing an approach which attempts to understand security not solely as a set of technical practices, but instead as also having social and human dimensions.

The third area that has informed the recent developments in HMPPS is security leadership, which has been described as critical to the professionalisation and effectiveness of the security sector (Button 2021). Although the security profession has matured over recent decades, it remains underdeveloped compared to other professions. Research on security management across different sectors has identified a shifting culture from 'traditionalist' to 'modern entrepreneurs' (Gill et al. 2007). A 'traditionalist' approach sees security as a service function rather than being strategically integrated, organised along command-and-control lines, and judgements of success are based on measures such as the number of arrests. 'Modern entrepreneurs' in contrast see security as an integrated part of the business process, drawing upon general business concepts, strategies and skills. This pattern can be seen to have been replicated in prisons, where a historically rooted and insular security culture saw a series of catastrophic failures in the 1990s (Woodcock 1994; Learmont 1995) and subsequently gave way to a more managerial approach with nationally prescribed standards enforced through a process of audits (Bennett 2015). In recent years, there has been an attempt to shift the approach by professionalising security through capability building, qualifications, research, connecting with external professional bodies and working more closely with other security and law enforcement organisations (Sturt and Gooch 2021; Button 2021).

This summary highlights three critical and interlinked theories that have informed the recent development of prison security. First, the focus of security has shifted to encompass ongoing criminality as much as escape and there has also been a reinvigorated interest in the capacity of security to be a social good, creating a safer community in which people can participate and find fulfilment. Second, the practices of security have been informed by an appreciation of their social and human dimensions as well as the need to foster legitimacy. Third, there is a shift in security leadership from traditionalist, to managerial and now to professionalisation. Together, these three approaches signal an intention to reimagine and develop prison security. This has been operationalised through the development of the 'state of security' model, which identifies the elements that contribute to effective prison security (Fig. 1).

The model is comprised of six elements. Three of the elements—security intelligence, physical security and procedural security—are the core technical and situational practices. Dynamic security was articulated by former prison administrator Ian Dunbar (1985) as an essentially social approach encompassing the quality of staff–prisoner relationships and access to meaningful activity for prisoners. Strategic integration

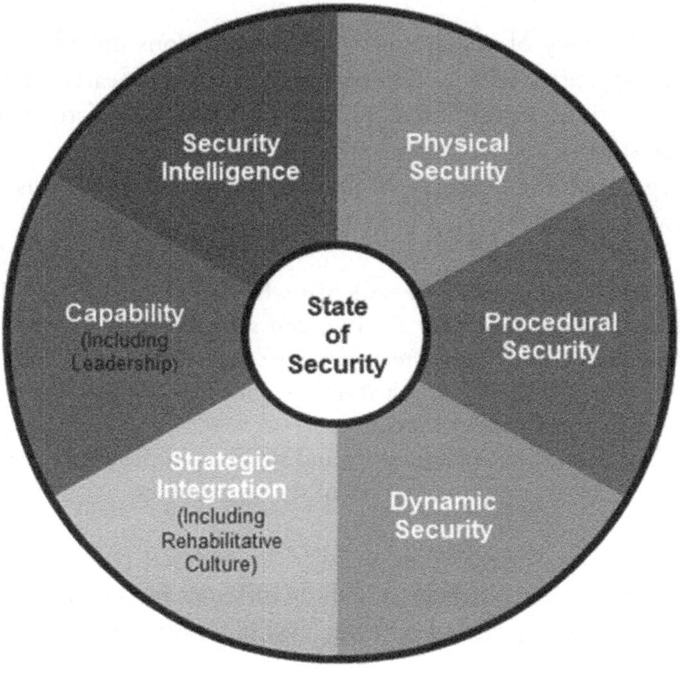

Fig. 1 State of security model

describes the degree to which leaders ensure that security is consistent with and reflect the broader aims of the organisation, including specifically the nurturing of rehabilitative cultures (Mann et al. 2018). Capability, including leadership, recognises the significance of investing in the professionalisation and development of people (Button 2021). The model is supported by tools including a process for self-assessment and improvement planning. It provides a framework for security leaders to adopt a more strategic approach by gathering information about different elements of security, evaluating strengths and weaknesses and developing improved local security strategies. The 'state of security' model intends to provide a practical vehicle for the incorporation of security research into practice.

3 Searching in Prisons

There are a variety of searches carried out in prisons including searches of people, property, vehicles and places such as cells. Searching is a core practice in prison security and will be used here to illustrate how the emerging 'state of security' approach is being applied.

The legal basis for searching of prisoners is set out in the Prison Rules 1999,[1] which state:

> 41.(1) Every prisoner shall be searched when taken into custody by an officer, on his reception into a prison and subsequently as the governor thinks necessary or as the Secretary of State may direct.
>
> (2) A prisoner shall be searched in as seemly a manner as is consistent with discovering anything concealed.
>
> (3) No prisoner shall be stripped and searched in the sight of another prisoner, or in the sight of a person of the opposite sex.

The processes for searching are detailed in national policy instructions (HMPPS 2016a; 2016b), which include different methods of searching, when they should be carried out, the level of authorisation required and

[1] Prison Rules 1999. Available at https://www.legislation.gov.uk/uksi/1999/728/contents. Accessed on 6 February 2022.

adaptations for reasons of sex, culture and religion and gender identity. The most frequent types of searching are rub-down searches, conducted by systematically feeling by hand on top of the clothing of the person being searched, to detect concealed items. Full searching, where the person being searched removes their clothing, is also used, albeit in a more limited set of circumstances. Intimate searching, conducting by looking or touching inside bodily orifices cannot lawfully be conducted by prison officers in England and Wales.

A range of aids are used in searching, including hand-held metal detectors, metal detecting arches and baggage scanners. More recently, significant investment has been made in x-ray body scanners, which can be used to detect items concealed internally within the body (HMPPS 2020b) and trace detection equipment, which can detect drugs on property (HMPPS 2021b). Specially trained dogs are also used to search for drugs, alcohol, mobile phones and arms or explosives (HMPPS 2021c).

National instructions set out the situations in which it is mandatory to conduct searching, but beyond that, it is for each prison to develop a local security strategy, which identifies the searching required to manage and mitigate risks in an individual prison (NOMS 2011). Local management should undertake regular assurance activity to ensure that the policies are being applied correctly (NOMS 2011) and there are also periodic corporate audits of security, which form part of the annual assessment of prison performance (Ministry of Justice 2020). The independent Inspectorate of Prisons include searching within their scrutiny, and their expectations state that: "Prisoners' well-being is safeguarded by effective intelligence and proportionate searching measures" (HM Inspectorate of Prisons 2017). The conduct of searching can also be the subject of grievances by prisoners or others, through the internal complaints process, externally to the Prison and Probation Ombudsman and can be the subject of litigation. Searching is therefore regulated, through policy and systems of scrutiny.

Searching in prisons is both necessary and effective. Annual data show that in the 12 months to March 2020, finds during searches included: 21,575 incidents of drugs being found; 11,792 incidents where mobile phones were confiscated; 5,510 incidents where SIM cards were retrieved and; 11,267 incidents where weapons were recovered (HMPPS 2020a).

That is not to say that searching is infallible. The rate of violence and positive drug tests in prisons, cited earlier, show that in itself searching is not eradicating the illicit economy. The evidence does, however, illustrate that searching is an important and effective security practice that can detect and reduce threats, and disrupt illicit activity. As with other settings, such as airports, effectiveness may be improved by using 'high reliability' techniques such as increased training, standardising practice and layering process for example by using physical searching accompanied by technological aids (Patankar and Holscher 2000).

Despite its regularity, apparent effectiveness and regulatory controls, searching is invasive and can be experienced as harmful or distressing by those subjected to it. In a poignant and insightful blog, Jason Warr (2020) estimated that during 12 years in prison he was subjected to 8,700 rub-down searches and over 1,000 strip searches. He describes how the imposition of "unwanted touch" was an exercise in power, which left him feeling angry, shamed and powerless. For all the legal and procedural apparatus, Warr describes that: "It doesn't take away that your nakedness, physical, emotional, psychological, is being coerced, under threat of punitive action". While Warr does not suggest that such practices should be eliminated, he highlights the lack of understanding of the effects upon those conducting as well as those subjected to searching, and the dehumanising processes when the practices becoming routinised and taken for granted. Warr also draws attention to how those who have experienced trauma and abuse, including sexual abuse may be affected in different, more intense and painful ways. This is a theme picked up in a trenchant critique by Jessica Hutchinson (2020) who has argued that women with a prior history of sexual victimisation experience searching as particularly harmful. Hutchinson goes on to describe strip searching as "state-inflicted sexual assault" (p. 168) as it is conducted under coercion in the context of a significant power imbalance between the parties involved. These two important contributions, rightly call attention to the subjective experiences of those being searched and the context of power relations in which searching is conducted.

Another area in which issues of fairness are most starkly highlighted is in relation to race and ethnicity. The conduct of searching, whether that is in airports (Lum et al. 2015) or by the police in street level stop and search (HMICFRS 2021), has been demonstrated to be disproportionately directed towards people from minority ethnic groups and this has generated a sense of unfairness. In prisons, concern has been expressed regarding unexplained disproportionality in security practices including the use of force and in the use of higher security categorisations (Lammy 2017), and again such disproportionality can undermine individual engagement and broader community cohesion.

So how can prison respond to these concerns about the use of searching and the subjective experience of individuals? Certainly, there is an arguable case that searching may be over-used and that local security strategies should be reviewed to ensure that they are proportionate to the risk and properly targeted. In addition, the approach taken in England and Wales acknowledges the problem of the subjective experience of people being searched and seeks to ameliorate the effects. This reflects the aim of the 'state of security' approach to pay attention to not only the technical and situational aspects of security but also to the social and human dimensions. One aspect of the 'state of security' model is to reconceptualise security as integrated with broader organisational strategy, including the fostering of rehabilitative cultures. HMPPS has produced a *Security and Rehabilitative Culture* sourcebook (HMPPS 2020c), which includes guidance on approaches that pay attention to the individual experiences and social effects of searching.

The first approach that is sponsored in the sourcebook is 'procedural justice' (Tyler 1990), which focuses on the procedural and relational aspects of decision-making. This approach suggests that people are more likely to accept the outcome of decisions, even if it is not favourable to them, if the process is perceived as legitimate. The key elements of procedural justice in practice are voice—that people have the opportunity to tell their story in their own words; respect—that is treating people with courtesy and politeness, and showing respect for their rights; neutrality—decision makers who make decisions based upon rules and not personal opinions, who apply legal rules consistently and are transparent about how they reach their decisions; and trust—a judgement on the character of the decision maker and whether they are acting honestly, trying to do what is right for everyone involved rather than being driven by personal prejudices (Tyler 2008). In relation to searching, the sourcebook provides examples of information notices and checklists that encourage this approach, such as prison officers explaining the purpose of the search and the basis for its authorisation (i.e. routine, random or targeted), listening to any comments or concerns and explaining the way in which the search will be conducted. The intention is not simply to develop practice that encounters less resistance but is intended to deploy the relational aspects of security practice to humanise the process for all parties involved.

The second approach in the sourcebook is to encourage trauma-informed or trauma-responsive practice. Trauma informed practice involves a commitment to adapting practices to meet the needs of people with a history of trauma (Bradley 2021). This approach is becoming more widely considered in prisons, particularly women's prisons, with training and organisational accreditation being offered to nurture more trauma-informed practice (Bradley 2021). People in prison are more likely to have experienced childhood trauma, including experiencing or witnessing abuse in the home, being taken into state care, and being excluded from school, as well as often being exposed to further traumatic experiences, including violence, as adults in the community or in prison (Williams et al. 2012; Bradley 2021). The sourcebook applies the key principles of trauma-informed practice to security activity including searching. The foundation is increasing staff awareness of the extent of trauma and possible responses by those being searched. Security staff are encouraged to adopt calm and open interpersonal engagement to foster a sense of safety; taking time to explain processes so as to establish trust; and encouraging collaboration and compliance so helping people to make positive choices—whether that be complying with a search or discussing any illicit items found to understand the context. The intention, again, is not simply to reduce resistance, but is intended to recognise and ameliorate the harmfulness of security practice, particularly where trauma responses may be triggered for trauma survivors.

The third relevant area that the sourcebook addresses is disproportionality. The sourcebook is clear that security leaders have a legal and moral duty to promote diversity and inclusion. Doing so can increase the legitimacy and effectiveness of security practice. Preventative measures include building the 'cultural competence' of staff through training and by diversifying the workforce. Structured decision-making such as the use of checklists to guide considerations in areas such as assessing intelligence and targeting security interventions, can reduce bias and support objectivity. Responsive actions include monitoring data on practices such as the conduct of searching, the use of complaints and other information, and subjecting this to scrutiny, where possible involving external representatives. The sourcebook encourages adopting the 'explain or reform' approach that was recommended by the most recent national review of disproportionality in the criminal justice system (Lammy 2017). The intention is to challenge the taken-for-granted quality of security practice and instead encourage critical questioning and engagement with wider attempts to tackle discrimination and nurture inclusivity.

The emerging approach, reflected in the 'state of security' model, situates security within the broader organisational strategy in prisons. It moves from an insular approach that views security practices as a series of technical, situational approaches, and instead gives greater attention to the social and human aspects of security, including the subjective experiences of people in prison. This approach consciously engages with the 'structuration' of security (Sparks et al. 1996) by ameliorating some of the harms and nurturing more legitimate practices.

4 Conclusion: The State of 'State of Security'

This chapter has described, discussed and reflected upon the emerging security strategy in England and Wales. The 'state of security' model has been informed by research on the concept of security, security practices and leadership models. It is intended to foster a progressive set of practices that are effective in responding to security threats, including organised crime in prison, but also sensitive to the subjective, relational and social aspects of security. In this model, the way in which security is practised should reflect the broader strategic aims of the organisation, including building more rehabilitative cultures. As the former Director of Security, Order and Counter Terrorism, Claudia Sturt described:

> …traditionally, people working within prison have almost had to choose which hat they are going to wear — whether they are focused on security or rehabilitation… What I absolutely urge people to think about is that you don't have to choose, because security serves rehabilitation. Good security should be helping the rehabilitation effort to happen safely and making a reality of it, not stopping it. (Sturt and Gooch 2021: 12)

From this perspective, security is a public good. Tackling organised crime not only reduces harm but also creates opportunities for individuals to engage in constructive activity and participate in the prison community. Further, the practices of security are being reframed as not only technical and situational but instead attention is being paid to the social and relational aspects. As has been described, this 'structuration' of security may offer a more legitimate and sustainable foundation.

At this point in time, the 'state of security' model is best seen as an articulation of a strategic intention. Work has taken place to communicate the model with senior leaders in prisons and particularly in security teams. The model has been incorporated into capability building such as training courses and other learning sessions, written communications, and is being used to inform policy development. There is also work being undertaken to integrate the model within organisational scrutiny, including audits and inspections. It must be acknowledged, however, that the implementation of the 'state of security' model is embryonic, inchoate and incomplete. As well as continuing to focus on turning strategic intention into action, there is also a need for research to understand whether the 'state of security' approach has the intended effects, including humanising and legitimising searching.

By engaging theory and applying it in practice, even if incomplete, HMPPS is responding to the challenge to make security practice more evidence-based (Button 2021). There is, however, relatively sparse attention given by criminologists to prison security practices and further attention could stimulate debate, discussion and reform. The work described and discussed in this chapter responds to Richard Sparks' invitation to deploy the criminological imagination to: "stimulate discourse, to promote conversation, and to connect distant and mutually separated settings and lives, and thereby to promote unanticipated solutions, to mediate conflict and misunderstanding and to serve the extension of democratic imagination and empathy" (Sparks 2019: 27–28). There is a hitherto underdeveloped opportunity to engage in a productive conversation between criminologists, practitioners and policy makers in the field of prison security. Such engagement offers no easy solutions but does initiate a quest in search of more effective and progressive security practices.

References

Alkire, S. 2002. *A Conceptual Framework for Human Security*. Oxford: Centre for Research on Inequality, Human Security and Ethnicity (CRISE). Available at http://citeseerx.ist.psu.edu/viewdoc/download?doi=10.1.1.580.2805&rep=rep1&type=pdf. Accessed on 5 February 2022.

Bennett, J. 2015. *The Working Lives of Prison Managers: Global Change, Local Culture and Individual Agency in the Late Modern Prison*. London: Palgrave Macmillan.

Bradley, A. 2021. Viewing Her Majesty's Prison Service through a Trauma-Informed Lens. *Prison Service Journal* 255: 4–11.

Bruster, B., and B. Peterson. 2013. Using Critical Incidents in Teaching to Promote Reflective Practice. *Reflective Practice: International and Multidisciplinary Perspectives* 14 (2): 170–182.

Button, M. 2021. Professionalising Prison Security: Developing a Model and Agenda Rooted in Research to Enhance the Delivery of Security in Prisons. *Prison Service Journal* 252: 3–8.

Drake, D. 2012. *Prisons, Punishment and the Pursuit of Security*. London: Palgrave Macmillan.

Dunbar, I. 1985. *A Sense of Direction*. London: Home Office.

Gill, M., A. Burns-Howell, G. Keats, and E. Taylor. 2007. *Demonstrating the Value of Security*. Leicester: Perpetuity Research & Consultancy International.

Gooch, K., and J. Treadwell. 2019. The Illicit Economy and Recovery—What We Need to Understand. *Prison Service Journal* 242: 56–63.

Gooch, K., and J. Treadwell. 2020. Prisoner Society in an Era of Psychoactive Substances, Organised Crime, New Drug Markets and Austerity. *British Journal of Criminology* 60 (5): 1260–1281.

Hasenstab, A. 2018. *The Thoughtful Security Practitioner: Exploring Reflective Practice in Security Risk Management*. PhD Thesis. University of Portsmouth.

Her Majesty's Inspectorate of Constabulary and Fire & Rescue Services. 2021. *Disproportionate Use of Police Powers: A Spotlight on Stop and Search and the Use of Force*. Available at https://www.justiceinspectorates.gov.uk/hmicfrs/wp-content/uploads/disproportionate-use-of-police-powers-spotlight-on-stop-search-and-use-of-force.pdf. Accessed on 6 February 2022.

HM Inspectorate of Prisons. 2017. *Expectations: Criteria for Assessing the Treatment of and Conditions for Men in Prisons. Version 5*. Available at https://www.justiceinspectorates.gov.uk/hmiprisons/wp-content/uploads/sites/4/2021/07/Expectations-FINAL-2021.pdf. Accessed on 6 February 2022.

HM Prison and Probation Service. 2016a. *Searching of the Person: PSI 07/2016a*. Available at https://assets.publishing.service.gov.uk/government/uploads/system/uploads/attachment_data/file/899420/psi-07-2016a-searching-of-the-person.pdf. Accessed on 6 February 2022.

HM Prison and Probation Service. 2016b. *Procedures for Searching Cells, Areas and Vehicles: PSI 09/2016b*. Available at https://assets.publishing.service.gov.uk/government/uploads/system/uploads/attachment_data/file/899419/psi-09-2016b-cell-area-vehicle-searching.pdf. Accessed on 6 February 2022.

HM Prison and Probation Service. 2019. *Serious and Organised Crime Policy Framework*. Available at https://assets.publishing.service.gov.uk/government/uploads/system/uploads/attachment_data/file/838763/serious-organised-crime-pf.pdf. Accessed on 5 February 2022

HM Prison and Probation Service. 2020a. *HMPPS Annual Digest 2019/20*. Available at https://assets.publishing.service.gov.uk/government/uploads/system/uploads/attachment_data/file/991704/HMPPS-annual-digest-2019-20.pdf. Accessed on 5 February 2022.

HM Prison and Probation Service. 2020b. *Use of X-Ray Body Scanners (Adult Male Prisons)*. Available at https://assets.publishing.service.gov.uk/government/uploads/system/uploads/attachment_data/file/886000/x-ray-body-scanners-use-pf.pdf. Accessed on 6 February 2022.

HM Prison and Probation Service. 2020c. *Security and Rehabilitative Culture: A Sourcebook for Managers at All Levels Leading Security in Prisons*. Unpublished internal document.

HM Prison and Probation Service. 2021a. *Safety in Custody Statistics, England and Wales: Deaths in Prison Custody to June 2021, Assaults and Self-Harm to March 2021*. Available at https://www.gov.uk/government/statistics/safety-in-custody-quarterly-update-to-march-2021/safety-in-custody-statistics-england-and-wales-deaths-in-prison-custody-to-june-2021-assaults-and-self-harm-to-march-2021. Accessed on 5 February 2022

HM Prison and Probation Service. 2021b. *Use of Narcotics Trace Detection Equipment on Correspondence Policy Framework*. Available at https://assets.publishing.service.gov.uk/government/uploads/system/uploads/attachment_data/file/1010436/use-narcotics-trace-detection-equipment-pf.pdf#:~:text=Background%20Narcotics%20trace%20detection%20equipment%20is%20utilised%20throughout,the%20detection%20of%20paper%20impregnated%20with%20illicit%20substances. Accesses on 6 February 2022.

HM Prison and Probation Service. 2021c. *HMPPS Prison Dogs Policy Framework*. Available at https://assets.publishing.service.gov.uk/government/uploads/system/uploads/attachment_data/file/1036983/prison-dogs-policy-framework.pdf. Accessed on 6 February 2022.

Hutchison, J. 2020. "It's Sexual Assault. It's Barbaric": Strip Searching in Women's Prisons as State-Inflicted Sexual Assault. *Affilia* 35 (2): 160–176.

Lammy, D. 2017. *The Lammy Review: An Independent Review into the Treatment of, and Outcomes for, Black, Asian and Minority Ethnic Individuals in the Criminal Justice System*. Available at https://assets.publishing.service.gov.uk/government/uploads/system/uploads/attachment_data/file/643001/lammy-review-final-report.pdf. Accessed on 6 February 2022.

Learmont, J. 1995. *Review of Prison Service Security in England and Wales and the Escape from Parkhurst Prison on Tuesday 3 January 1995*. London: HMSO.

Loader, I., and N. Walker. 2007. *Civilising Security*. Cambridge: Cambridge University Press.

Lum, C., P. Crafton, R. Parsons, D. Beech, T. Smarr, and M. Connors. 2015. Discretion and Fairness in Airport Security Screening. *Security Journal* 28: 352–373.

Mann, R.E., F. Fitzalan Howard, and J. Tew. 2018. What Is a Rehabilitative Prison Culture? *Prison Service Journal* 235: 3–9.

Ministry of Justice. 2020. *Annual Prison Performance Ratings 2019/20*. Available at https://assets.publishing.service.gov.uk/government/uploads/system/uploads/attachment_data/file/913004/annual-prison-performance-ratings-2019-20-bulletin.pdf. Accessed on 6 February 2022.

National Crime Agency. 2018. *National Strategic Assessment of Serious and Organised Crime 2018*. Available at National Strategic Assessment of Serious and Organised Crime 2018 v1.1 (nationalcrimeagency.gov.uk) accessed on 2 February 2022.

National Offender Management System. 2011. *Management of the Local Security Strategy (LSS): PSI 63/2011*. Available at https://assets.publishing.service.gov.uk/government/uploads/system/uploads/attachment_data/file/900756/psi-63-2011-local-security-strategy.pdf. Accessed on 6 February 2022.

Patankar, M., and L. Holscher. 2000. Accessibility vs Security: The Challenge to Airport Security System. *Security Journal* 13: 7–19.

Schon, D. 1983. *The Reflective Practitioner*. New York: Basic books.

Sparks, R. 2019. *Beyond the Rendez-vous: Criminology, Critique, Connection.* Public Lecture, Leuven 29 April 2019. Available at https://www.law.kuleuven.be/apps/leden/storage/content/docs/c7f9d2b9b0ca8e6562023f9005bb3751.pdf. Accessed on 6 February 2022

Sparks, R., A. Bottoms, and W. Hay. 1996. *Prisons and the Problem of Order*. Oxford: Clarendon Press.

Sturt, C., and K. Gooch. 2021. Leading Prison Security: Interview with Claudia Sturt, Executive Director for Security, Order and Counter Terrorism. *Prison Service Journal* 252: 9–14.

Tyler, T.R. 1990. *Why People Obey the Law*. New Haven: Yale University Press.

Tyler, T.R. 2008. Procedural Justice and the Courts. *Court Review* 44: 26–31.

Warr, J. 2020. The Power of Touch. *Sensory Criminology*. Available at https://sensorycriminology.com/tag/search/. Accessed on 6 February 2022.

Williams, K., V. Papadopoulou, and N. Booth. 2012. *Prisoners' Childhood and Family Backgrounds: Results from the Durveying Prisoner Crime Reduction (SPCR) Longitudinal Cohort Study of Prisoners*. London: Ministry of Justice. Available at https://assets.publishing.service.gov.uk/government/uploads/system/uploads/attachment_data/file/278837/prisoners-childhood-family-backgrounds.pdf. Accessed on 5 March 2022.

Woodcock, J. 1994. *Report of an Inquiry into the Escape of Six Prisoners from the Special Secure Unit at Whitemoor Prison in Cambridgeshire on Friday 9 September 1994*. London: HMSO.

Zedner, L. 2009. *Security*. London: Routledge.

Strip Searches: A Risky Practice That Needs to Be Monitored

Barbara Bernath

1 Introduction

Ensuring the safety and security of all persons who are living, working and accessing prisons is part of the State's responsibility when depriving someone of his or her liberty. However, security needs to be balanced with dignity and this difficult balancing exercise is perfectly illustrated with the issue of body searches. Body searches may be justified to prevent the entry of illegal goods into prison but due to their intrusive nature and their infringement on a person's privacy, they inherently come with risks of humiliation, abuses or even ill-treatment.

Body searches take different forms including pat-down or frisk searches that include physical contact but no nudity, strip searches that

B. Bernath (✉)
Association for the Prevention of Torture, Geneva, Switzerland
e-mail: bbernath@apt.ch

T. Daems (ed.), *Body Searches and Imprisonment*, Palgrave Studies in Prisons and Penology,
https://doi.org/10.1007/978-3-031-20451-7_4

include nudity but no contact and body cavity searches that are a physical examination of body orifices.[1]

'All types of body search can be intimidating and degrading, and the more intrusive the method, the stronger the feeling of invasion will be' (APT and PRI 2015: 1). International human rights law has initially overlooked the inherent risks of infringement of person's dignity and privacy that come with the conduct of body searches in prisons. This practice has however been more and more regulated and international human rights standards have recently limited its use and clarified the modalities of its conduct. However, even if the adoption of international norms and standards regulating body searches is a welcome development, it is not enough in itself to reduce the risks inherent in such a practice.

The domestication of international standards needs to be reviewed and more importantly, the way the norms are implemented in practice needs to be monitored. Monitoring bodies that regularly visit places of detention—such as the European Committee for the Prevention of Torture (CPT) and especially National Preventive Mechanisms (NPM) established under the Optional Protocol to the UN Convention Against Torture (OPCAT)[2]—have a key role to play in ensuring transparency and accountability of prison procedures and functioning in general and the use of body searches in particular.

This chapter therefore proposes to look at the importance of monitoring the conduct of body searches. It focuses on strip searches. Out of the three types of searches, it is the one where the balancing exercise between the pursuit of a legitimate purpose and the use of '… a very invasive and potentially degrading measure' (CPT 2018a: 7) is very challenging. From a prevention of torture perspective, strip searches represent a typical grey zone that needs to be carefully regulated and closely monitored.

[1] These are prohibited by the 'Principles and Best Practices on the Protection of Persons Deprived of Liberty in the Americas' (Inter-American Commission on Human Rights, Resolution 1/08), principle XXI: 'Intrusive vaginal or anal searches shall be forbidden by law'.

[2] Optional Protocol to the Convention against Torture and other Cruel, Inhuman or Degrading Treatment or Punishment, adopted 18 December 2002 by the fifty-seventh session of the General Assembly of the United Nations by resolution A/RES/57/199.

This chapter will first look at the context and existing international legal framework regulating body searches as well as oversight mechanisms. It will then focus on the role of monitoring bodies in questioning why strip searches are being used. The final section discusses the role of monitoring bodies in examining how strip searches are conducted in practice.

2 Context and Legal Framework: Development of International Standards on Body Searches and on Oversight Bodies

International and regional standards have been progressively developed to regulate the use of body searches. In parallel, the international legal framework also provides oversight mechanisms that can monitor the implementation of the legal framework in practice.

2.1 International Standards Define and Regulate the Use and Modalities of Body Searches

The inherent tension between the security objective of body searches and the risks inherent in the conduct of a practice involving nudity has led to the development of international and regional standards reiterating the importance of the respect for dignity when performing searches.

The use of body searches also has to respect the absolute prohibition of torture and other cruel, inhuman and degrading treatment and punishment under international law that is not only enshrined in many treaties but also recognized as a norm of customary law.[3]

[3] Article 5 of the Universal Declaration of Human Rights, Article 7 of the International Covenant on Civil and Political Rights, Article 1 of the UN Convention Against Torture, Article 3 of the European Convention on Human Rights.

In addition, human rights international law also provides for the right for detainees to be '…treated with humanity and with respect for the inherent dignity of the human person'.[4]

The 2015 revised UN Standard Minimum Rules on the Treatment of Prisoners (the Nelson Mandela Rules)[5] also reaffirm this in its new Rule 1, stating that

> All prisoners shall be treated with the respect due to their inherent dignity and value as human beings. No prisoner shall be subjected to, and all prisoners shall be protected from, torture and other cruel, inhuman or degrading treatment or punishment, for which no circumstances whatsoever may be invoked as a justification. The safety and security of prisoners, staff, service providers and visitors shall be ensured at all times.

In addition, taking into account the fact that body searches are a particularly risky practice, the Nelson Mandela Rules also add specific provisions reaffirming the need to respect human dignity in the conduct of body searches. The 2010 UN Rules for the Treatment of Women Prisoners and Non-Custodial Measures for Women Offenders (the Bangkok Rules)[6] also provide additional protection for women detainees. Rule 19 states the following: 'Effective measures shall be taken to ensure that women prisoners' dignity and respect are protected during personal searches'.[7]

Nelson Mandela Rule 50 specifies that 'Searches shall be conducted in a manner that is respectful of the inherent human dignity and privacy of the individual being searched, as well as the principles of proportionality, legality and necessity'. Rule 51 adds that 'Searches shall not be used to harass, intimidate or unnecessarily intrude upon a prisoner's privacy'. European Prison Rule 54.4 further specifies that 'Persons being searched shall not be humiliated by the searching process'.[8]

---

[4] Article 10 of the International Covenant on Civil and Political Rights.

[5] 70th session of the UN General Assembly in Resolution A/RES/70/175, adopted on 17 December 2015.

[6] 65th session of the UN General Assembly in Resolution A/RES/65/229, adopted on 16 March 2011.

[7] On heightened risks faced by persons in situation of vulnerability, see also APT (2018, 2022).

[8] Recommendation Rec(2006)2-rev of the Committee of Ministers to member States on the European Prison Rules (Adopted by the Committee of Ministers on 11 January 2006, at the

In addition, international and regional standards have also defined and clarified modalities to limit the inherent risks and ensure respect for dignity in practice. First 'Intrusive searches, including strip and body cavity searches, should be undertaken only if absolutely necessary' (Nelson Mandela Rule 52). They shall respect the 'principles of proportionality, legality and necessity' (Nelson Mandela Rule 50)[9] and procedures need to be properly regulated (Bangkok Rule 19; European Prison Rule 54.2).

Norms have also clarified that body searches can only be conducted by staff of the same gender that is adequately trained to conduct searches (Nelson Mandela Rule 52; Bangkok Rule 19; European Prison Rule 54.5). In addition, body cavity searches shall not be conducted by prison staff but '...only by qualified health-care professionals other than those primarily responsible for the care of the prisoner or, at a minimum, by staff appropriately trained by a medical professional in standards of hygiene, health and safety' (Nelson Mandela Rule 52.2; see also European Prison Rule 54.3). The modalities have also been clarified in terms of need for respect for privacy. Last but not least, international standards recommend the use of alternatives to intrusive searches (Nelson Mandela Rule 52.1; Bangkok Rule 20).

2.2 The Role and Powers of Independent Monitoring Bodies Are Being Recognized

Prisons have long been places closed to outside scrutiny and ruled by the principles of opacity and secrecy, allowing for torture and ill-treatment to occur. Therefore, the Association for the Prevention of Torture (APT) has been promoting since the late 1970s, a shift towards transparency through the creation of a system of regular and unannounced visits to places of detention (see APT 2007). This advocacy led to the progressive

952nd meeting of the Ministers' Deputies and revised and amended by the Committee of Ministers on 1 July 2020 at the 1380th meeting of the Ministers' Deputies).

[9] See also Principle XXI of the Principles and best Practices on the Protection of Persons Deprived of Liberty in the Americas.

acceptance of transparency and adoption of treaties providing access to places of detention by external independent bodies.

A system of regular visits to all places of deprivation of liberty was first established within the Council of Europe with the adoption, in 1987, of the European Convention for the Prevention of Torture creating the European Committee for the Prevention of torture (CPT). Since its first visits in 1990, the CPT has not only proven to play a very valuable role in improving treatment and conditions of detention but has also developed a corpus of standards that serve as a reference for the prevention of torture beyond the Council of Europe. Based on its preventive mandate, the CPT has regularly looked at the issue of the risks of ill-treatment linked with the conduct of body searches.

In 2002, the United Nations adopted the Optional Protocol to the UN Convention against Torture (OPCAT) which creates a system of visits at two levels, by an international body, the UN Subcommittee on Prevention of Torture (SPT), and by national bodies. State Parties have to create or designate a National Preventive Mechanism (NPM) mandated to visit any place of deprivation of liberty at any time (Articles 3 and 17 OPCAT). The SPT has a double mandate of conducting visits to places of detention in the State Parties and advising and supporting NPMs (Article 11 OPCAT). This innovative treaty is not creating any new norms but is establishing a monitoring system based on a unique tripartite relation between the State, the SPT and the NPMs aimed at better-protecting persons deprived of their liberty (see Articles 1, 11b, 12 and 20f OPCAT).

With the OPCAT extensive powers of a national body have for the first time been anchored and guaranteed by an international legally binding treaty: NPMs have powers of access to all places of deprivation of liberty and all facilities within the place; can conduct interviews in private with detainees of their choice and have access to all documentation and information (Article 19 OPCAT). Following their visits NPMs submit reports and recommendations to the authorities which have an obligation to examine them and enter into dialogue on their implementation (Article 22 OPCAT). At the time of writing (July 2022), there are 91 State Parties to the OPCAT worldwide and 75 NPMs are operational in different regions. The OPCAT does not prescribe any specific form for these NPMs but in most countries, the existing National Human Rights Institution or Ombuds Institution has been designated as NPM.[10]

The important preventive role played by monitoring bodies has led to a strengthening of the provisions related to prison inspection in the 2015 Nelson Mandela Rules. The Mandela Rules provide for a twofold inspection system: in addition to the internal inspection conducted by the prison administration, there shall also be external inspections conducted by an independent body (Nelson Mandela Rule 83.1).

The extensive powers entrusted to external inspections by the Nelson Mandela Rules are very similar to the powers foreseen by the OPCAT. Indeed, Nelson Mandela Rule 84.1 not only provides access to all places of detention but also the power to conduct unannounced visits. External inspection bodies have access to information including records and the power to conduct interviews in private with staff and detainees.

The objective of the inspection is to ensure that prisons are managed '…in accordance with existing laws, regulations, policies and procedures, with a view to bringing about the objectives of penal and corrections services, and that the rights of prisoners are protected' (Nelson Mandela Rule 83.2). Following visits, external inspection bodies submit a written report, with recommendations, that could be made public. Authorities '…shall indicate, within a reasonable time, whether they will implement the recommendations resulting from the external inspection' (Nelson Mandela Rule 85.2).

With the inclusion of external inspections in the Nelson Mandela Rules, the importance of independent monitoring is recognized and applicable beyond States that have ratified the OPCAT. Monitoring bodies, either international, regional or national established under the OPCAT or under the Nelson Mandela Rules, play a key role in monitoring the respect of international and domestic standards in practice. Thanks to their presence inside places of detention they play a deterrent role. More importantly, through their direct access and private interviews with persons deprived of their liberty, they can get first-hand information about the reality of the treatment and daily life in prisons. They also get information from the authorities as they can conduct interviews with

[10] See APT OPCAT Database www.apt.ch.

the staff. In addition, they can examine all documents, registers, records and other types of information relevant and available in order to cross-check the information collected from detainees. This enables oversight bodies to conduct a complete and systemic analysis of the functioning of the prison as an institution. This is essential to understand how risky practices such as strip searches are regulated and conducted in practice. Thanks to their extensive powers, monitoring bodies, in particular, NPMs, can question practices and offer needed external scrutiny and accountability. As mentioned by the Italian NPM ('Garante nazionale dei diritti delle persone detenute o private della libertà personale'), oversight and observation means "...to exercise a form of democratic control (...) and (...) to provide help to those who act in various ways within the 'microcosm' represented by each total institution" (Garante 2020: 123).[11]

3 Why? The Role of Monitoring Bodies in Reviewing the Legality, Necessity and Proportionality of Body Searches

Body searches can play a legitimate role in ensuring safety and security in prisons but this has to be balanced with respect for the dignity of all persons. The use of body searches therefore needs to come with a series of safeguards. In this regard, international human rights law has carefully defined limitations and clarified the important principles that need to govern the use of body searches in prisons. The Nelson Mandela Rules recall that searches shall be conducted in a manner that is respectful of the overarching '...principles of proportionality, legality and necessity' (Nelson Mandela Rule 50). Oversight bodies play, thanks to their extensive powers, a crucial role in monitoring the respect of these principles in practice.

[11] The Garante is quoting M. Palma *L'idea della pena nel mondo globalizzato,* in Rassegna penitenziaria e criminologica 2015, no. 2, pp. 215 and ff.

3.1 Role of Monitoring Bodies in Checking the Legality of Strip Searches

International standards only specify that body searches have to be necessary but leave it to national law to define the '...situations in which such searches are necessary' (European Prison Rule 54.2). This means that strip searches need to be regulated by national legislation or other forms of regulation, such as internal circulars or guidelines.

As part of their broad mandate and powers, monitoring bodies and NPMs need to examine the legality of strip searches and assess the existence of the national legal framework and its conformity with international standards. The Italian NPM, for example, has called upon the prison authorities to respect the provisions of circular 3542/5992 issued by the Prison Department (Garante 2018: 105). In Norway, the NPM criticized the fact that the Guidelines to the Execution of Sentences Act provide for body searches to be conducted 'as far as practically possible' by a staff member of the same sex (Sivilombudsmannen 2018: 21). This is not in conformity with existing international standards which stipulate that searches be conducted by persons of the same gender (Nelson Mandela Rule 52; Bangkok Rule 19; European Prison Rule 54.5). In France, Article 57 of the 2009 Penitentiary Law introduced a restrictive approach to the use of strip searches, allowing them only on the basis of an individual assessment.[12] However, in 2015, governmental amendments to Article 57—as part of a draft law against organized crime and terrorism—proposed to open up the possibilities of strip searches in certain places, for a certain period, independently of the personality of the detainee. The French General Controller of Places of Deprivation of Liberty ('Contrôleur général des lieux de privation de liberté' [CGLPL]), the French NPM, expressed concerns about opening up the justifications for body searches in a letter to Members of Parliamentary Committee examining the bill (CGLPL 2016). The amendments were eventually adopted.

Monitoring the domestic legal framework is therefore an important task for NPMs in order to limit the circumstances and the situations

---

[12] On this, see the chapter by Falxa, this volume.

where strip searches could be considered legitimate in the pursuit of security. Legal norms are often subject to interpretation, and it is important for monitoring bodies to call for a restrictive interpretation of the legal basis (CGLPL 2019: 42).

Finally, monitoring bodies can make observations and comments on existing legislation or propose new legislation (Art 19 OPCAT). Moreover, they can also promote good practices as part of a general or thematic standard setting exercise based on their practice. The French NPM has published minimum recommendations to respect the dignity and fundamental rights of people deprived of liberty (CGLPL 2019). The Italian NPM published a recommendation called 'elementary' rather than 'minimal' on the rights of persons deprived of liberty in prisons[13] where it compiled its recommendations on different issues, including body searches. In the UK, Her Majesty's Inspectorate of Prisons (HMIP) published so-called 'Prison Expectations' which specifies the standards against which it conducts its monitoring and formulates its recommendations (HMIP 2017, 2021). Such standards and recommendations serve as a useful reference for all prison authorities regarding strip searches, independently of any specific visit or report.

3.2 Role of NPMs in Monitoring the Respect of the Principle of Necessity

According to the Nelson Mandela Rules 'Intrusive searches, including strip and body cavity searches, should be undertaken only if *absolutely* necessary' (Nelson Mandela Rule 52.1; emphasis added). The role of monitoring bodies is therefore also to question the general assumption made by prison authorities that strip searches are necessary to ensure security and prevent the entry of prohibited items or substances.

[13] 'The distinction between minimum and elementary is not secondary. A minimum standard is limited to indicating the threshold below which a particular aspect of detention is unacceptable and risks becoming an "inhuman or degrading treatment" – and a possible breach of article 3 of the European Convention on Human Rights. Thus, a downward target. An elementary standard indicates a reachable and accessible target and at the same time, indicates that change is possible, toward progressive improvement' (Garante 2018: 6).

Strip searches are usually considered as necessary by the prison authorities following contacts between the detainees and the outside world or with other persons, i.e. in situations such as:

- upon arrival
- when detainees are placed in isolation or a security cell
- when returning from leave
- after family visits
- after contacts with lawyers or doctors, in principle only when detainees have been left unsupervised
- after return from workshops, activities and outdoor exercise.

Such a rather long list of generic moments or situations where strip searches could be applied systematically to all detainees, as a blanket policy, may not respond to the criteria of necessity. It comes with a risk of arbitrariness and disproportionality, and it is important for monitoring bodies to keep the objective of strip searches in mind during their visits.

Monitoring bodies can review the respect of the principle of necessity by questioning the systematic use of body searches as well as the use of random searches. Indeed, in the case of Roth v. Germany, where random strip searches were applied systematically prior and after receiving visitors to every detainee out of five, the European Court of Human Rights (ECtHR) concluded that the

> ...feeling of arbitrariness and the feelings of inferiority and anxiety often associated with them, as well as the feeling of serious affront to dignity indisputably prompted by the obligation to undress in front of another person and submit to inspection of the anus, resulted in a degree of humiliation exceeding the - unavoidable and hence tolerable - level that strip-searches of prisoners inevitably involve.[14]

The CPT has therefore constantly recommended a change from a blanket systematic policy towards an individualized approach. In its report on the 2020 visit to Monaco, it argued, for example, that the use of body searches must be based on an individual risk assessment and subject to

[14] *Roth v. Germany*, App. No. 6780/18 and 30776/18, 22 October 2020, para 72.

criteria of appropriateness and proportionality (CPT 2021a: 28). The Italian NPM has also considered that 'personal searches, sometimes even squatting, cannot constitute a routine practice and method for maintaining internal order, not even when conducted periodically and at random' (Garante 2018: 105). In Norway, the NPM has also criticized the practice of routine body searches involving full removal of clothes when inmates were placed in security cells. Such a practice is not in line with the recommendation for an individualized approach (Sivilombudsmannen 2018: 18).

Monitoring bodies can also review and question the rationale behind strip searches, i.e. the actual link between the objective of preventing the illegal entry of goods and its actual reality. In its 2016 letter to Members of Parliament, the French Controller mentioned that there is no evidence for a link between a restrictive use of body searches and an increase in the introduction of prohibited items (CGLPL 2016). The French NPM analysed the number of searches and the seizure of illegal items following searches: the success rate was quite low (for example, in Marseille 3.15% for searches following visits and 1.23% for searches in other circumstances [CGLPL 2020c: 104]). In its report following the visit to the Penitentiary Centre of Villefranche-sur-Saône, the NPM published statistics and tables showing that there is little correlation between the number of strip searches and the level of seizure of prohibited goods. Indeed, the level of seizure is much higher in the case of ad hoc searches based on suspicion which are less numerous than systematic searches applied to specific detainees or specific situations (CGLPL 2020b: 71–72).

There are sometimes positive developments regarding a more individualized approach of searches, such as in the case of Monaco where systematic searches of detainees following meetings with their lawyers, judicial agents ('auxiliaire de justice') or consular authority were stopped following the CPT visits and recommendations (CPT 2021a).

However, there are sometimes also setbacks. In 2019 amendments to Article 57 of the 2009 Penitentiary Law in France introduced two exceptions to the principle of individualization of body searches. First, the prison director can authorize systematic searches of some detainees when required by the necessity of public order or the constraints of public service for a (renewable) period of 3 months. The French NPM is now closely monitoring the respect of the limits placed by the amended Article 57. With these new powers, prison directors can identify 'specific detainees' ('détenus particulièrement signalés' [DPS]) who have to undergo systematic strip searches following family visits. The NPM is carefully monitoring that such decisions are limited in time and reviewed every 3 months (CGLPL 2020a: 65–66) and that prisoners are properly informed and decisions adequately motivated (see e.g. CGLPL 2021a: 41). In addition, the French NPM is also reminding the authorities that being put on this list cannot be used as a form of punishment (CGLPL 2020b: 70–74).

Second, the prison director can also order searches independently from personal circumstances when there are serious reasons to suspect the introduction of items or substances that are prohibited or that constitute a threat to the security of persons or of goods. The French NPM is stating 'its opposition in principle' to the possibility of planned searches for a group of persons in a place or for a specific activity (CGLPL 2021b: 73). In addition, in its 2019 Minimum Recommendations, it is also stressing that the use of checks and searches should not '...constitute a systematic response to transgressive behaviour, much less a systematic response to general risks' (CGLPL 2019: 41). In its report on the 2019 visit to France the CPT recommended to take necessary measures to ensure, in law and practice, that strip searches be conducted following an individual risk assessment (CPT 2021b: 62–63).

More could be done by monitoring bodies in analysing and questioning the necessity of strip searches and especially their usefulness in achieving their intended purpose of prohibiting the entry of illicit items in prisons.

3.3 The Role of Monitoring Bodies in Reviewing the Proportionality of Strip Searches

Monitoring bodies can also review the proportionality of strip searches. This relates both to the frequency as well as to the requirement of selecting the least intrusive method to achieve the intended security objective. In Monaco, the CPT considered that the number and frequency of searches was very high: in 2019 each detained person had on average been subjected to 54 searches, more than one every two days (CPT 2021a: 28). In Slovakia, in one prison, detainees had to undergo up to four searches in a day when transferred to Court. The CPT was of the opinion that such a '…resort to multiple strip-searches …appears to be disproportionate' (CPT 2019a: 29).

Monitoring bodies should also monitor that strip searches are a measure of last resort and that less intrusive alternatives are chosen when these are available. However, in the UK, where most prisons are equipped with body scanners or metal detectors, Her Majesty's Inspectorate of Prisons observed that all detainees are—in addition to the use of searching technology—routinely subjected to strip searches (HMIP 2022a: 18; 2022c: 19; 2022e: 20), a measure that is disproportionate and not in line with the requirement of last resort.

4 How? The Role of Monitoring Bodies in Reviewing the Way Strip Searches Are Conducted in Practice

Even when strip searches respect the principle of legality, necessity and proportionality, the way they are conducted in practice may present risks of ill-treatment.

As mentioned above, international standards have better defined the modalities of conducting strip searches and clarified who, how and where searches should be conducted. Oversight bodies in general, and NPMs, in particular, have extensive powers of access to places, to information, and to persons, and they should make full use of these powers to monitor whether the norms are respected and how strip searches are conducted in practice. In addition, through their regular visits, NPMs have a comparative overview of the reality in different prisons and can question any differences in the implementation of the legislation.

NPMs have access to 'all information' referring to the treatment of persons deprived of their liberty in places of detention '… as well as their conditions of detention' (Article 20 OPCAT). During their visits, NPMs can examine the existence and maintenance of registers and records, as requested by Nelson Mandela Rule 51. Examining such registers provides important information about the respect of legal norms. Carefully examining registers is also an important source of information to cross-check information received from detainees during interviews in private and ensure a triangulation of information. In the UK, Her Majesty's Inspectorate of Prisons is conducting anonymous surveys before the actual visit and one of the question is 'When you were searched in reception, was it done in a respectful way?'. The vast majority of the response is positive but a proportion varying between 14 and 24% of the detainees usually respond negatively (for example, HMIP 2022b: 8, 2022d: 8; 2022f: 8).

During its visits, the French NPM noted that recording varied in practice and that not all types of searches were properly and electronically recorded. Searches conducted following family visits were properly recorded, even if the motivation of the searches was often very vague. However, searches conducted when detainees returned to their cells from the courtyard were not well recorded (CGLPL 2020a: 66). The lack of traceability of the different searches has been criticized by the French NPM.

As registers should also record the name and identity of the staff conducting searches, NPMs can, for example, monitor whether the searches are conducted by staff of the same gender as the detainee. This remains an issue in Norway, where the NPM reports that documentation '... showed that body searches of female inmates in security cells had been carried out with male prison officers present' and vice versa (Sivilombudsmannen 2018: 21; see also CPT 2018a, b: 106). In another prison, both staff and inmates '... confirmed that it was standard practice to have both a male and a female officer present. Inmates confirmed that the female officer was supposed to turn her back to the inmate during the last part of the undressing process, but some found the presence of female staff in that cramped room to be intrusive' (Sivilombudsmannen 2017: 35).

As strip searches come with a '...feeling of serious affront to dignity indisputably prompted by the obligation to undress in front of another person',[15] it is important to make sure that '...every time a strip search is deemed necessary that it be carried out in a manner so as to limit embarrassment and preserve the dignity of the person' (CPT 2020: 30; see also CPT 2021a: 28; 2021c: 43; 2019c: 35).

One of the modalities, recommended by the CPT, is to make sure that the searches are conducted in two phases. 'The prisoner who are searched should not normally be required to remove all their clothes at the same time, e.g. a person should be allowed to remove clothing above the waist and get dressed again before removing further clothing' (CPT 2019b: 101; 2019c: 84, 2020: 55). However, in several recent visits, the CPT noted that this is not respected in practice (CPT 2019c, 2020, 2021c). During its visit to Ila prison, the Norwegian NPM was informed that the prison had considered such two-stage body searches, but that it did not wish to introduce them. The NPM therefore recommended that 'Ila should consider introducing two-stage body searches or other similar methods to make the body search process as non-invasive as possible' (Sivilombudsmannen 2017: 8).

During their visits, monitoring bodies have access to all the facilities and rooms within a prison and can therefore also examine the equipment and location of the rooms where body searches are conducted. The UK NPM, for example, has examined searches upon arrival and has sometimes been critical about the lack of privacy in the area (HMIP 2022a: 18, 2022c: 19). The French NPM has looked at the equipment, cleanliness and privacy of the room where searches are conducted. It has systematically included photos of the rooms used for searches in the arrival/visit area in its visit reports (see e.g. CGLPL 2020a: 67; 2020b: 73; 2020c: 104).

However, NPMs have to be alert to the fact that searches are not conducted only upon arrival or following leave or extraction. When strip searches are conducted following return from courtyard or in association with cell searches, they can be conducted in other places.

During its visit to Villefranche-sur-Saône Penitentiary Centre, the French NPM noted that body searches conducted together with the weekly cell searches, were conducted in the showers, and in a collective

[15] *Roth v. Germany*, App. No. 6780/18 and 30776/18, 22 October 2020, para 72.

way, in groups of 5 detainees, in the presence of several prison officers, including female staff (CGLPL 2020b: 73). During these searches, several mistreatments and inappropriate behaviours took place, including inappropriate touching and verbal humiliation. The French NPM therefore recommended that collective searches be prohibited and stressed that such measures should not give rise to any humiliating practice (CGLPL 2020b: 74).

Interviews in private are one of the most important powers of the NPMs aimed at collecting information and testimonies about the actual practice of body searches and also about their impact on persons deprived of liberty. 'Several inmates said that they were apprehensive about body search situations and therefore chose not to work in the garden nursery outside the prison because this entailed daily body searches' (Sivilombudsmannen 2017: 35). Interviews, out of hearing and possibly out of sight of the staff, enable NPMs to establish trust with the detainees and collect sensitive information and testimonies, such as humiliating practices, gestures or comments. These may be difficult to verify but when they are both frequent and precise, NPMs can call on the authorities to monitor and address the situation.

Finally, monitoring bodies also have a general role in monitoring other aspects of the conduct of strip searches. In particular, they can monitor the consequences of refusing to undergo body searches and the use of disciplinary sanctions. In many situations, a refusal to undergo strip searches may lead to the placement in isolation cells. NPMs can examine the registers of placement in solitary cells, as part of their overall monitoring. In the case of Milka v. Poland, the European Court of Human Rights considered that the placement in solitary cell, as sanction following the third refusal to undergo strip searches, is of a serious nature.[16]

As part of their overall review of the institutional functioning of prisons, oversight bodies can also look at the issue of training and how the staff is trained in conducting strip searches. European Prison Rule 54.3 stipulates that 'Staff shall be trained to carry out these searches in such a way as to detect and prevent any attempt to escape or to hide

[16] *Milka v. Poland*, App. No. 14322/12, 15 September 2015.

contraband, while at the same time respecting the dignity of those being searched and their personal possessions'.

Thanks to their extensive powers during their prison visits, oversight bodies play a key role in monitoring how strip searches are conducted in practice and make recommendations to improve the modalities and the respect for the dignity of the detainees.

References

APT. 2007. *Letting in the light: 30 years of Torture Prevention.* Geneva: APT. https://www.apt.ch/sites/default/files/publications/apt30years.pdf.

APT. 2018. *Towards the effective protection of LGBTI persons deprived of liberty: A monitoring guide.* Geneva: APT. https://www.apt.ch/en/resources/publications/towards-effective-protection-lgbti-persons-deprived-liberty-monitoring-guide.

APT. 2022. *Women in detention: Body searches. Improving protection in situations of vulnerability.* Geneva: APT. https://www.apt.ch/en/resources/publications/women-detention-body-searches

APT and PRI. 2015. *Body searches: Addressing risk factors to prevent torture and ill-treatment*, 2nd ed. London: PRI. https://cdn.penalreform.org/wp-content/uploads/2016/01/factsheet-4-searches-2nd-v5.pdf

CGLPL. 2016. *Lettre à la Commission mixte paritaire, Assemblée nationale, 3 mai 2016.* http://www.cglpl.fr/wp-content/uploads/2016/05/Lettre-fouilles_CMP.pdf.

CGLPL. 2019. *Contrôleur Général des Lieux de Privation de Liberté's Minimum Recommendations to Respect the Dignity and Fundamental Rights of People Deprived of Liberty.* Paris: CGLPL. https://www.cglpl.fr/wp-content/uploads/2020/07/CGLPL-Minimum-Recommendations_EN.pdf.

CGLPL. 2020a. *Rapport de visite: 3 au 11 décembre 2020 – 2ème visite Centre pénitentiaire de Beauvais (Oise).* Paris: CGLPL. https://www.cglpl.fr/wp-content/uploads/2022/02/Rapport-de-la-deuxi%C3%A8me-visite-du-centre-p%C3%A9nitentiaire-de-Beauvais-Oise.pdf.

CGLPL. 2020b. *Rapport de visite: 30 novembre au 7 décembre 2020 – 3ème visite Centre pénitentiaire de Villefranche-sur-Saône (Rhône).* Paris: CGLPL.

https://www.cglpl.fr/wp-content/uploads/2021/12/Rapport-de-la-troisi%C3%A8me-visite-du-centre-p%C3%A9nitentiaire-de-Villefranche-sur-Sa%C3%B4ne-Rh%C3%B4ne.pdf.

CGLPL. 2020c. *Rapport de visite: 2 au 13 mars 2020 – 2e visite Centre pénitentiaire des Baumettes à Marseille (Bouches-du-Rhône).* Paris: CGLPL. https://www.cglpl.fr/wp-content/uploads/2021/09/Rapport-de-la-deuxi%C3%A8me-visite-du-centre-p%C3%A9nitentiaire-des-Baumettes-%C3%A0-Marseille-Bouches-du-Rh%C3%B4ne.pdf.

CGLPL. 2021a. *Rapport de visite: 11 au 15 janvier 2021 – 2ème visite Centre pénitentiaire d'Aiton (Savoie).* Paris: CGLPL. https://www.cglpl.fr/wp-content/uploads/2022/02/Rapport-de-la-deuxi%C3%A8me-visite-du-centre-p%C3%A9nitentiaire-dAiton-Savoie.pdf.

CGLPL. 2021b. *Rapport de visite: 1er au 5 et 8 au 10 février 2021 – 2ème visite Centre Pénitentiaire de Lille-Loos-Sequedin (Nord).* Paris: CGLPL. https://www.cglpl.fr/wp-content/uploads/2021b/12/Rapport-de-la-deuxi%C3%A8me-visite-du-centre-p%C3%A9nitentiaire-de-Lille-Loos-S%C3%A9quedin-Nord.pdf.

CPT. 2018a. *Factsheet: Women in prisons*, CPT/Inf (2018) 5. Strasbourg: Council of Europe. https://rm.coe.int/168077ff14.

CPT. 2018b. *Report to the Norwegian Government on the visit to Norway carried out by the European Committee for the Prevention of Torture and Inhuman or Degrading Treatment or Punishment (CPT) from 28 May to 5 June 2018.* CPT/Inf (2019) 1. Strasbourg: Council of Europe. https://rm.coe.int/1680909713.

CPT. 2019a. *Report to the Slovak Government on the visit to the Slovak Republic carried out by the European Committee for the Prevention of Torture and Inhuman or Degrading Treatment or Punishment (CPT) from 19 to 28 March 2018.* CPT/Inf (2019) 20. Strasbourg: Council of Europe. https://rm.coe.int/168094fd71.

CPT. 2019b. *Report to the Danish Government on the visit to Denmark carried out by the European Committee for the Prevention of Torture and Inhuman or Degrading Treatment or Punishment (CPT) from 3 to 12 April 2019.* CPT/Inf (2019) 35. Strasbourg: Council of Europe. https://rm.coe.int/1680996859.

CPT. 2019c. *Report to the Estonian Government on the visit to Estonia carried out by the European Committee for the Prevention of Torture and Inhuman or Degrading Treatment or Punishment (CPT) from 27 September to 5 October 2017.* CPT/Inf (2019) 31. Strasbourg: Council of Europe. https://rm.coe.int/168098db93.

CPT. 2020. *Report to the Portuguese Government on the visit to Portugal carried out by the European Committee for the Prevention of Torture and Inhuman or Degrading Treatment or Punishment (CPT) from 3 to 12 December 2019.* CPT/Inf (2020) 33. Strasbourg: Council of Europe. https://rm.coe.int/1680a05953.

CPT. 2021a. *Rapport au Gouvernement de la Principauté de Monaco relatif à la visite effectuée à Monaco par le Comité européen pour la prévention de la torture et des peines ou traitements inhumains ou dégradants (CPT) du 15 au 18 septembre 2020.* CPT/Inf (2021) 12. Strasbourg : Council of Europe. https://rm.coe.int/1680a2851d.

CPT. 2021b. *Rapport au Gouvernement de la République française relatif à la visite effectuée en France par le Comité européen pour la prévention de la torture et des peines ou traitements inhumains ou dégradants (CPT) du 4 au 18 décembre 2019.* CPT/Inf (2021) 14. Strasbourg: Council of Europe. https://rm.coe.int/1680a2f0a0.

CPT. 2021c. *Report to the Spanish Government on the visit to Spain carried out by the European Committee for the Prevention of Torture and Inhuman or Degrading Treatment or Punishment (CPT) from 14 to 28 September 2020.* CPT/Inf (2021) 27. Strasbourg: Council of Europe. https://rm.coe.int/1680a47a76.

Garante. 2018. *Norms and normativity, standards for the enforcement of adult sentencing; Collection of recommendations, 2016–2017.* Rome. Garante. https://www.garantenazionaleprivatiliberta.it/gnpl/resources/cms/documents/d7716fed68164b657b6bb0a41db176ea.pdf.

Garante. 2020. *Report to Parliament 2020.* Rome. Garante https://www.garantenazionaleprivatiliberta.it/gnpl/resources/cms/documents/1a914f80cdad973aeaee49fbe15b2acd.pdf.

HMIP. 2017. *Expectations: Criteria for assessing the treatment of and conditions for men in prisons.* https://www.justiceinspectorates.gov.uk/hmiprisons/wp-content/uploads/sites/4/2021/07/Expectations-FINAL-2021.pdf.

HMIP. 2021. *Expectations: Criteria for assessing the treatment of and conditions for women in prison.* https://www.justiceinspectorates.gov.uk/hmiprisons/wp-content/uploads/sites/4/2021/08/Womens-Expectations-FINAL-July-2021-1.pdf.

HMIP. 2022a. *Report on an unannounced inspection of HMP Durham by HM Chief Inspector of Prisons 15 and 22–26 November 2021.* https://www.justiceinspectorates.gov.uk/hmiprisons/wp-content/uploads/sites/4/2022a/03/Durham-web-2021.pdf.

HMIP. 2022b. *Prisoner survey methodology, results and analyses HMP Durham November 2021.* https://www.justiceinspectorates.gov.uk/hmiprisons/wp-content/uploads/sites/4/2022b/03/Durham-combined-survey-methodology-and-results.pdf.

HMIP. 2022c. *Report on an unannounced inspection of HMP Altcourse by HM Chief Inspector of Prisons 1–2 and 8–12 November 2021.* https://www.justiceinspectorates.gov.uk/hmiprisons/wp-content/uploads/sites/4/2022c/02/Altcourse-web-2021.pdf.

HMIP. 2022d. *Prisoner survey methodology, results and analyses HMP Altcourse November 2021.* https://www.justiceinspectorates.gov.uk/hmiprisons/wp-content/uploads/sites/4/2022d/02/Altcourse-combined-survey-methodology-and-results.pdf.

HMIP. 2022e. *Report on an unannounced inspection of HMP Swaleside by HM Chief Inspector of Prisons 18–19 and 25–29 October 2021.* https://www.justiceinspectorates.gov.uk/hmiprisons/wp-content/uploads/sites/4/2022e/02/Swaleside-web-2021-1.pdf.

HMIP. 2022f. *Prisoner survey methodology, results and analyses HMP Swaleside October 2021.* https://www.justiceinspectorates.gov.uk/hmiprisons/wp-content/uploads/sites/4/2022f/02/Swaleside-combined-survey-methodology-and-results.pdf.

Sivilombudsmannen. 2017. *Visit report: Ila Detention and Security Prison, 6–9 March 2017.* https://www.sivilombudet.no/wp-content/uploads/2017/03/Visit-report-2017-Ila-Detention-and-Security-Prison.pdf.

Sivilombudsmannen. 2018. *Visit report: Bergen prison, 2–4 May 2018.* https://www.sivilombudsmannen.no/wp-content/uploads/2019/03/Bergen-Prison.pdf.

Strip Searches Through the Lens of the Prohibition of Inhuman and Degrading Treatment in European Human Rights Law

Natasa Mavronicola and Elaine Webster

1 Introduction

It has been twenty years since the European Court of Human Rights ('ECtHR' or 'the Court') first found that a body search amounted to a violation of Article 3 of the European Convention on Human Rights ('ECHR'), which provides that: "No one shall be subjected to torture or to inhuman or degrading treatment or punishment".[1] In its judgment in

[1] Council of Europe, *European Convention for the Protection of Human Rights and Fundamental Freedoms, as amended by Protocols Nos 11 and 14* (1950) ETS 005.

N. Mavronicola (✉)
University of Birmingham, Birmingham, UK
e-mail: n.mavronicola@bham.ac.uk

E. Webster
University of Strathclyde, Glasgow, UK
e-mail: elaine.webster@strath.ac.uk

T. Daems (ed.), *Body Searches and Imprisonment*, Palgrave Studies in Prisons and Penology, https://doi.org/10.1007/978-3-031-20451-7_5

Valašinas v Lithuania, the ECtHR centred on the search alone—a strip search—despite the applicant's argument that *both* his general conditions of imprisonment and the search he had been subjected to were incompatible with the right.[2] Finding that the detention conditions did not violate Article 3, the ECtHR focused on what it was about the search, in which the applicant was searched naked in front of a female officer and was asked to squat while his genitals and food were examined by officers not wearing gloves, that brought the experience within the scope of the Article 3 prohibition. The Court described this constellation of factors as having 'diminished' the applicant's human dignity.[3]

Making judgements about what respect for dignity demands has become critical in the context of body searches, as in the treatment of prisoners more generally in international[4] as well as European human rights law.[5] There is a single reference to respect for human dignity in the original (1955) UN Standard Minimum Rules for the Treatment of Prisoners ("The regime of the institution should seek to minimize any differences between prison life and life at liberty which tend to lessen the responsibility of the prisoners or the respect due to their dignity as human beings").[6] This principle was integrated into the original iteration of the Council of Europe's European Prison Rules in 1973, and these rules accorded an even more prominent role to respect for human dignity as a basic principle. The rules state that imprisonment "…shall be effected in material and moral conditions which ensure respect for human dignity".[7] Moreover, with reference to Article 3 ECHR especially,

---

[2] *Valašinas v. Lithuania*, App. No. 44558/98, 24 July 2001.

[3] *Valašinas*, ibid., para. 117.

[4] See, e.g. UN General Assembly, International Covenant on Civil and Political Rights, 16 December 1966, 999 UNTS 171, Article 10; UN General Assembly, United Nations Standard Minimum Rules for the Treatment of Prisoners (Nelson Mandela Rules) 17 December 2015, A/RES/70/175; UN General Assembly, Convention Against Torture and Other Cruel, Inhuman or Degrading Treatment or Punishment, 10 December 1984, 1465 UNTS 85.

[5] E.g. *Kudła v. Poland* [GC], App. No. 30210/96, 26 October 2000, para. 92.

[6] United Nations, Standard Minimum Rules for the Treatment of Prisoners (n 4) para. 60(1).

[7] Council of Europe Committee of Ministers, European Standard Minimum Rules for the Treatment of Prisoners, Resolution no. R(73)5, adopted 19 January 1973, para. 5(3) and para. 3 and 58; see also Council of Europe Committee of Ministers, Recommendation Rec(2006)2-rev of the Committee of Ministers to Member States on the European Prison Rules [1], 11 January 2006, revised and amended 1 July 2020.

European human rights law has come to provide a relatively rich foundation for understanding the line between treatment that respects human dignity and treatment that does not.

The doctrine that has been developed by the ECtHR provides a significant lens for understanding—and questioning—the practice of body searches within carceral contexts and their significance for human dignity. The Court's baseline is that body searches are not inherently incompatible with Article 3.[8] We can thereby draw from the case law a number of insights which reflect push and pull factors, moving body searches above or below a line of respect for human dignity according to the ECtHR. We can also draw insights from the case law around the nexus between respect for human dignity and justifications for body searches in the name of prison security. In its line of judgments since 2001, the Court has mediated between ideas of necessity and appropriateness of conduct, within assessments of the 'nature and context'[9] of body search practices.

The Article 3 perspective is especially interesting because the relevant doctrine has been developed against the backdrop of Article 3's 'absolute' character. That is, Article 3 ECHR enshrines a right which cannot be displaced by extraneous considerations. The absolute character of Article 3 is tied to its significance in safeguarding human dignity. As the ECtHR has repeatedly underlined, "respect for human dignity forms part of the very essence of the Convention",[10] and Article 3 represents a commitment that is "…closely bound up with respect for human dignity".[11] Besides the complexity arising in the concretisation of human dignity in the context of body searches, the ECtHR's assessment of the compatibility of body searches with Article 3 raises questions relating to this right's absolute character. Notably, if body searches are rationalised as being necessary in the pursuit of security or 'order', how can such rationales be squared with Article 3's non-displaceability? Features of body searches and their assessment by the ECtHR may also be seen to raise

---

[8] *Frérot v. France*, App. No. 70204/01, 12 June 2007, para 38.

[9] See, e.g. *Garabayev v. Russia*, App. No. 38411/02, 7 June 2007, para 75.

[10] *Bouyid v. Belgium* [GC], App. No. 23380/09, 28 September 2015, para 89.

[11] *Bouyid*, ibid., para 81.

further questions with respect to Article 3's absolute character: Can an activity so ubiquitous—so 'banal' even, in the eyes of those who execute it—be deemed to violate an absolute right? Given that body searches are predominantly (considered) justified in their application to those imprisoned, does this call the unconditionality of Article 3's protection into question? By unpacking the ECtHR's approach we can begin to provide clarity in answer to such questions, and to assess the response of human rights courts to body search practices.

In national legal and policy contexts across the Council of Europe, the demands of Article 3 ECHR constitute, or should constitute, one key element of regulating search practices. Glimpses of the relevance of Article 3 to shaping regulatory standards and practices in national contexts are indeed visible within Article 3 case law and related sources.[12] Such glimpses indicate the relevance of the Strasbourg case law to shifting policy discourse (see also Daems 2014). Beyond the Council of Europe, the ECtHR's interpretation of Article 3 is significant for other international human rights monitoring bodies. It is the Strasbourg Court that has had the most extensive opportunities to develop the interpretation of the 'inhuman and degrading treatment' elements of the broader Article 3 prohibition of torture (Webster 2018: 4–5). Article 3 jurisprudence can therefore form an important part of the discourse around body searches. At the same time, we recognise, as other scholars have long observed, that rules based on 'dignity' and 'abstract' human rights are not easily translated into practice by those with the power to institute change, or into improved outcomes for those who are imprisoned (Liebling 2011; Daems 2014). Nevertheless, the approach of the ECtHR should be examined for the influential role that it plays within the development of these rules. And while high profile examples regarding body searches from within the ECtHR's case law on the prohibition of inhuman and degrading treatment (and the protection of private life)[13] may be well known, this chapter offers an in-depth look beyond the surface of the

[12] See spate of cases against the Netherlands in 2006: *Sylla v. Netherlands*, App. No. 14683/03, 6 July 2006; *Baybaşın v. Netherlands*, App. No. 13600/02, 6 July 2006; *Salah v. Netherlands*, App. No. 8196/02, 6 July 2006; see, too, the European Committee for the Prevention of Torture reports cited therein and in much of the rest of the case law we refer to in this chapter.

[13] *Wainwright v. UK*, App. No. 12350/04, 26 September 2006.

ECtHR's case law, from the perspective of an holistic view of Article 3 jurisprudence, and by drawing upon extensive research on the Court's interpretation of this right (inc. Webster 2018; Mavronicola 2021).

In this chapter, we outline key aspects of the ECtHR's doctrine, on Article 3 in general and body searches in prisons in particular.[14] We identify *strip searches* as the core of the Article 3 case law on body searches (on the scope of the term 'body searches', see Daems, Chapter 1 in this volume). We draw out three principles relating to strip searches: (1) strip searches must not be routine and must be justified on protective grounds, (2) strip searches must not be conducted with intent to humiliate, debase, or cause distress, and (3) strip searches must be performed in a dignity-respecting manner. We unpack each of these principles in turn, examining the elements of strip searches and their contextual settings that should be understood as either constitutive of inhuman and/or degrading treatment, or as compatible with human dignity (and, by implication, Article 3). This process necessarily incorporates our own interpretation since only so much is visible in the doctrine about the nature of the wrongs captured in the text of Article 3 (Webster 2016). A further challenge is that the Court is not always precise about how particular experiences are characterised (as inhuman or degrading or both). Filling the space in the doctrine is of heightened importance when we want to understand prospectively whether something would fall within the scope of inhuman and/or degrading treatment. Our starting point is that the interpretation of these wrongs, by the Court or by others, including us, is a "morally loaded evaluative endeavour" (Mavronicola 2021: 56). This view is underpinned by certain understandings of how the ECtHR judges, and we as interpreters outside of the judicial context, do or should operate as actors interpreting the legal text (Webster 2018: 11–12). Presently, this implies that we outline what is visible in the Court's case law and that we then go beyond this to explain, or interpret, the doctrine. This process provides a basis for engaging critically

[14] The ECtHR has addressed body searches outside of prisons. Two recent examples are *Aghdgomelashvili and Japaridze v. Georgia*, App. No. 7224/11, 8 October 2020 (strip searches during a police raid of office premises of an LGBTQ organisation) and *Safi and others v. Greece*, App. No. 5418/15, 7 July 2022 (outdoor strip searches of a group of persons under the control of state authorities in a migration context).

with the Court's approach, and for contemplating how it may evolve in the future.

2 The Doctrine

2.1 Article 3 ECHR: An Unconditional, Context-Sensitive Standard

It is firmly established in Strasbourg doctrine that Article 3 ECHR enshrines an 'absolute right'.[15] To explain what this signifies, the ECtHR has juxtaposed Article 3 with rights that permit legitimate interference,[16] or can be departed from during public emergencies 'threatening the life of the nation',[17] or whose protection can be limited because of someone's wrongful conduct. The Court has underlined that "even in the most difficult circumstances, such as the fight against terrorism and organised crime, the Convention prohibits in absolute terms torture and inhuman or degrading treatment or punishment, irrespective of the conduct of the person concerned" and that "[t]he nature of the offence allegedly committed by the applicant is therefore irrelevant for the purposes of art. 3".[18] The fact that Article 3 makes no provision for lawful interference for the fulfilment of a legitimate aim, does not allow for any derogation even in a public emergency, and protects everyone unconditionally, makes it an invaluable source of protection for persons who have been found to have committed criminal offences warranting a term of imprisonment.

These 'components' of absoluteness reflect the idea that the right's protection is not *displaceable* on the basis of extraneous considerations (Mavronicola 2021). This non-displaceability entails that the *content* of the right is of the utmost significance. The determination

[15] *Derman v. Turkey*, App. No. 21789/02, 31 May 2011, para 27.

[16] See, e.g. Articles 8(2), 9(2), 10(2), 11(2) ECHR.

[17] *Ireland v. UK* [Plenary], App. No. 5310/71, 18 January 1978, para 163. Article 15(2) ECHR provides: 'No derogation from Article 2, except in respect of deaths resulting from lawful acts of war, or from Articles 3, 4(1) and 7 shall be made under this provision'.

[18] *Gäfgen v. Germany* [GC], App. No. 22978/05, 1 June 2010, para 87.

of whether something amounts to inhuman and/or degrading treatment or punishment draws the line between potentially lawful treatment and conclusively unlawful treatment (Webster 2018: 1; Mavronicola 2012).

The Court delineates what it often refers to as the Article 3 'threshold' primarily by reference to what it calls a 'minimum level of severity': according to the Court, "ill-treatment must attain a minimum level of severity if it is to fall within the scope of Article 3".[19] It has frequently been repeated that the assessment of whether the particular circumstances evince an Article 3 violation "is, in the nature of things, relative; it depends on *all the circumstances of the case*, such as the duration of the treatment, its physical or mental effects and, in some cases, the sex, age and state of health of the victim, etc." (emphasis added).[20] Within the 'all the circumstances' umbrella, the Court has also referred to "the nature and context of the treatment or punishment, the manner and method of its execution",[21] as well as to "whether the victim [was] in a vulnerable situation".[22]

The criteria of 'nature and context' of the treatment[23] may be seen as the overarching factors operating in the ECtHR's 'relative' assessment of severity, forming the basis for considering relevant contextual factors that determine the relational and qualitative severity at issue. The 'nature' of the treatment, in particular, offers a gateway for considering the intent, purpose, and/or attitude of those engaging in the act or omission under consideration. The criterion of 'context', in turn, enables a consideration of various contextual factors that shape the experience of relevant actors and any vulnerabilities and power asymmetries at issue.

By way of general guidance on its assessment—or what Waldron refers to as 'benchmarks' (Waldron 2010: 273) of inhuman treatment/punishment and degrading treatment/punishment—the Court has observed that treatment or punishment "has been held ... to be

[19] *Ireland v. UK* (n 17) para 162.

[20] Ibid.; see also, e.g. *Svinarenko and Slyadnev v. Russia* [GC], App. No. 32541/08 and 43441/08, 17 July 2014, para 114.

[21] See, e.g. *Garabayev* (n 9) para 75.

[22] See, e.g. *Khlaifia and others v. Italy* [GC], App. No. 16483/12, 15 December 2016, para 160.

[23] See, for example, *Garabayev* (n 9) para 75.

'inhuman' because, *inter alia*, it was premeditated, was applied for hours at a stretch and caused either actual bodily injury or intense physical and mental suffering".[24] It has described degrading treatment or punishment as that which "…humiliates or debases an individual showing a lack of respect for, or diminishing, his or her human dignity or arouses feelings of fear, anguish or inferiority capable of breaking an individual's moral and physical resistance".[25] The Court has suggested that the 'public nature' of treatment or punishment "may be a relevant or aggravating factor in assessing whether it is 'degrading' within the meaning of Article 3".[26] The Court has also on occasion referred to treatment or punishment "driving the victim to act against his will or conscience"[27] or as having "adversely affected his or her personality in a manner incompatible with Article 3"[28] as degrading. As discussed below, both inhuman and degrading treatment/punishment can be understood as capturing dignity harms that encompass the denial of "the status owed to human beings" (Vorhaus 2021: 434).

While it may be assumed that 'punishment' can be subsumed within the term 'treatment', we should not overlook significant dimensions of punishment and "treatment associated with it".[29] Punishment carries the implication of something undesirable or unpleasant being meted out in response to a behaviour considered to be unacceptable (see, generally, the nuanced account in Duff 2001). According to the Court, in order "…for a punishment or treatment associated with it to be 'inhuman' or 'degrading', the suffering or humiliation involved must go beyond that inevitable element of suffering or humiliation connected with a given form of legitimate treatment or punishment".[30] The Court appears to consider the legally permitted or mandated loss of liberty as 'legitimate',

---

[24] See, e.g. *Stanev v. Bulgaria* [GC], App. No. 36760/06, 17 January 2012, para 203; *Jalloh v. Germany* [GC], App. No. 54810/00, 11 July 2006, para 68.

[25] *Pretty v. UK*, App. No. 2346/02, 29 April 2002, para 52. See also *Ireland v. UK* (n 17) para. 167.

[26] *Svinarenko and Slyadnev v. Russia*, App. No. 32541/08 and 43441/08, 17 July 2014, para 115.

[27] *Keenan v. UK*, App. No. 27229/95, 3 April 2001, para 110.

[28] *Iacov Stanciu v. Romania*, App. No. 35972/05, 24 July 2012, para 165.

[29] *A and others v. UK* [GC], App. No. 3455/05, 19 February 2009, para 127.

[30] *A v. UK*, ibid para 127.

and has accordingly repeatedly indicated that, in respect of measures imposed on persons in detention, Article 3 only captures measures that subject persons to "distress or hardship exceeding the unavoidable level of suffering inherent in detention".[31] In determining what exceeds this level of suffering, the Court relies on the context-sensitive assessment it employs to delineate the Article 3 'threshold'.

2.2 The ECtHR's Position on Body Searches

The ECtHR's starting point in respect of body searches is that they are not contrary to Article 3 ECHR per se.[32] However, at least since its landmark judgment in *Valašinas*,[33] the ECtHR has viewed body searches with suspicion, on the understanding that they are likely to raise an issue under Article 3. It therefore specifically looks for the justification underpinning the search, as well as examining the manner in which the search is performed, and the wider context in which it occurs. The Court's approach in this respect may be likened to its attitude to other 'suspect' measures taking place within carceral contexts, such as the imposition of (additional) restrictions on movement and interaction. The Court accepts that a degree of restrictive incarceration may be applied in a way which remains respectful of the dignity of the person insofar as it is applied solely and only to the extent necessary to avert risks posed by the acts of the person subjected to it, with due safeguards for that person's health and wellbeing, and with the onus of demonstrating both justification and safeguards resting on the State authorities (Mavronicola 2015).

Article 3 judgments on body searches concern strip searches, in which individuals were partially undressed[34] or fully undressed.[35] They have

[31] *Kafkaris v. Cyprus* [GC], App. No. 21906/04, 12 February 2008, para 96.

[32] *Frérot* (n 8) para 38.

[33] *Valašinas* (n 2). The Court's former sister body, the European Commission on Human Rights, had previously considered body searches. See *McFeeley and Others v. UK* (Commission Decision), App. No. 8317/78, 15 May 1980. This Decision concerned routine, intrusive body searches, which were found not to amount to inhuman or degrading treatment.

[34] E.g. *Iwańczuk v. Poland*, App. No. 25196/94, 15 November 2001.

[35] E.g. *Savičs v. Latvia*, App. No. 17892/03, 27 November 2012.

tended to include visual anal inspections (including when individuals have been directed to bend over or squat)[36] and sometimes have included the touching of genitals, as well as visual genital inspections.[37] The Court has described strip searches involving anal and/or genital inspections as 'full body' searches.[38]

The ECtHR has repeatedly indicated that it accepts that "strip-searches may be necessary on occasions to ensure prison security or to prevent disorder or crime".[39] So even though the Court recognises that strip searches are likely, by their nature, to be experienced as invasive and humiliating,[40] and 'humiliation' evokes the Court's characterisation of degrading treatment, the Court does not consider strip searches to be conclusively unlawful. It nonetheless shows a readiness to scrutinise the (purported) necessity of such searches, and the Court's suspicion and consequent scrutiny of the particular measure or practice deepen in line with the degree of intrusion involved in the search.[41] Moreover, according to the Court, strip searches must be performed in a way that is 'appropriate' and does not lead to suffering or humiliation which goes "beyond the inevitable element of suffering or humiliation connected with this form of legitimate treatment".[42] The latter aspect of the Court's delimitation of Article 3-compliant strip searches, which relies on an assumed understanding of what suffering or humiliation is 'inevitable' within a 'legitimate' strip search, somewhat begs the question.

The flip side of the Court's acceptance that strip searches which are justified by considerations of necessity may not violate Article 3, is that the Court is not prepared to accept the *routine* and thereby not clearly justified performance of strip searches. In *Piechowicz*, it found that where a strip search "was carried out as a matter of routine and was not linked

---

[36] E.g. *Sylla v. The Netherlands*, App. No. 14683/03, 6 July 2006; *Frérot* (n 8); *Michał Korgul v. Poland*, App. No. 36140/11, 21 March 2017; *Roth v. Germany*, App. No. 6780/18 and 30776/18, 22 October 2020.

[37] E.g. *Valasinas* (n 2); *Wainwright v. UK*, App. No. 12350/04, 26 September 2006.

[38] E.g. *Michał Korgul* (n 36), para 42.

[39] *Lorsé and others v Netherlands*, App. No. 52750/99, 4 February 2000, para 72. See also *Iwańczuk* (n 34) para 59.

[40] *Frérot* (n 8) para 38 (citations omitted).

[41] *Frérot* (n 8) para 38 (citations omitted).

[42] Ibid.

to any concrete security needs, nor to any specific suspicion concerning the applicant's conduct", it was bound to "have diminished [the applicant's] human dignity and caused him feelings of inferiority, anguish and accumulated distress which went beyond the unavoidable suffering and humiliation involved in the imposition of detention", and accordingly violated Article 3.[43]

The ECtHR is sensitive to the presence of what it deems as *arbitrariness* in the practice of strip searches, both in terms of undue uniformity (in the sense of routine strip searching), and in terms of undue variability. In *Frérot*, for example, the Court was "struck by the fact that the application of the most intrusive procedures in terms of physical intimacy varied from one place of detention to another in the applicant's case".[44] It noted that the most intrusive inspections (in the form of anal inspections) had not been clearly shown to have been "based each time on strong and specific suspicions".[45] The ECtHR found that the element of arbitrariness added to the feelings of inferiority and anxiety associated with the strip search to make the humiliation experienced go beyond what the Court called "the – unavoidable and hence tolerable – level that strip-searches of prisoners inevitably involve".[46] The Court therefore treats the absence of tailored justification as giving rise to an arbitrariness that pushes the treatment over the Article 3 'threshold'.

Even if a strip search is justified and not deemed arbitrary by the Court, the *manner* in which it is conducted may bring it within the scope of the prohibition under Article 3. The Court has elaborated that strip searches "should be carried out in an appropriate manner with due respect for human dignity".[47] An additional relevant factor, which the Court sees as shaping the character of the treatment, is the intention on the part of those conducting the search. While the Court has confirmed that the position of principle that an intention to humiliate or cause distress is not an essential component of ill-treatment under

[43] *Piechowicz v Poland*, App. No. 20071/07, 17 April 2012, para 176.

[44] *Frérot* (n 8) para 46.

[45] Ibid., para 47.

[46] Ibid.

[47] *Dejnek v. Poland*, App. No. 9635/13, 1 June 2017, para 60.

Article 3 applies to strip searches, it is sensitive to any intent to humiliate or cause distress. In *Iwanczuk*, for example, the Court indicated that "regard must be had to the intentions of the persons inflicting [the treatment], namely whether they acted with a deliberate intention to degrade or humiliate".[48] The Court noted that the applicant had been "insulted and derided"[49] by the guards performing the strip search before it made a finding of degrading treatment. The Court has also treated as an aggravating factor the presence of a particularly coercive element in respect of intrusive searches: in *Frérot*, it indicated that "the humiliation felt by the applicant was aggravated by the fact that on a number of occasions his refusal to comply with such measures led to his being placed in a punishment cell".[50]

The baseline then, is that although strip searches are not incompatible with Article 3 per se, they are *prima facie* suspect. There are several principles we may distil from the ECtHR's case law that can act as guidelines to avoid strip searches being characterised as inhuman and/or degrading within the meaning of Article 3. Strip searches must not: (1) be routine and must be justified on relevant grounds, (2) be motivated by an intent to humiliate (including as a means to an end, for example to intimidate or punish), and (3) be conducted in a manner that is incompatible with human dignity. If an incident or regime falls foul of any one of these requirements, it is likely to be found to be contrary to Article 3. A closer look at these principles allows us to better understand what it is about such features of strip searches that are problematic from the perspective of Article 3, and why.

---

48 *Iwańczuk* (n 34) para 57.

49 Ibid.

50 *Frérot* (n 8) para 47.

3 The Principles

3.1 Strip Searches Must Not Be Routine and Must Be Justified on Relevant Grounds

For the ECtHR to deem the performance of strip searches compatible with Article 3 ECHR, a necessary—but not sufficient—requirement is that such searches be justified on what the ECtHR considers appropriate grounds that render such a search necessary. If strip searches take place as a matter of *routine* rather than necessity grounded in appropriate justification, the Court is likely to find them to be insufficiently justified and hence incompatible with Article 3 ECHR. In this section, we draw out two interconnected points in relation to 'justification': The first aims to clarify how we should understand what the Court means when it refers to, and permits, justification in this context. The second aims to clarify *why* searches that are justified on relevant grounds may be compatible with Article 3, and conversely, why searches that are not justified on relevant grounds may be incompatible with Article 3.

What are 'appropriate' grounds for undertaking a strip search, in the Court's view? While we are not given a comprehensive treatment of this issue within the doctrine, it is clear from the Court's approach that, to be Article 3-compatible, strip searches must be performed for reasons relating to the protection and safety of persons within the prison context, as opposed to reasons or motives associated with purposes such as intimidation or further punishment. In *Iwanczuk*, which concerned the strip search of a prisoner exercising his right to vote, the ECtHR placed emphasis on the applicant's "...peaceful behaviour during the entire period of his detention and the fact that he was not charged with a violent crime and had no previous criminal record", and determined that there were no "grounds on which to fear that he would behave violently"[51] and thereby justify the strip search, concluding that he had been subjected to degrading treatment. The reasoning of the Court indicates that there must be a *protective* justification for such a

---

[51] *Iwańczuk* (n 34) para 56.

search—notably to protect (a) person(s) from violence or harm (see also Spalding 2021: 461–462).

Moreover, the strip search must be *necessary* in the sense that only such a search can perform the protective role assigned to it—accordingly, if less intrusive measures may sufficiently fulfil the purpose of ensuring protection, and such measures are available to or indeed pursued by the authorities, the Court may find the implementation of strip searches unnecessary and thereby incompatible with Article 3. This is illustrated in *Piechowicz*, in which the Court reasoned as follows:

> Having regard to the fact that the applicant was already subjected in addition to several other strict surveillance measures, that the authorities did not rely on any concrete convincing security needs and that, despite the serious charge against him, he apparently did not display any disruptive, violent or otherwise dangerous behaviour in the remand centre, the Court considers that the practice of daily strip-searches applied to him for two years and nine months must have diminished his human dignity and caused him feelings of inferiority, anguish and accumulated distress which went beyond the unavoidable suffering and humiliation involved in the imposition of detention...[52]

The Court concluded that Article 3 had been violated in the circumstances of the case.

Article 3 does not establish a prohibition on using force or invading bodily integrity per se. Rather, the Court's context-sensitive assessment determines whether an act which forcibly or non-consensually impinges upon another's body is, or is not, inhuman or degrading. For example, the Court has repeated that Article 3 'does not prohibit' the use of force in narrow, 'well-defined circumstances', insofar as the Government proves that such force is indispensable and not excessive in repelling violence.[53] The Court has, in addition, indicated that incursions on bodily integrity that amount to medically necessary treatment

---

52 *Piechowicz* (n 43) para 175–176 (citations omitted).

53 *Güler and Öngel v. Turkey*, App. No. 29612/05 and 30668/05, 4 October 2011, para 28. This is the approach in *Rehbock v. Slovenia*, App. No. 29462/95, 28 November 2000, para 72. See also Mavronicola (2013).

may, provided certain conditions are met, be compatible with Article 3.[54] The Court has also stated that a medical procedure, such as the taking of saliva samples, performed in defiance of the will of the individual subjected to it for the purposes of obtaining evidence of their involvement in a criminal offence, is not 'as such' prohibited by Article 3.[55]

The question arises of whether the Court is, in effect, justifying inhuman or degrading treatment in the context of strip searches and thereby contradicting the absolute character of Article 3 ECHR. A key textbook on the ECHR takes precisely this view in relation to the use of force, suggesting that case law such as that outlined above effectively establishes "recognized exceptions to the absolute nature of Article 3" (Harris et al. 2009: 70). The Court might appear to be *qualifying* Article 3's protection, by carving out circumstances in which 'indispensable' ill-treatment is lawful. Yet what the doctrine confirms instead is that justification may play a role in determining whether a treatment or punishment is inhuman or degrading in character. To make sense of this, the criterion of 'severity' delineating Article 3's 'threshold' must be understood as qualitative and as attaching to the *wrong* rather than purely to the harm at issue.

The 'minimum level of severity' appears to delimit Article 3 by means of a requirement that a certain quantum of suffering or humiliation be established in order for a finding of violation of Article 3 to be made (see Farrell 2015). This warrants reconsideration. Rather than being a merely quantitative concept attached to the degree of harm at issue, severity is tied to the *wrong* in inhuman and in degrading treatment or punishment. It attaches to the character of the act, omission, or situation and not simply to its consequences for the victim(s) (see Mavronicola 2021). Accordingly, severity goes beyond the degree of humiliation or anguish suffered. Two lines of case law that illustrate this most clearly are cases in which the Court is prepared to recognise that the infliction

---

[54] See, for example, *Nevmerzhitsky v. Ukraine*, App. No. 54825/00, 5 April 2005, para 94; *Herczegfalvy v. Austria*, App. No. 10533/83, 24 September 1992, para 82; *Naumenko v. Ukraine*, App. No. 42023/98, 10 February 2004, para 112.

[55] *Jalloh* (n 24) para 67–74.

of considerable suffering may *not* be inhuman or degrading if the relevant act, omission, or situation is respectful of human dignity; and cases in which an act that has only minor—or even what some might label trivial[56]—harmful impact on an individual is nonetheless found to reach the 'minimum level of severity'. The case law on the justified use of force exemplifies the former, while the case of *Bouyid*[57] exemplifies the latter.

Bouyid concerned single slaps in the face inflicted on two young men by local police officers while they were detained at a police station. In a Chamber judgment, the ECtHR found that the "threshold of severity has not been reached in the present case".[58] The majority (14 judges) in the Grand Chamber disagreed. They stressed that Article 3 is "closely bound up with respect for human dignity"[59] and that

> in respect of a person who is deprived of his liberty, or, more generally, is confronted with law-enforcement officers, any recourse to physical force which has not been made strictly necessary by his own conduct diminishes human dignity and is, in principle, an infringement of the right set forth in Article 3.[60]

The ECtHR found that the applicants' allegedly disrespectful attitude was "certainly insufficient to establish such necessity".[61] The Court therefore found that the applicants' human dignity had been undermined and there had been a breach of Article 3.[62]

Bouyid potently illustrates that 'severity' does not stem straightforwardly from the degree of harm or suffering inflicted, but relates to the character of the treatment at issue. The violation inflicted on the applicants in *Bouyid* was an abuse of power that may be viewed as a microcosm of the totalitarianism found in torture (see Luban 2014:

[56] *Bouyid* (n 10) Dissenting Opinion of Judges De Gaetano, Lemmens and Mahoney, para 7.
[57] *Bouyid* (n 10).
[58] Ibid., para 51.
[59] Ibid., para 81.
[60] Ibid., para 88, citations omitted.
[61] Ibid., para 102.
[62] Ibid.

48).[63] Its severity pertained to its character and not merely to its consequence.

Many instances of forcible—meaning, for our purposes, not freely consented to—impingement upon one's body may be inhuman or degrading, but not all are. This is what the ECtHR means when it states that Article 3 'does not prohibit' the use of force in certain circumstances. The overarching reasoning of the Court in regard to the use of force emerges in *Muradova*—according to the Court: "Recourse to physical force which has not been made *strictly necessary* by a person's own conduct diminishes human dignity and is in principle an infringement of the right set forth in Article 3 of the Convention" (emphasis added).[64]

The Court's position is that only force which has been made strictly necessary by the individual's conduct can potentially be understood as respecting rather than brutalising the person (see Waldron 2005: 1726–1727). The strict necessity assessment the ECtHR employs also shows sensitivity to relevant context, notably to the power asymmetry at play in situations where persons are confronted by State agents. The Court places an onus on the State to demonstrate the strict necessity of forcible impingement upon a person's body.[65]

All of this is relevant in unpacking the way that justification impacts on the Article 3 compatibility of strip searches. As *Bouyid* demonstrates, a person's dignity can be disrespected, and their right under Article 3 violated, even if they have not been gravely harmed. This is particularly the case where, in a situation of substantial power asymmetry, someone's bodily integrity is forcibly impinged upon without any justification grounded in the strict necessity of fending off violence and/or protecting the person subjected to the intervention or any other person. The ECtHR's approach suggests that wholly unjustified or insufficiently justified strip searches, which often equate to routine strip searching, constitute inhuman or degrading treatment. This appears to reflect the

---

[63] On torture's totalitarianism, see Luban (2014: 48).

[64] *Muradova v. Azerbaijan*, App. No. 22684/05, 2 April 2009, para 109. See also *Bouyid* (n 10) para 88.

[65] See, in this regard, the Court's reasoning in *Güler* (n 61) para 28–29; and in *Bouyid* (n 10) para 102.

view that unnecessary, *routine* strip searches, which effectively express the notion that the person being searched can be intruded upon at will, are fundamentally not respectful of dignity.

By insisting on justification demonstrating the concrete and current necessity of performing a strip search upon one's person, the Court delineates a baseline of respect demanded by Article 3 ECHR. What is also apparent from case law going as far back as *Valašinas,* is that while justificatory reasoning rooted in *protection* will tend to be accepted in principle by the Court, problematic reasons or purposes that are tied to, for example, punishment, intimidation, control, or humiliation will tend to be deemed a basis for making a finding of an Article 3 violation. The role of *appropriate* justification in this context is therefore to distinguish Article 3-incompatible intrusions from potentially Article 3-compatible intrusions, subject to the additional criteria we outline in the following sections.

3.2 Strip Searches Must Not Be Conducted with Intent to Humiliate

Within Article 3 ECHR, intention to "degrade or humiliate"[66] is a non-essential but relevant characteristic of inhuman and/or degrading treatment or punishment. Clarifying why intent is non-essential simultaneously illuminates why it is nevertheless relevant. The discussion below will suggest that in the context of strip searches, the relevance of intent lies in what it communicates within the relationship between the agent who conducts the search and the person subjected to the search. If there is evidence of an agent's intent to humiliate, debase, or cause distress in the conduct of a strip search, this can be understood to communicate active denial of the person's dignity.

Article 3 case law indicates that intent relates differently to degrading treatment compared to inhuman treatment. The relevance of intent in the Court's degrading treatment case law emerged specifically in relation

[66] *Iwańczuk* (n 34) para 57.

to the 'humiliation and debasement' benchmarks of degrading treatment.[67] It is well-established that the Court may arrive at a finding of degrading treatment while accepting that the actors in question showed no intent to humiliate or debase.[68] Even active non-intent does not eliminate the possibility of the Court recognising humiliation or debasement.[69] This is because degradation from the perspective of Article 3 must be understood as a social fact judged with reference to social norms; a judgement as to whether a person has been subjected to degradation is influenced but not determined by the subjective perspective of the agent conducting the search (Webster, 2018: 69–72).

The relationship between intent and inhuman treatment is somewhat opaque in the case law. The benchmarks of inhuman treatment remain based on a description of the circumstances in one early case[70] in contrast to the broader range of benchmarks that have developed in relation to degrading treatment. Inhuman treatment is characterised as treatment that is, *inter alia*, premeditated, applied for hours and causes bodily injury or intense physical and mental suffering.[71] If treatment is premeditated and prolonged, one can assume an inherent intent on the part of the actor(s) responsible. However, inhuman treatment is not a closed category ('*inter alia*') and the Court has also accepted that treatment can be characterised as inhuman in the absence of intent.[72] The place of intent can be clarified by reflecting on the conceptual underpinnings of inhuman treatment in light of the Court's jurisprudence as a whole, in particular when seen in relation to degrading treatment and torture (Webster 2018: 125–126). Inhuman treatment tends to be characterised by relations of power asymmetry, and to involve a relational interaction of some kind (in contrast to degrading treatment; Webster, 2018: 131–135). Within such asymmetric relationships, indifference on the part of the power-holder (including a set of actors forming part of a

---

[67] *Raninen v. Finland*, App. No. 20972/92, 16 December 1997, para 55; *T v UK* [GC], App. No. 24724/94, 16 December 1999, para 69.

[68] *T v. UK*, ibid., para 69; see also *Bouyid* (n 10) para 86.

[69] *Farbtuhs v. Latvia*, App. No. 4672/02, 2 December 2004.

[70] *Ireland v. UK* (n 17) para 167.

[71] Ibid.

[72] *Mahmut Kaya v. Turkey*, App. No. 22535/93, 28 March 2000, para 118.

public authority) towards the humanity (human status) of the powerless person can give rise to inhuman treatment (Webster, 2018: 132–134). In this reading, indifference as an attitude of disregard (Webster, 2018: 132–135) may be deliberately aimed at dehumanising the person but it need not be. The intent is not an essential feature.

Nevertheless, for both inhuman and degrading treatment, intent—where it is present—matters. This is the key point for understanding the principle that strip searches must not be conducted with an intent to humiliate, debase, or cause distress. When determining the presence or absence of intent, the Court tends to examine the reported speech and conduct of the actors inflicting the treatment[73] and whether the treatment was carried out in public[74] (i.e. where 'in public' means 'with witnesses'; this is discussed in relation to humiliation specifically by Silver et al. 1986: 278–279). If the Court considers that there is evidence of intent to humiliate, debase, or cause distress on the part of those involved in conducting the search, this factor forms part of the Court's holistic 'context-sensitive, relational and qualitative' assessment (Mavronicola 2021: 105) of whether a strip search will be specified as, or will form part of broader conditions (such as a high security regime or generalised detention conditions) specified as, inhuman and/or degrading. Going back to its reasoning in *Valašinas*, it appears that the Court sees an intent to humiliate or cause distress (including as a means to an end, such as intimidation) as indicative of active and deliberate dignity denial. In summary, searches conducted with the intent to humiliate or cause distress will point towards an expression of denial of a person's human status, and will likely cross the Article 3 threshold.

---

[73] *Iwańczuk* (n 34) para 57, 59.

[74] *Raninen* (n 67) para 55.

3.3 Strip Searches Must Not Be Conducted in a Manner That Is Incompatible with Human Dignity

In addition to concern with *why* strip searches are carried out, the case law reflects a core concern with *how* they are carried out. A recurring part of the assessment of strip searches in Article 3 case law relates to the 'manner' in which strip searches are conducted.[75] The ECtHR has stated that strip searches "should be carried out in an appropriate manner with due respect for human dignity".[76] Similar language is found in recommendations of the European Committee for the Prevention of Torture and Inhuman or Degrading Treatment or Punishment, which has stipulated that strip searches must be "carried out in a manner respectful of human dignity" (CPT 2011: 38). In a sense, the requirement that strip searches must be conducted in a way that respects human dignity can be seen as an overarching requirement, like the requirement that conditions of detention should be compatible with human dignity. However, 'appropriate manner' also points towards something more specific regarding *conduct*, and the precise manner in which officials undertake searches can be determinative of the acceptability or unacceptability of a search from a dignity perspective. To safeguard against dignity disrespect, Article 3 case law establishes certain red lines for the conduct of strip searches: they must be conducted in a private setting in which the person searched is only visible to those searching them, and they must be conducted by persons of the same sex. Explaining these red lines in the Court's approach means explaining why these specific features are relevant and how they might be seen to protect against dignity disrespect.

'Conduct' is best understood to refer to the process of an interaction between an agent who conducts a search and the person subjected to the search. This interaction, and the way in which it unfolds, is the space in which dignity-communication takes place. What happens within the interaction itself is significant when judging whether dignity has been disrespected, distinct from how that interaction might be perceived by

---

[75] E.g. *Valasinas* (n 2) para 117; *Iwanczuk* (n 34) para 59; *Savičs* (n 35) para 133.

[76] *Dejnek v. Poland*, App. No. 9635/13, 1 June 2017, para 60.

those actually involved in conducting or being subjected to a search. As discussed in relation to 'intent to humiliate', the specification of a strip search as inhuman or as degrading (in 'social fact') is not necessarily determined by the attitude of the person(s) conducting the search. Similarly, the specification of a strip search as inhuman or degrading is not determined by the subjective perspective of the person subjected to a search (Webster 2018: 70–71; see also Vorhaus 2021: 437–441). In other words, neither the subjective perspective of the agent, nor the subjective perspective of the person subjected to the search displaces the significance of the interaction itself. A focus on 'conduct' should be understood as a focus on the interaction, and on how this occurrence or process might communicate dignity disrespect.

Interactions need not have an obviously 'severe' effect or even a physical component to be deemed to communicate dignity disrespect. We can understand the communication, or expression, of dignity disrespect to have an intrinsic symbolic dimension. 'Symbolic' should not be interpreted in this context as less-than-real, or as having no impact. Rather, as Kuch argues in discussing the 'rituality of humiliation', to say that humiliation is symbolic is to say that it is intrinsically constituted at least in part by a symbolic dimension (Kuch 2011: 50). This dimension is not an incidental feature of treatment that is incompatible with human dignity, but a constitutive one (Kuch 2011: 50–52; Vorhaus 2021: 455–456). Dignity disrespect is always a symbolic wrong (Vorhaus 2021) in the sense that it *represents* exclusion from the human community (Webster 2018: 85). The manner in which a strip search is conducted is problematic from an Article 3 perspective when it can be judged to symbolise such exclusion.

A key idea in unpacking the Court's red lines regarding private settings and searches being undertaken by persons of the same sex is the idea of 'humiliation', which is at the core of the ECtHR's approach to interpreting degrading treatment. Humiliation is a term used in everyday language but within Article 3 it must be seen to have a circumscribed meaning which fits with the text of the Article as a whole and its overarching purpose. In this context, humiliation is best understood with reference to a person's regard towards themselves as a human being and the way in which this basic form of self-respect can be eroded by experiences of profound powerlessness. (Webster 2018: 64–76 drawing on the work of a range of scholars, including Isaiah Berlin, Avishai Margalit, William Ian Miller, and Maury Silver et al.). Self-respect is tied up with social norms, and thus with social judgements about occurrences of humiliation. It is "a self-regarding attitude that is developed and sustained or undermined in the social environment" (Webster 2018: 73). This aligns with an understanding of dignity itself as essentially relational (Malpas 2007).

A person's regard towards themselves as a human being can be undermined by the loss of an ability to live up to social standards befitting human persons (Webster 2018: 74–75), and this inability to protect 'basic interests' (Margalit 1996: 211) symbolises extreme powerlessness. Strip searches, already taking place within a context of physical power asymmetry in interpersonal relationships with prison staff (Margalit 1996: 268), communicate something about a person's basic ability to protect intimate interests. These intimate interests are 'personal boundaries', which are commonly related, in literature, to profound powerlessness (see discussion in Webster 2018: 75). The violation of personal boundaries can communicate profound powerlessness, and in turn, symbolic exclusion from the human community, i.e. a violation of human dignity (Webster 2018: 75–76). Humiliation always communicates a 'gesture of exclusion' (Kuch 2011: 48). In his discussion of privacy, Margalit writes that "violation of privacy can serve as an extreme form of humiliation in that those whose privacy is violated are shown that they lack even minimal control over their lives [...]" (Margalit 1996: 207). Vorhaus, writing on degradation in the penal context, refers to denial of 'opacity respect' (Vorhaus 2021: 453). A prisoner, including in the context of a 'full-body strip search', is "deprived of control [...] over how she presents herself, over what she chooses to reveal to others" (Vorhaus 2021: 454). This is seen to culminate in a symbolic dignitary harm in that it symbolises less-than-human status (Vorhaus 2021: 454–455).[77] Referring specifically to intimate body

[77] Vorhaus discusses this point through the lens of experiences which have, and are often deliberately intended to have, public witnesses (Vorhaus 2021: 453) but, arguably, the point

searches, Margalit describes "searching people's private parts against their will" as "the prototypical example of a humiliating gesture" (Margalit 1996: 210–211).

Experiences of profound powerlessness, then, can be understood to have the capacity to erode basic self-respect. Since humiliation (and degradation) is judged with reference to social norms, whether humiliation occurs with or without witnesses is relevant but not determinative. The presence of witnesses is inherently relevant because even one witness may create a context (or a dynamic; Klein 1991: 101) which can reinforce an individual's perception of what they are experiencing as humiliating (Silver et al. 1986: 278–279). In other words, the presence or absence of witnesses can alter the experience of the person even if it does not determine whether we, from the outside, view the situation as humiliating in social fact. Restricting witnesses thereby removes one potentially aggravating factor. Further, the presence of witnesses is relevant because it can reveal an intent to humiliate on the part of those conducting a search. The Article 3 case law associates strip searches carried out in public with the intent to humiliate[78] because deliberate conduct of a strip search before witnesses ('in public') can be seen as a way of expressing active dignity denial towards the person being searched. This helps to make sense of the principle visible in the case law that strip searches must be conducted in a private setting in which the person searched is only visible to the person(s) conducting the search.

The principle regarding the conduct of strip searches by persons who are not of the same sex similarly concerns a potential aggravating factor. It is not obvious from Article 3 case law whether strip searches conducted by persons not of the same sex are seen to be capable of constituting a dignity violation in and of themselves, or as giving rise to an unacceptable risk of sexual violence, or both.[79] Assuming that such searches are

is equally relevant for thinking about strip search situations where the person conducting the search is the only other person present; see below.

[78] *Iwańczuk* (n 34) para 57–59.

[79] On this point, the explanatory notes to the Bangkok Rules, pertaining specifically to the treatment of women, view the conduct of searches by persons not of the same sex as problematic in and of themselves. This comes across in the view that "[s]pecial sensitivity should be demonstrated in the case of women [...] because they are likely to feel the humiliation of undergoing intimate searches particularly" (Footnote omitted). UN General Assembly, *United Nations*

inherently capable of constituting a dignity violation, taken alone or in combination with other treatment, this principle must be approached with reference to social norms, not only around powerlessness but also around gender and the social significance of intimate searches by persons of the opposite sex. Bernstein, for example, places 'sex-differentiated' (Bernstein 2015: 152) norms as central to his philosophical examination of the moral injury constituted by rape. This account accords a foundational significance to a connection between self-respect and an ability to exercise autonomy in terms of self-presentation of different aspects of embodiment, which, he argues, are deeply rooted in ideas projected onto female embodiment specifically (in particular, Bernstein 2015: 293–299). Such perspectives may point towards possible understandings of the relevance of sex in the body search context. Some such account is necessary to make sense of the Court's stance on the acceptability of strip searches conducted by persons of the same sex as distinct from strip searches conducted by persons not of the same sex; in other words, to make sense of why the former might be more readily seen to constitute a symbolic expression of denial of a person's human status than the latter.

Indeed an account like Bernstein's, while suggesting a rationale for the relevance of social norms around sex, at the same time makes a distinction on this basis problematic. This is fundamentally because human dignity is understood to be coextensive with the body, i.e. all bodies. Bernstein describes the body as a morally bounded and protected sphere, captured by the notion of 'bodily integrity' (e.g. Bernstein 2015: 60–61). Powerlessness has a foundational connection to the loss of bodily integrity, and so to a violation of bodily autonomy (Bernstein 2015: 327). Bernstein (2015: 60) writes: "Bodily integrity involves recognizing the body as a limit, so that to physically interfere with a person's body—to touch, to mark, to directly manipulate, to invade, to violate the body—involves crossing an absolute moral boundary". This is a challenge from the point of view of the ECtHR's approach—and indeed all

---

Rules for the Treatment of Women Prisoners and Non-custodial Measures for Women Offenders (the Bangkok Rules), A/RES/65/229, 16 March 2011, Rule 19). This refers to the conduct of the search itself and not a risk of further violence.

approaches that start from the position that strip searches are not inherently degrading. Ultimately, Bernstein's perspective might underpin an argument that all strip searches have a particular symbolic significance when combined with a lack of consent and structural power imbalance. The ECtHR has not gone so far as to recognise this symbolic significance as rendering all such searches incompatible with Article 3.

The use of 'dignity' language to represent a yardstick for the acceptability of strip searches, and the expression of this in baseline safeguards, aligns with other regional and international law standards and interpretations.[80] Together, the elements that make up the conduct of strip searches negotiate the line between dignity respect and disrespect. Ultimately, as Skinns et al. (2020) point out, in these loaded circumstances what remains fundamental is a person's sense of being treated as someone of equal worth to those with whom they are interacting: a sense of being 'treated like a human being'.

4 Strip Searches in (Carceral) Context

One dimension of the Court's approach to strip searches is that, in assessing whether they are necessary for protective purposes, it will take into account other measures contributing to safety and reducing the likelihood that any dangerous items will be in a detained person's possession. Besides examining strip searches in their wider context, the Court also often opts for assessing the cumulative conditions of detention to determine compliance with Article 3. It therefore frequently considers the performance of strip searches as part of a detention regime that it then deems contrary to Article 3 as a whole.[81] In such cases, a finding of an Article 3 violation on the basis of the applicant's cumulative conditions or experience of detention makes it challenging to establish whether the

[80] See Inter-American Commission on Human Rights, *Principles and Best Practices on the Protection of Persons Deprived of Liberty in the Americas*, 13 March 2008, No. 1/08, Principle XXI; UN General Assembly, *United Nations Standard Minimum Rules for the Treatment of Prisoners (the Nelson Mandela Rules)*, 8 January 2016, A/RES/70/175, Rule 50.

[81] See, e.g. *Piechowicz* (n 43).

strip searches would have been found to have violated Article 3 on a free-standing basis. Nonetheless, the Court's doctrine in 'cumulative' cases suggests that strip searches are often recognised as being a key part of an environment that oppresses and dehumanises persons in prison.

A challenge that arises in determining whether the conditions of detention within which strip searches occur may reach the Article 3 'threshold' is the Court's repeated assertion that, for such a finding to be made, the distress or hardship experienced must "go beyond that inevitable element of suffering or humiliation connected with a given form of legitimate treatment or punishment"[82] and, specifically within a detention context, be "of an intensity exceeding the unavoidable level of suffering inherent in detention".[83] The notion of suffering that is 'inherent in detention' raises significant questions from a penological perspective, which the Court has not explicitly confronted. Nonetheless, some parameters of the Court's thinking in this area can be discerned from the case law (see, further, Mavronicola 2015).

First, it is clear that, for the Court, the lawful deprivation of liberty must entail bounded, rather than potentially boundless, suffering (Mavronicola 2021: 114). The ECtHR's doctrine indicates that while it considers lawfully ordained imprisonment and its attendant suffering to be prima facie 'legitimate', a number of factors may augment the severity involved to a degree that crosses the Article 3 'threshold'. These include situational factors or personal characteristics that place the person detained in a particularly vulnerable position, such as illness, disability, advanced age, or other circumstances (consider, for example, sexual orientation or gender expression that does not conform to cis-heteronormative expectations) that may deepen one's vulnerability in the prison environment.[84] Additionally, it is clear that the ECtHR considers the violent treatment of persons in detention, including physical, sexual, and mental abuse, as not being 'inherent in detention'—indeed it

---

[82] *A v. UK* (n 29) para 127.

[83] *Savičs* (n 35) para 146.

[84] See, e.g. *Farbtuhs* (n 69) para 61; *Helhal v. France*, App. No. 10401/12, 19 February 2015, para 63.

often finds the intentional and purposeful infliction of abuse in such circumstances to amount to torture.[85]

Moreover, regimes of detention that essentially *extinguish* liberty—by being highly restrictive and/or intrusive—will tend to be found to violate Article 3 ECHR. The Court treats with particular suspicion regimes of imprisonment that suppress human interaction. It has repeatedly underlined that total sensory and social isolation is incompatible with Article 3 per se: according to the Court, "…[c]omplete sensory isolation coupled with total social isolation can destroy the personality and constitutes a form of inhuman treatment which cannot be justified by the requirements of security or any other reason".[86] Other restrictions on interaction which "fall short of complete sensory isolation" may still violate Article 3, according to the Court, which has suggested that "[w]hile prolonged removal from association with others is undesirable, whether such a measure falls within the ambit of Article 3 of the Convention depends on the particular conditions, the stringency of the measure, its duration, the objective pursued and its effects on the person concerned".[87] Moreover, the ECtHR has made it clear that even where such regimes may be deemed justified, their harmful effects should be counteracted through positive measures, including taking steps to provide 'mental or physical stimulation'.[88]

The Court's approach to conditions of detention which are highly restrictive as well as intrusive is demonstrated in some of the case law on strip searches, given that such searches are often part of a broader 'regime' of surveillance and control. It has repeatedly found that certain regimes involve an *overreach* of restriction and intrusion, which cannot be deemed necessary for people's protection. In a series of cases concerning the 'dangerous detainee' prison regime in Poland, for example, the ECtHR held that:

---

85 See, among many cases, for example, *Karabet and others v. Ukraine*, App. No. 38906/07 and 52025/07, 17 January 2013; *Dedovskiy and others v. Russia*, App. No. 7178/03, 15 May 2008.

86 *Öcalan v. Turkey* [GC], App. No. 46221/99, 12 May 2005, para 191; *Onoufriou v. Cyprus*, App. No. 24407/04, 10 December 2009, para 69.

87 *Onoufriou*, ibid para 69.

88 *Piechowicz* (n 43) para 173.

> taking into account the cumulative effects of the "dangerous detainee" regime on the applicant, the Court finds that the authorities did not provide sufficient and relevant reasons which could justify, in the circumstances of the case, the severity of the measures taken. In particular, the authorities failed to show that the impugned measures were necessary in their entirety to attain the legitimate aim of ensuring prison security.[89]

Given the growing centrality of rehabilitation as the overarching criterion by which dignity-compliance is determined in the prison context post-*Vinter*[90] (analysed in Mavronicola 2015: 737–743), it seems reasonable to predict that the circumstances in which highly restrictive and/or intrusive prison regimes will be deemed Article 3-compliant will increasingly narrow and require both frequent and ever more robust justification rooted in protection, as well as positive measures mitigating the harm that such regimes tend to cause.

Nonetheless, the idea that a (substantial) degree of suffering is a 'normal' aspect of imprisonment and that it is only aberrations from this norm that bring the experience(s) of imprisonment over the Article 3 threshold not only begs the question, but also suggests that common elements of the prison experience may be unduly presumed legitimate and shielded from scrutiny. An enduring question is the extent to which the ECtHR may ultimately come to question, on a 'wholesale' basis, prison itself (Mavronicola 2021: 118). The growth in penal abolitionist thinking (e.g. Coyle and Scott 2021) is relevant in this respect: it invites at the very least a more sweeping interrogation of what is understood as acceptable, 'tolerable' or to-be-tolerated suffering or distress in the penal context, by not taking the legitimacy of the prison as 'a given'.[91]

---

[89] *Karykowski v. Poland*, App. No. 653/12, 12 January 2016, para 39; *Prus v. Poland*, App. No. 5136/11, 12 January 2016, para 38; *Romaniuk v Poland*, App. No. 59285/12, 12 January 2016 para 46. See also *Filas v. Poland*, para 36.

[90] *Vinter and others v. UK* [GC], App. No. 66069/09, 130/10 and 3896/10, 9 July 2013. On the centrality of rehabilitation in determining prison regimes' compliance with Article 3, see, for example, *Harakchiev and Tolumov v. Bulgaria*, App. No. 15018/11 and 61199/12, 8 July 2014, para 264–267.

[91] See text in n 30 above.

5 Conclusion

The assessment of whether a practice is contrary to the right not to be subjected to inhuman or degrading treatment or punishment is, within the parameters of the European Convention and the ECtHR's interpretation of the Convention, a high-stakes determination of the lawfulness of State action and of State authorities' compliance with the demands of human dignity. Given the right's absolute character in particular, the ECtHR's doctrine provides an important lens for examining how ideas of necessity mediate against judgements of appropriateness of conduct. Crucially, the right's absolute character also means that its protection is acutely significant for those who are most vulnerable to the heavy hand or cruel indifference of the State. We have sought to examine the application of Article 3 to body searches, notably strip searches, with this in mind.

We have observed that the Court does not consider strip searches to cross the 'threshold' set by Article 3 in all their manifestations. Yet while the Court's approach involves conducting a context-sensitive assessment of whether Article 3 is violated in any given case, it is possible to distil from the Court's reasoning and findings a set of principles that can serve to guide norm-appliers and other stakeholders on an *ex ante* basis. The Court's approach is that a strip search that is undertaken for protective purposes and is necessary to achieve such purposes may be respectful of the dignity of the person being intruded upon if conducted in a dignity-respecting manner. Conversely, unnecessary, routine strip searches are fundamentally not respectful of that person's dignity; strip searches intended to humiliate or cause distress are not respectful of the person's dignity; and strip searches performed in ways that convey dignity disrespect, including when carried out in public and by persons of the opposite sex, are unlawful. We have sought to unpack and flesh out these criteria in some detail, based on a holistic view of the ECtHR's doctrine, to provide an enhanced insight into the relationship between them and the substance of each.

Besides the utility of distilling these principles for the purposes of guidance, what we hope we have offered is an account of the dignity dimensions of Article 3's application to strip searches within the carceral context and an attempt to make sense of the Court's approach in light of these dimensions, but also a clearer basis for engaging critically with the Court's thinking and its concrete implications. A particular issue ripe for critique is the way legitimacy and acceptability are assumed in respect of common elements of the prison 'experience' within the reasoning of the Court. We believe that there is considerable scope for reflecting further on the direction(s) that the doctrine will, or should, take in this regard, in light of the increasing centrality of the rehabilitative aim within imprisonment since the Grand Chamber judgment in *Vinter v UK*[92] and the case law that has followed it. In particular, what can be deemed the "unavoidable level of suffering [and humiliation] inherent in detention", and its relationship to practices such as strip searches, should be seen as continuously evolving in light of rehabilitation's ascendancy within European human rights law, and as being potentially subject to more radical transformation alongside a growth in penal abolitionist thinking and campaigning.

References

Bernstein, J.M. 2015. *Torture and dignity: An essay on moral injury*. Chicago: University of Chicago Press.

Coyle, M.J., and D. Scott, eds. 2021. *The Routledge international handbook of penal abolition*. London: Routledge.

CPT. 2011. *Report to the Polish Government on the visit to Poland carried out by the European Committee for the Prevention of Torture and Inhuman or Degrading Treatment or Punishment (CPT) from 26 November to 8 December 2009*. CPT/Inf (2011) 20. Strasbourg: Council of Europe.

Daems, T. 2014. 'Ceci N'est Pas Une Fouille À Corps': The Denial of Strip Searches in Belgian Prisons'. In *Punishment and Incarceration: A Global Perspective (Sociology of Crime, Law and Deviance, Vol. 19)*, ed. M. Deflem, 75–94. Bingley: Emerald Group Publishing.

[92] *Vinter* (n 90).

Duff, A. 2001. *Punishment, communication, and community*. Oxford: Oxford University Press.

Farrell, M. 2015. Just how ill-treated were you? An investigation of cross-fertilization in the interpretive approaches to torture at the European Court of Human Rights and in International Criminal Law. *Nordic Journal of International Law* 84: 482–514.

Harris, D.J., M. O'Boyle, E.P. Bates, and C.M. Buckley. 2009. *Harris, O'Boyle & Warbrick: Law of the European Convention on Human Rights*. Oxford: Oxford University Press.

Klein, D.C. 1991. The humiliation dynamic: An overview. *The Journal of Primary Prevention* 12 (2): 93–121.

Kuch, H. 2011. The rituality of humiliation: Exploring symbolic vulnerability. In *Humiliation, degradation, dehumanization: Human dignity violated*, ed. P. Kaufmann, H. Kuch, C. Neuhäuser, and E. Webster, 37–56. Dordrecht: Springer.

Liebling, A. 2011. Moral performance, inhuman and degrading treatment and prison pain. *Punishment & Society* 13 (5): 530–550.

Luban, D. 2014. *Torture, power and law*. Cambridge: Cambridge University Press.

Malpas, J. 2007. Human dignity and human being. In *Perspectives on human dignity: A conversation*, ed. J. Malpas and N. Lickiss, 19–25. Dordrecht: Springer.

Margalit, A. 1996. *The decent society*. Cambridge: Harvard University Press.

Mavronicola, N. 2012. What is an "absolute right"? Deciphering absoluteness in the context of Article 3 of the European Convention on Human Rights. *Human Rights Law Review* 12 (4): 723–758.

Mavronicola, N. 2013. *Güler and Öngel v Turkey*: Article 3 of the European Convention on Human Rights and Strasbourg's discourse on the justified use of force. *Modern Law Review* 76 (2): 370–382.

Mavronicola, N. 2015. Crime, punishment and Article 3 ECHR: Puzzles and prospects of applying an absolute right in a penal context. *Human Rights Law Review* 15 (4): 721–743.

Mavronicola, N. 2021. *Torture, inhumanity and degradation under Article 3 of the ECHR: Absolute rights and absolute wrongs*. Oxford: Hart Publishing.

Skinns, L., A. Sorsby, and L. Rice. 2020. "Treat them as a human being": Dignity in police detention and its implications for "good" police custody. *British Journal of Criminology* 60 (6): 1667–1688.

Silver, M., R. Conte, M. Miceli, and I. Poggi. 1986. Humiliation: Feeling, social control and construction of identity. *Journal for the Theory of Social Behaviour* 16 (3): 269–283.

Spalding, A. 2021. Strip-searching for nationality documents. *Modern Law Review* 84 (3): 456–476.

Vorhaus, J. 2021. Bringing people down: Degrading treatment and punishment. *New Criminal Law Review* 24 (3): 433–466.

Waldron, J. 2005. Torture and positive law: Jurisprudence for the White House. *Columbia Law Review* 105 (6): 1681–1750.

Waldron, J. 2010. Inhuman and degrading treatment: The words themselves. *Canadian Journal of Law and Jurisprudence* 23: 269–286.

Webster, E. 2016. Interpretation of the Prohibition of Torture: Making sense of 'dignity' talk. *Human Rights Review* 17 (3): 371–390.

Webster, E. 2018. *Dignity, degrading treatment and torture in human rights law: The ends of Article 3 of the European Convention on Human Rights*. London: Routledge.

Body Searches and Vulnerable Groups: Women and LGBTQI+ People in Prison

Aurore Vanliefde

1 Introduction

While body searches are inherently invasive procedures for all prisoners, some vulnerable groups (e.g. women, LGBTQI+ people, children, people with disabilities and/or any religious/ethnic/cultural minorities in a specific prison context) might be significantly more affected by its degrading character. This chapter examines how body searches are experienced by vulnerable groups, with a focus on women and LGBTQI+ people in prison.

Like most practices in prison, initial guidelines on body searches have been developed with mainly male, cisgender and straight people in mind. Because the specific needs and sensibilities of women and/or LGBTQI+ people are not always considered, these searches can be experienced

A. Vanliefde (✉)
KU Leuven, Leuven, Belgium
e-mail: Aurore.vanliefde@kuleuven.be

T. Daems (ed.), *Body Searches and Imprisonment*, Palgrave Studies in Prisons and Penology, https://doi.org/10.1007/978-3-031-20451-7_6

as particularly degrading or humiliating by women and/or LGBTQI+ people in prison. This is especially the case when the search is conducted by prison staff of the opposite sex/gender, or for more invasive body cavity searches.

This chapter confronts recommendations on conducting body searches on vulnerable groups with how body searches are experienced by vulnerable groups based on literature and reports from the European Committee for the Prevention of Torture and Inhuman or Degrading Treatment or Punishment (CPT). The chapter proposes a more gendered and queer perspective on body searches, with specific attention to the gendered dynamics that shape the experience of body searches, the experience of searches as humiliation or sexual abuse by some prisoners and recommendations on conducting body searches on vulnerable populations in prison.

2 Women and LGBTQI+ People in Prison: A Vulnerable Group

Women and LGBTQI+ (lesbian, gay, bisexual, transgender, queer, intersex and self-identifying members of the community) people have been repeatedly identified as particularly vulnerable in prison settings (United Nations Office on Drugs and Crime [UNODC] 2009). This vulnerability is related to one's sexual orientation, gender identity, gender expression and/or sex characteristics (SOGIESC). This section defines key concepts further, before defining the concept of vulnerability.

2.1 On Sexual Orientation, Gender Identity, Gender Expression and Sex Characteristics (SOGIESC)

The 'LGB' part of the LGBTQI+ acronym refers to one's sexual orientation. Sexual orientation is "...each person's capacity for profound emotional, affectional and sexual attraction to, and intimate and sexual relations with, individuals of a different gender or the same gender or more than one gender".[1] People who have a different sexual orientation than the societal expectation for men and women to relate heterosexually to each other (heteronormativity) are usually called lesbian (L: women x women), gay (G: men x men), or bisexual (B: men x multiple genders; women x multiple genders) (Sauer and Podhara 2013).

When referring to people as 'men' or 'women', we refer to their gender identity. Gender is used here to describe the socially constructed characteristics and expectations of women and men, such as norms, behaviours and roles associated with a certain gender. Gender differs from biological sex, which is determined by physical characteristics (chromosomes, hormones, internal and external genitalia and secondary sex characteristics). Gender identity refers to "...each person's deeply felt internal and individual experience of gender, which may or may not correspond with the sex assigned at birth including the personal sense of the body (...) and other expressions of gender, including dress, speech and mannerisms".[2] People whose gender identity does not match their biological sex such as assigned at birth are called transgender (or trans) people (Blight 2000). When a person's gender identity corresponds with their biological sex, they are referred to as cisgender. The term 'transgender' includes trans men,[3] trans women,[4] transvestites[5] and people who identify as non-binary (Stryker 2017). Gender (identity) is often conceptualised in a male–female binary. However, across cultures and history, significant amounts of people have identified outside this binary and still do

---

[1] Yogyakarta Principles (November 2006) on the Principles on the Application of International Human Rights Law in Relation to Sexual Orientation and Gender Identity (2007). Available at: http://yogyakartaprinciples.org/, note 1.

[2] Yogyakarta Principles (November 2006) on the Principles on the Application of International Human Rights Law in Relation to Sexual Orientation and Gender Identity (2007). Available at: http://yogyakartaprinciples.org/, note 2.

[3] People who were assigned as female at birth (biological sex), but identify as a man (gender identity).

[4] People who were assigned as male at birth (biological sex), but identify as a woman (gender identity).

[5] People who regularly or sporadically express their inner lived (sub)gender identity through clothing, language, behaviour, attitude, etc. This is usually temporary and dependent on the context.

(Herdt 1996). 'Non-binary' is used as an umbrella term[6] for these gender identities (Richards et al. 2016). Where 'gender identity' refers to one's internally experienced gender, 'gender expression' refers to one's external presentation of gender (behaviour, mannerisms, interests and appearance that are associated with gender or within the categories of femininity or masculinity).

Intersex people are born with sex characteristics that are not typically either male or female (Sauer and Podhara 2013). Despite the potential ambiguity of physical characteristics, most intersex people identify within the traditional gender binary (Richards and Barker 2013).

While 'queer' is sometimes used interchangeably with the LGBTQI+ acronym, 'queer' also refers to a distinct group of people. '(Gender)queer' or 'questioning' people actively question or critique the man–woman dichotomy in gender identity and heteronormative societal norms on a more ontological level (Richards et al. 2016; Matsuno and Budge 2017). Most empirical research on the experiences of LGBTQI+ people is limited to LGBT people. There is little research on incarcerated intersex and queer people, because of the relative invisibility of the first group and the varying definitions given to the latter group. The acronym 'LGBTQI' is non-exhaustive, as people across cultures and time periods have used diverse language to express the wide range of sexual orientations, gender identities, gender expressions and sex characteristics. Therefore, this chapter will use the term 'LGBTQI+' for inclusivity.

2.2 Vulnerability as a Collective Experience?

Women and LGBTQI+ people have consistently been described as vulnerable prisoners with special needs. Vulnerable prisoners are those who face an increased risk to their safety, security, or well-being as a result of imprisonment because of their class, ethnicity, gender, age,

[6] 'Non-binary' includes a wide variety of gender identities. Some people's androgynous or mixed gender identity may consistently include both male and female elements, while genderfluid people have a more changing, fluid experience of gender over time. There are also people who identify as third gender or other gender, while others are genderless, agender, or gender-neutral. Some people also prefer the term 'pangender' to refer to their complex and fluid understanding of their gender identity (see e.g. Matsuno and Budge 2017; Richards et al. 2016).

illness, disability and sexual preferences, legal or political status (adapted from Penal Reform International [PRI] 2003; Liamputtong 2007). This group can include juveniles, women and mothers, LGBTQI+ people, the mentally ill or developmentally disabled, physically disabled or ill persons, foreigners, minorities or indigenous peoples, the elderly and those held in pre-trial detention or under sentence of death (PRI 2003).

This chapter focuses on incarcerated women and LGBTQI+ people. However, the different characteristics from the definition above are not mutually exclusive. When overlapping (e.g. a foreign trans woman from an ethnic minority), these characteristics add up to a layered form of vulnerability. While the scope of this chapter is limited to women and LGBTQI+ people, different other traits may add to this vulnerability when understood from an intersectional perspective. The term intersectionality, coined by Kimberlé Crenshaw (1989, 1991), refers to the combination of minority characteristics that can add up to a complex and layered vulnerability.

The vulnerability of detained women and LGBTQI+ people in prison is twofold. On the one hand, all prisoners are institutionally vulnerable because they are under the formal authority of the criminal justice system and the prison administration and staff (Gordon 2020). On the other hand, LGBTQI+ people as a group are particularly vulnerable to discrimination and violence because of their sexual orientation and/or gender identity (Sauer and Podhara 2013; Blanc 2015, 2021). This is also very true for women in prison settings, as will be discussed further in this chapter. 'Vulnerability' is not inherent to the vulnerable prisoners themselves but must always be understood within the specific context of norms and values. The vulnerability of women and LGBTQI+ people is not inherent to their gender identity/sexual orientation in itself, but must be understood in relation to particular contexts (such as prisons) where particular forms of masculinity prevail, and where misogyny, homophobia and transphobia are prevalent (Blanc 2015).

Despite the significant differences between those different categories and their individual lived experience and needs, the concept of vulnerability is helpful to understand the context in which the practice of body searches exists for detained women and LGBTQI+ people in prison.

Indeed, the institutional and social vulnerability of this group of prisoners highlights the asymmetrical power dynamics in the prison settings that are inherent to the practice of body searches.

3 Experiences of Searches by Women and LGBTQI+ People

Body searches are part of the functioning of most prisons and are usually conducted for safety reasons: the aim is to identify and remove items that are not allowed in the prison (such as weapons, drugs and other contraband). Different forms of body searches can be distinguished and the invasiveness of the searches varies. The first kind is pat-down (or 'frisk') searches, where prisoners are searched over their clothes. Secondly, strip searches require the prisoner to remove their clothing for prison staff to visually examine their body. Lastly, the visual inspection and probing of bodily orifices constitute body cavity searches. There are differences in how these practices are precisely defined in research and practice and these categories are not always used by prisoners in their testimonies (Scraton and Moore 2005; Wahidin 2016).

Depending on the applicable rules, body searches can be conducted routinely or when there is reason to believe a prisoner is hiding the item in their clothing, on their body or inside their body. Body searches are more likely to be carried out at times when the likelihood of object transfer or dissimulation is considered to be higher. Routine pat-down searches are often conducted when (re-)entering the prison, before and/or after visits with physical contact with relatives or certain professionals, when being transferred to a segregation cell or after movements within the prison (e.g. work, education, exercise or meals in collective spaces) (PRI and APT 2015; APT 2022). One of the key principles of the case law of the European Court of Human Rights (ECtHR) is that strip searches and body cavity searches should not be carried out routinely and must be individually motivated.[7] When there are no rules

[7] See Mavronicola & Webster's chapter in this book for further discussion on ECtHR case law and this principle.

on the precise conditions when body searches are indicated, prison staff can conduct searches at any given time (PRI and APT 2015). Even when carried out by a staff member of the same gender, arbitrarily conducted body searches may cause severe humiliation (APT 2022).

Due to their invasive nature, body searches have the potential to infringe upon the dignity of detainees.[8] This is especially the case when searches are conducted routinely or systematically, or in a disproportionate, humiliating or discriminatory manner (PRI and APT 2015). Such applications of body searches can therefore be interpreted as inhuman or degrading treatment. These go against international norms applicable to all prisoners (such as the United Nations Standard Minimum Rules for the Treatment of Prisoners (the Nelson Mandela Rules) and the European Prison Rules[9]) or elaborated specifically for women (the Bangkok Rules[10]). While there are no internationally binding norms regarding LGBTQI+ people in prison (yet), a group of international human rights experts formulated a series of principles on the application of binding international human rights law to the issues of sexual orientation and gender identity: the Yogyakarta Principles.[11] While these principles are non-binding, they interpret and clarify states' obligations according to human rights law to protect the rights of LGBTQI+ persons in general, and LGBTQI+ prisoners in particular (Blanc 2015; PRI and APT 2015). The values of respect for the prisoner's dignity and freedom from inhuman or degrading treatment are central

---

[8] Dignity is one of the key concepts in the revised United Nations Standard Minimum Rules for the Treatment of Prisoners (the Nelson Mandela Rules), adopted by the UN Commission on Crime Prevention and Criminal Justice on 22 May 2015, endorsed by the Economic and Social Council on 9 September 2015, UN-Doc. E/RES/2015/20 and adopted by UN General Assembly Third Committee on 5 November 2015. Hereafter: Standard Minimum Rules for the Treatment of Prisoners.

[9] Recommendation Rec(2006)2-rev of the Committee of Ministers to Member States on the European Prison Rules, adopted by the Committee of Ministers on 11 January 2006 and revised and amended by the Committee of Ministers on 1 July 2020 (Hereafter: the European Prison Rules).

[10] United Nations Rules on the Treatment of Women Prisoners and Non-custodial Measures for Women Offenders (the Bangkok Rules).

[11] Yogyakarta Principles (November 2006) on the Principles on the Application of International Human Rights Law in Relation to Sexual Orientation and Gender Identity (2007). Available at: http://yogyakartaprinciples.org/.

in these recommendations and can serve as a benchmark to analyse the practice of body searches, in particular for vulnerable groups.

Searches can also indirectly impact the social ties detained women and LGBTQI+ people have with people outside of prison. On the one hand, they might refuse visits themselves to avoid being searched after the visit (Goldblatt and Steele 2019; McCulloch and George 2008). On the other hand, (frisk) searches conducted on visitors in certain facilities, might deter friends and family from visiting women and/or LGBTQI+ people in prison. Deprivation of social contact with family and friends often affects women more severely than men (Crewe et al. 2017) and is especially detrimental to their mental health (Harner and Riley 2013; Douglas et al. 2009). For LGBTQI+ people, maintaining social ties with people outside of prison may already be more difficult because of weakened social ties prior to detention as a result of outing their gender identity and/or sexual orientation, and limited visit access in some prisons for same-sex couples (James et al. 2016; National Center for Transgender Equality [NCTE] 2018; UNODC 2009). Imposing searches on visitors can thus impact women and LGBTQI+ people disproportionately by having fewer visits and degrading their relationships with families and friends.

3.1 Body Searches and Harm

Even when conducted under the best possible circumstances, body searches constitute a severe infringement of one's privacy (APT 2022). Regardless of one's gender identity, it has been well-established that prisoners are likely to feel humiliation when undergoing any kind of search in general, and intimate searches in particular. The forced display of the prisoner's body to prison staff with asymmetrical power relations created opportunities for potential (gendered) violence and abuse (Wahidin 2016). Touching and inspecting the body of the prisoner might be experienced as particularly humiliating because it forcefully and completely invades the little intimacy a detainee has left in the prison context (Baker 2003). This loss of privacy and violation of bodily integrity reinforces the prisoner's awareness of their powerlessness in the prison (Wahidin 2016).

This feeling of powerlessness and the lack of autonomy and freedom of action is characteristic of prisons as total institutions, as described by Sykes (1958).

Furthermore, body searches can result in psychological and physical harm.[12] Body searches can induce psychological distress or trauma due to the experience of feeling ashamed, violated, humiliated and sexualised, especially in people who have had traumatising or negative sexual experiences in the past (APT 2022; Reyes 2006; Psutka and Sheehy 2016; Wahidin 2016). By doing so, the practice may perpetuate the cycle of trauma and abuse that women and LGBTQI+ people have endured during their lives (Shalev 2021). Body cavity searches can result in physical injury (of the mouth, vagina, anus or rectum) when performed by staff without medical training (PRI and APT 2015; Reyes 2006).

Apart from being dehumanising and isolating, body searches are especially humiliating for people with active uteruses[13] during menstruation and pregnancy (Marcoux Rouleau 2021; Hutchison 2019; Psutka and Sheehy 2016; Goldblatt and Steele 2019; McCulloch and George 2008; Wahidin 2016). Prisoners who menstruate are often asked to remove their sanitary items and dispose of them before the search is conducted. They are not always provided with new sanitary items after the search or must pay for one themselves, which adds up to other inequalities related to menstruation prisoners might face (Goldblatt and Steele 2019). Body searches may even cause physical harm in the case of pregnancy and other medical conditions, especially if carried out by staff who have not received proper training.[14]

Finally, searches can be used as intimidation, threat or additional punishment. Body searches then are part of penal 'mechanisms of fear' used to exercise control over prisoners (Wahidin 2016; PRI and APT 2015; Poulantzas 1978: 83). Research by Wahidin (2016) and Scraton

[12] Statement of the World Medical Association (WMA) on body searches of prisoners, adopted by the 45th World Medical Assembly, Budapest, Hungary, October 1993, editorially revised at the 170th Council Session, Divonne-les-Bains, France, May 2005 and revised by the 67th WMA General Assembly, Taipei, Taiwan, October 2016. (https://www.wma.net/policies-post/wma-statement-on-body-searches-of-prisoners/, consulted 21 February 2022), paragraph 12.

[13] This formulation was chosen to include all women as well as trans, intersex and non-binary people who do not identify as women, but bear an active uterus.

[14] Statement of the WMA on body searches of prisoners, op. cit., paragraph 8.

and Moore (2005, 2007, 2014) on the experiences of incarcerated ex-combatant women in Northern Ireland, described body searches as gender differentiating and sexualising tools to abuse women's bodies and break their spirit. In this particular setting, women described the use of body searches as a gendered and sexualised form of punishment (Scraton and Moore 2005, 2007, 2014; Wahidin 2016).[15]

3.2 Body Searches as State-Inflicted Sexual Assault

Strip searches and body cavity searches may be experienced as sexual assault or rape by the person undergoing them (George 1993; Marcoux Rouleau 2021; Hutchison 2020; Scraton and Moore 2005; Wahidin 2016; McCulloch and George 2008). Indeed, the acts constituting a body search would be considered sexual assault were they not legally defined and conducted by a state official in a prison setting (George 1993; Marcoux Rouleau 2021). Furthermore, body searches can create facilitating conditions for staff to perform acts of sexual violence (Arkles 2009; Davis 2003, 2005; Psutka and Sheehy 2016). Forms of sexual violence can differ greatly and range from inappropriate comments regarding the prisoner's body, gender identity, gender expression or sexual orientation, inappropriate touching and groping (unnecessary to the means of the search) and even rape (Scraton and Moore 2005; McCulloch and George 2008). The experience of sexual violence through a body search in turn can create fear, pain and even terror in victims (Wahidin 2016).

Incarcerated women and LGBTQI+ people have among the highest rates of sexual victimisation (Hutchison 2020; Beck et al. 2013; Meyer et al. 2017; NCTE 2018; Reyes 2006). Body searches can induce psychological trauma in people who have had traumatising or negative sexual experiences in the past (Reyes 2006). Invasive body searches may thus constitute the next step in the cycle of harm and (sexual) violence

[15] There are numerous other contexts where searches and sexualised forms of punishments were used as a control mechanism for women. For example, sexual violence has been used as a colonial subjugating and controlling strategy on Indigenous and enslaved Black women and has racial, colonial and cultural implications to the present day (See e.g. Davis 2003; Marcoux Rouleau 2021; McCulloch and George 2008).

for many detained women and LGBTQI+ people (Shalev 2021). The important difference is that the author of the violence is the state, *in casu* of prison staff and authorities (George 1993). Even if women and LGBTQI+ people consent to a search, this consent must be understood within the coercive environment searches occur in, the power imbalance between staff and prisoners and the risk of further punishment or other measures (Hutchison 2020; McCulloch and George 2008; Wahidin 2016). In these conditions, body searches can be understood as a form of ritualised state-inflicted violence against women, 'sexual coercion' or even 'sexual terrorism' (Wahidin 2016: 182; McCulloch and George 2008: 121–122).

The acknowledgement that non-consented acts of touching intimate parts or penetration during a search constitute a form of rape is fairly recent. In academic literature, George (1993: 31) was one of the first to argue that even "...some 'legal' strip searches fall under the definition of sexual assault". Improper touching during pat-downs and searches was then considered a form of sexual assault by the Special Rapporteur on violence against women in 1999[16] (Penal Reform International 2003). The 2008 report of the then Special Rapporteur on torture and other cruel, inhuman or degrading treatment or punishment, Manfred Nowak,[17] documented the broadening of the scope of crimes of sexual violence that can be prosecuted as rape, especially in prison settings. It refers to the conclusion of the Inter-American Court of Human Rights that "...the acts of sexual violence to which an inmate was submitted under an alleged finger vaginal 'examination' constituted sexual rape that due to its effects constituted torture".[18]

While prisoners might experience body (cavity) searches as a form of sexual assault, body searches remain a part of the normal functioning of prisons to ensure the safety of the prisoners and the prison staff.

---

[16] Report of the Special Rapporteur on violence against women of the mission to the United States of America on the issue of violence against women in state and federal prisons, E/CN.4/1999/68/Add.2, 4 January 1999, paragraphs 55 and 58.

[17] Report of the Special Rapporteur on torture and other cruel, inhuman or degrading treatment or punishment to the Human Rights Council, A/HRC/7/3, 15 January 2008, paragraph 35 and footnote 18.

[18] Miguel Castro-Castro Prison v. Peru, Inter-American Court of Human Rights judgement of 25 November 2006, paragraph 312.

This blurs the line between the extraordinary character of body searches and their ordinary use in penal settings (Carlton 2007; Wahidin 2016; Balfour 2017). According to Angela Davis (2003: 81; 2005), incorporating body (cavity) searches in prison policy can lead to the routinisation or normalisation of sexual abuse.

3.3 LGBTQI-Specific Issues with Body Searches

As documented above for women, body searches entail a risk of humiliation, abuse and violence for LGBTQI+ people because of their gender identity and/or sexual orientation. Because of the pronounced culture of hyper-masculinity in many male prisons or wings, male prisoners strongly hold on to their heterosexual identity, accentuate heterosexual norms (heteronormativity) and develop negative (homophobic and transphobic) attitudes towards homosexual, bisexual and transsexual persons (Ricordeau 2004, 2008; UNODC 2009; Carr et al. 2016; Wacquant 1999). This culture of hyper-masculinity is sometimes expressed in a deep fear of sexual assault by other prisoners of the same sex, where gay prisoners are potentially viewed as a threat or sexual predators (Reyes 2006; Ricordeau 2004). In turn, lesbian, gay and bisexual prisoners might choose to hide their sexual orientation, while trans and non-binary people might be more visible when they show or express traits of other genders (Robinson 2011; Carr et al. 2016).

Negative attitudes or curiosity towards LGBTQI+ people by staff members can shape the experience of body searches. During body searches, trans people are often the subject of jokes, mockery, misgendering[19] or denigrating remarks on their physical appearance or gender identity (Ghosh and Bourothu 2021; Maycock 2020; Sevelius and Jenness 2017; Routh et al. 2017; Stohr 2015; Maras et al. 2021). Repeated unjustified and/or voyeuristic body searches on trans, intersex and non-binary prisoners may occur with the intent of humiliating the prisoner, but also of satisfying the staff's curiosity or sexual arousal

[19] Misgendering refers to numerous (intentional or unintentional) ways in which trans people are not recognised in their gender identity. This includes using the wrong gender terms (pronouns, forms of address) and/or name (deadnaming).

regarding the prisoner's body (Arkles 2009; Brockmann et al. 2019). In countries where homosexuality is not culturally accepted and/or illegal, several cases of forced body cavity searches used to humiliate gay prisoners have been documented (Human Rights Watch 2004; Reyes 2006).

When in doubt about conducting a search on a trans or non-binary person, protocols for staff members who conduct body searches vary greatly. Some prisons rely on the sex of the person as registered on their identity documents, or on their physical attributes to decide whether a male or female staff member will conduct the search. Even then, directives can differ from case to case. For example, the French National Preventive Mechanism (NPM) (Contrôleur général des lieux de privation de liberté: CGLPL) reports that male staff members conduct searches on trans women (even if they have developed breasts), while some prison directors refuse that female staff members conduct searches on trans women with male genitalia (CGLPL 2021). Another practice is conducting searches with both a male and a female staff member present. For example, a trans woman who has not had gender reassignment surgery might be searched by a woman for their top half and by a man for their bottom half (Blanc 2021; Maras et al. 2021; Federale Ombudsman 2019). This practice relies entirely on the concept of anatomical sex and might re-enforce feelings of gender dysphoria in trans people. Gender dysphoria is the significant distress trans people experience because of the incongruence between their inner experienced gender identity and their physical characteristics (American Psychiatric Association [APA] 2013). As we will see later on in the recommendations, the gender identity and the preference of the prisoner being searched should be the primary argument for selecting staff conducting the search.

Because women and LGBTQI+ people often have been subjected to forms of discrimination and violations of their dignity during their lifetime, respecting deontological principles and prisoners' dignity when conducting body searches on trans people is especially important to avoid perpetuating the cycle of trauma and abuse that women and LGBTQI+ people have endured during their lives (Shalev 2021; CGLPL 2021).

4 A Gendered and Queer Understanding of Body Searches Within Gender Binary Prisons

As with most practices in prison, body searches were conceived for and are conducted on mainly male, cisgender and straight prisoners. The heteronormative and binary organisation of prisons, separating men from women in distinct wings or institutions, is closely related to the practice of body searches. These assumptions are especially problematic for trans, non-binary and intersex people, and there is a lack of consistent policy on body searches that takes the sensibilities of these groups of people into consideration (Gorden et al. 2017; Routh et al. 2017). The European Court of Human Rights has ruled that respecting the gender identity of a person, whether or not it is different from the gender they are officially registered as, is essential for safeguarding human dignity because it is one of the most basic elements of one's self-determination.[20] In practice, however, trans people are often allocated to a male or female prison based on their physical characteristics (Observatoire International des Prisons—Section Française [OIP-SF] 2021).

On the one hand, the decision to assign the prisoner to a facility based on their biological sex or physical characteristics, instead of one that conforms to their gender identity, is often justified by the perceived risk of sexual assault or even pregnancy (OIP-SF 2021; Lamble 2012). As a result, trans women are also sometimes put into a male facility or segregated from other prisoners. This portrayal of trans women as dangerous to other women or as sexual predators is highly problematic as it is rooted in transphobic beliefs and anecdotal incidents which received disproportionate media attention (Lamble 2012, 2019). On the other hand, this segregation is meant to prevent so-called 'gender panics'[21] by fellow inmates and correctional staff in women's prisons, and often relies on identifying prisoners based on their biological sex as attributed at birth,

[20] *Van Kück v. Germany*, App. No. 35968/97, 12 September 2003, para 73.

[21] A deep, cultural fear that occurs when the "naturalness" of a male–female gender binary is challenged (Schilt and Westbrook 2009; Schilt and Westbrook 2014).

or on their physical characteristics (Murray and Hunter Blackburn 2019; Westbrook and Schilt 2014).

This focus on physical attributes as a determinant for placement is closely related to the practice of body searches. Indeed, strict placement according to the physical (external) genitalia of detainees means that trans or intersex individuals might be subjected to a naked search of their genitalia upon entry into a prison, in order to determine in which (male or female) prison or wing the detainee will be placed (Jenness et al. 2019; Lamble 2012; Sumner and Jenness 2014). This focus on external sex attributes within the sex segregation policy in turn constructs and reiterates binary categories of 'sex', with no acknowledgement of variation in gender identity or sexual characteristics (Pemberton 2013). These assumptions further condition the prisoners in a gendered, heterosexual and cisgender organisational logic (Balfour 2017), which they will also carry in their day-to-day lives outside of the criminal justice system after their release. As Pemberton (2013) argues, sex segregation enables gendered prison regimes that contribute to the (re)production of specific forms of masculinity and femininity among prisoners. According to Kirkup (2009: 107), "...strip searches exist as part of a larger system of power, a system in which bodies, genders, and sexualities outside the socially constructed 'norm' are routinely subjected to discipline and punishment". Body searches might be the ultimate expression of how the prison system constantly recreates and reinforces masculine, cisnormative and heteronormative values regarding gender and sexuality.

5 To Reform or to Abolish

When assessing the lived experience of body searches by women and LGBTQI+ people against the key concept of dignity, one of the keystones of multiple standards on treating prisoners, several recommendations can be formulated. The recommendations that have been issued by academics, NGOs and human rights institutions are often of a reformist nature, meaning they tolerate the existence of the practice and propose changes to adapt and improve it. The first part of this section formulates (a non-exhaustive overview) of recommendations with the intent of minimising harm and respecting women and LGBTQI+ prisoners' dignity and privacy as much as possible whenever body searches have to be conducted. Other authors have argued for the complete abandonment of body searches, given how much it affects prisoners' dignity and its risks. The abolitionist view will be discussed before concluding the chapter.

5.1 Reformist Recommendations Specific for Women and LGBTQI+ People

Even when conducted for safety reasons, body searches can result in many other indirect and unintentional consequences (e.g. serve as a disciplining measure, humiliation, state-inflicted sexual assault). Therefore, a careful balancing exercise must be made when considering conducting a body search where the potential benefits for security must be weighed against the known adverse effects it can have. Several general recommendations to reduce harm caused by body searches have been formulated in international human rights standards and reports. Such recommendations include that body searches must not be conducted unless absolutely necessary[22] and follow the principles of legality, proportionality and necessity[23] (PRI and APT 2015; UNDP 2020; APT 2022). These principles entail that body searches can only be conducted within a fixed legal framework and after a careful risk assessment with regard to safety for the prison, its staff and its residents. Other unwritten goals and consequences of body searches (such as humiliation, enforcing power relations or using it as a punishment) cannot be used to motivate the body search. Instead, the known negative consequences of body searches on women and LGBTQI+ detainees must be taken into consideration in

[22] Rule 50 of Standard Minimum Rules for the Treatment of Prisoners; Commentary to Rule 19 of the Bangkok Rules.

[23] The *legality principle* states that the nature of body searches, the reasons for conducting them and the procedures should be defined by national law. The *principle of proportionality* refers to whether the invasive body search is proportionate with regard to the perceived risk (of the prisoner carrying an object) for the prisoner themselves, other prisoners or prison staff. This is closely linked to the final *principle of necessity*; whether the body search is necessary based on the perceived safety risk.

the proportionality and necessity check when considering conducting a body search. Furthermore, strip and more invasive body cavity searches should never be conducted on a routine basis.[24] To reduce harm, alternatives to body searches with physical contact (e.g. magnetometers, body scanners, ultrasound, ...) are recommended by the Bangkok Rules and the European Committee for the Prevention of Torture and Inhuman or Degrading Treatment or Punishment (CPT) (Tschanz 2016; PRI and APT 2015; APT 2022; Blanc 2021).[25] The CGLPL (French NPM) specifically recommends the use of a magnetometer over clothing for conducting searches on trans people, as this method is less intrusive and might be used by officers of all genders (CGLPL 2021).

The CPT (2018: 7) issued three recommendations with respect to a 'gender-sensitive' approach to personal searches in their 2018 factsheet on women in prison. The focus of this chapter on women and LGBTQI+ people aims to broaden this concept to sexual orientation, gender identity, gender expression and sex characteristics (SOGIESC). First, *body searches should be conducted by staff members of the same gender identity as the person deprived of their liberty.*[26] Generally, search procedures include specifications about the search to be conducted by a staff member of the same anatomical sex as the searched detainee (e.g. CPT 2018: 7). By using the term 'sex', legal texts and procedural directives do not account for trans, non-binary and intersex people (Blanc 2021). While some institutions might let the notion of 'gender' overrule the concept of 'sex' in practice (CGLPL 2021), it is preferred to use 'gender' in the codification of these procedures as well. Prison authorities should take the gender with which the prisoner identifies themselves into account and not the sex category as registered on identification documents (Kirkup

---

[24] Commentary to Rule 19 of the Bangkok Rules; The recommendation that strip and body cavity searches should never be conducted routinely is also one of the key principles of ECtHR case law on this matter. See Mavronicola and Webster's chapter in this book for further discussion on ECtHR case law and this principle.

[25] Rule 20 of the Bangkok Rules; Statement of the WMA on body searches of prisoners, op. cit., paragraph 12; CPT (2018: 7).

[26] Rule 19 of the Bangkok Rules; Rule 54.2 of the European Prison Rules; Statement of the WMA on body searches of prisoners, op. cit., paragraph 11.

2009).[27] Blanc (2021) notes that a search should never be used to determine the biological sex of a prisoner based on their sex characteristics. It is recommended to invite trans (and non-binary) people to express their preferences regarding the gender of the guard(s) who will conduct searches on them prior to the search and respect this preference (UNDP 2020; Blanc 2021; CGLPL 2021). The possibility of expressing a preference regarding the gender identity of the staff conducting the search should be notified to trans and non-binary prisoners and can be codified in a short written agreement.[28]

Second, full nudity must be avoided during strip and body cavity searches to minimise embarrassment and the degrading nature of the procedure. *People deprived of their liberty should be allowed to cover parts of their body in a way that does not interfere with the search.* Different options are possible: two-step strip searches (where the person undresses in two phases), providing a towel or sheet the person can use to cover parts of their body that are not being searched at that specific moment, letting the person hide their breasts or their genitals with their hands,—(PRI and APT 2015; APT 2022; CPT 2017: 30; CPT 2018: 7; CGLPL 2021).

Third, *body cavity searches should preferably not be carried out* (APT 2022). Apart from severely infringing on a person's privacy and dignity, body cavity searches can also result in physical or psychological injury for the person being searched.[29] Cases of body cavity searches being used to humiliate or sexually assault women and LGBTQI+ people emphasise the need to provide alternatives to this practice. Supervising the prisoners closely until potential forbidden items are naturally expelled from the body may suffice in most cases (PRI and APT 2015; Enggist et al. 2014). However, supervision is not synonymous with prolonged segregation. The forced administration of laxatives for the sake of accelerating

[27] Statement of the WMA, op. cit., paragraph 11.

[28] For example, this is part of voluntary agreements for transgender residents in prisons in England and Wales, which also includes rules on showering, living space, laundry, dress code and the ownership of certain items related to one's gender expression. See HMPPS Diversity and Inclusion Team (2020). The Care and Management of Individuals who are Transgender: Operational Guidance. London: Her Majesty's Prison & Probation Service.

[29] Commentary to Rule 20 of the Bangkok Rules; Statement of the WMA on body searches of prisoners, op. cit., paragraph 12.

the process of eliminating the suspected forbidden object, as has been observed by the CPT (2012: 24) in Greece in 2011 for women who refused to undergo a vaginal exam, cannot be justified. *In the case they are carried out, body cavity searches should be conducted by (external) qualified medical professionals or staff* trained to conduct these searches safely and knowledgeable of standards of women's and trans hygiene, health and safety (Lehtmets and Pont 2014; Reyes 2006; Enggist et al. 2014).[30]

Fourth, staff must be trained to conduct pat-down and strip searches appropriately (APT 2022).[31] This training should allow staff to detect and retrieve any hidden items, while at the same time respecting the dignity of those being searched.[32] *Training should also focus on professionalism and sensitivity towards diversity in sexual orientation, gender identity, gender expression and sex characteristics (SOGIESC)*, both for women and LGBTQI+ people deprived of their liberty and visitors.[33] Prison policy and staff should be aimed at combatting "...violence, discrimination and other harm on grounds of sexual orientation, gender identity, gender expression or sex characteristics faced by persons who are deprived of their liberty, including with respect to such issues as (...) body or other searches".[34]

Security and safety considerations, prison organisation and issues with staff (understaffing, lack of training, unavailability of sufficient people

30 Rule 52, Standard Minimum Rules for the Treatment of Prisoners; Rule 54.6 of the European Prison Rules. Because body cavity searches are a security procedure and not a medical care procedure, the normal patient-care provider relationship does not exist. This entails that medical confidentiality does not apply, as the results of the search are communicated with the prison authorities. This puts the medical professional in a particularly difficult position regarding their relationship with their patient. By participating in the prison's security system (e.g. by conducting a body (cavity) search), physicians' obligation to provide medical care to prisoners can be compromised. The nature of a physician's relationship with a prisoner should first and foremost be one between a physician and a patient, with the patient's best clinical interest at heart. Therefore, it is recommended that vaginal, anal or other intrusive searches are conducted by medical staff who are not the ones primarily responsible for the care of the prisoner. The World Medical Association (WMA) also states that forced body cavity searches (without the consent of the person undergoing the search) are ethically unacceptable, like any other clinical action without consent. See Statement of the WMA on body searches of prisoners, op. cit., paragraphs 6, 8, 9 and 10; See also Enggist et al. (2014),Lehtmets and Pont (2014).

31 Rule 19, Bangkok Rules; Rule 54.3 of the European Prison Rules.

32 Rule 54.3 of the European Prison Rules.

33 Rule 21 of the Bangkok Rules; Rule 81.3 of the European Prison Rules.

34 Principle 9, H of the Yogyakarta Principles.

from the requested gender,...) are all factors that might impact the implementation of such recommendations. Suggested practices do not entail a significant increase in workload or preferential treatment for women and/or LGBTQI+ people. Instead, they constitute a natural adaptation from standards on dignity that must be translated to fit the specific needs of vulnerable groups. Prisons must put practices in place that guarantee a neutral look on vulnerable prisoners' exposed bodies, reduce harm and respect the prisoners' dignity and privacy as much as possible (United Nations Development Programme [UNDP] 2020; CGLPL 2021).

5.2 An Abolitionist Take on Body Searches

Recommendations and human rights standards on body searches might reduce harm, but the negative consequences resulting from body searches can only be eliminated by abolishing the practice entirely (Hutchison 2020). While pragmatic steps towards reducing the degrading nature of body searches are encouraged by some moderate and pragmatic abolitionists, the ultimate ideological goal within abolitionism is to abolish carceral institutions altogether (Marcoux Rouleau 2021). By dismantling the prison system in which body searches exist, the practice and its negative consequences would disappear with it. Indeed, one of the main criticisms from abolitionists towards reformist recommendations, is that reforms tolerate the existence of the practice of body searches, and legitimise its use by 'improving' the way it is conducted.

As the experience of body searches by the ones undergoing them largely depends on factors outside of their control and can have severe consequences, abolitionists argue that body searches can simply not be conducted in a more humane way because of their fundamentally degrading and harmful nature (Marcoux Rouleau 2021). Furthermore, the continuation of the practice is hard to justify if body searches are experienced by women as a state-inflicted form of sexual violence (Hutchison 2020; Marcoux Rouleau 2021). As Marcoux Rouleau (2021: 323) notes, "...it is hypocritical for states and governments to incarcerate some people for committing sexual assaults while simultaneously inflicting this form of violence daily". The degree of harm caused by body searches, as described in this chapter, naturally induces a reflection on the existence of the practice itself and the institution of the prison where body searches are part of daily functioning. This rationale can also be found in Carlen's (1990) work on alternatives to women's imprisonment. She argued that if imprisonment in itself is so harmful to women, women should not be placed in prisons and the priority should be to look at alternatives to women's imprisonment (Carlen 1990). Therefore, is the abolition of body searches the next step in the civilising process, as skilfully articulated by Norbert Elias (1994)? Similarly to the nineteenth-century shift in punishment from the physical infliction of pain to the deprivation of liberty, the twenty-first century might see the abolition of body searches or the prison system as a whole as we know them today, in favour of other practices that are deemed more humane and civilised. However, there is no indication of such civilising process regarding body searches as they continue to be widely practised. The abolitionist discussion on body searches with a focus on women and LGBTQI+ people leads to a more radical gendered and queer reflection on the penal system, where normative assumptions on heterosexuality and binary cisgender identities are deconstructed (Stanley and Smith 2011).

6 Conclusion

While all prisoners are vulnerable to some degree because they are under the formal authority of the criminal justice system while being deprived of their liberty, detained women and LGBTQI+ people are particularly vulnerable to discrimination and violence because of their sexual orientation and/or gender identity. Body searches are the product of the prison system, which was born from and constantly reiterates cisnormative and heteronormative views on gender and sexuality.

Women and LGBTQI+ people may experience body searches as particularly invasive, humiliating and as a violation of dignity, privacy and bodily integrity. Women and LGBTQI+ prisoners can experience body (cavity) searches as sexual assault or rape, and the conditions under which searches are conducted can facilitate acts of sexual violence by prison staff. Because of the visibility and focus on the prisoner's body, searches offer opportunities for jokes, mockery or denigrating remarks on women's and LGBTQI+ people's physical appearance, gender identity and/or sexual orientation. Body searches can be particularly humiliating and harmful to trans people, non-binary and intersex people when their gender identity and preference regarding the staff members conducting the search are not taken into consideration. Searches have also been used as a disciplining method where the body is used to exercise power and control over the prisoner through the inspection and manipulation of their (naked) body. Negative experiences of body searches can perpetuate the cycle of trauma and abuse that women and LGBTQI+ people endure during their lives outside of prison.

Depending on how they are conducted, body searches can be extremely traumatising and harmful for women and LGBTQI+ people in particular and all prisoners in general. As always in discussions about punishment and penitentiary practices, the discussion on dignity and humane treatment is weighed against security considerations. Naturally, penal establishments must have some way of checking for potentially dangerous objects to promote the safety and protect the physical integrity of prisoners themselves, other prisoners and prison staff. Practitioners may nuance the harm caused by body searches by stating 'not all body searches'[35] are traumatising and harmful. As we have discussed in this chapter, the general (prison culture, protocols for conducting searches, training of staff) and immediate (language use of the staff conducting the search, contact with the body, privacy) context in which the search is conducted are major determinants for how the procedure is experienced by the person undergoing the search. This chapter formulated recommendations on these determinants that might reduce the risk of harm whenever body searches have to be conducted. These recommendations formulated for women and LGBTQI+ people can be regarded as good practices in general, regardless of one's gender identity or sexual orientation. Technological improvements may constitute stepping stones towards limiting physical contact and risks of humiliation and

---

[35] Reference to the 'not all men' argument (or #NotAllMen) that is used as a response in discussions of feminist issues like rape culture, sexual assault, gender income inequality to deflect attention away from these topics.

degradation, but other policy changes are necessary to safeguard vulnerable populations from discrimination, harm and the perpetuation of (gendered) trauma and abuse. From an abolitionist perspective however, body searches can no longer be justified given their degrading nature and severe consequences, especially for women and LGBTQI+ people. Reforms and safeguards can help to reduce harm, but might contribute to legitimising the practice. Therefore, abolitionists propose that dismantling the prison system as we know it is the only way to eliminate the harm resulting from its practices, with body searches only being one of many.

Despite the narrow focus of this chapter, the experiences and recommendations formulated above do not solely apply to women and LGBTQI+ people. Indeed, all prisoners are vulnerable to some extent, if only because they are deprived of their liberty. Male, straight and cisgender prisoners may also encounter infringements against their dignity and experience humiliation when undergoing body searches. By focusing on women and LGBTQI+ people, this chapter aimed to make gendered, heteronormative and cisnormative dynamics more visible through the practice of body searches. By doing so, this chapter hopes to serve as an invitation to reflect on the assumptions of heterosexuality and binary gender identity that perspire through body searches and are deeply embedded in prison settings.

References

American Psychiatric Association [APA]. 2013. *Diagnostic and Statistical Manual of Mental Disorders (DSM-5).* American Psychiatric Association.

Arkles, G. 2009. Safety and Solidarity Across Gender Lines: Rethinking Segregation of Transgender People in Detention. *Temple Political & Civil Rights Law Review* 18 (2): 515–560.

Association for the Prevention of Torture [APT]. 2022. *Women in Detention: Body Searches Factsheet*. Geneva: Association for the Prevention of Torture.

Baker, C. 2003. *Pourquoi faudrait-il punir? Sur l'abolition du système pénal (version abrégée).* Lyon: Tahin Party.

Balfour, G. 2017. Searching Prison Cells and Prisoner Bodies: Redacting Carceral Power and Glimpsing Gendered Resistance in Women's Prisons. *Criminology & Criminal Justice* 18 (2): 139–155.

Beck, A. J., M. Berzofsky, R. Caspar, and C. Krebs. 2013. *Sexual Victimization in Prisons and Jails Reported by Inmates, 2011–2012*. Washington, DC: Bureau of Justice Statistics.

Bès, F. 2021. Femmes trans en prison, ostracisées et discriminées. *Dedans-Dehors* 112: 25–29.

Blanc, J.-S. 2015. Minorités sexuelles en détention: De l'invisibilité à la stigmatisation. In *Vulnérabilité et risques dans l'exécution des sanctions pénales*, ed. N. Queloz, T. Noll, L. von Mandach, and N. Delgrande, 149–171. Bern: Stämpfli Verlag.

Blanc, J.-S. 2021. *La prise en charge des personnes LGBTIQ+ en détention*. Fribourg: CSCSP.

Blight, J. 2000. *Transgender Inmates*. Canberra: Australian Institute of Criminology.

Brockmann, B., S. Cahill, T. Wang, and T. Levengood. 2019. *Emerging Best Practices for the Management and Treatment of Incarcerated Lesbian, Gay, Bisexual, Transgender, and Intersex (LGBTI) Individuals*. Boston: The Fenway Institute.

Carlen, P. 1990. *Alternatives to Women's Imprisonment*. Buckingham: Open University Press.

Carlton, B. 2007. *Imprisoning Resistance—Life and Death in an Australian Supermax*. Sydney: Institute of Sydney Criminology Press.

Carr, N., S. McAlister, and T. Serisier. 2016. *Out on the Inside: The Rights, Experiences and Needs of LGBT People in Prison*. Dublin: Irish Penal Reform Trust.

CGLPL. 2021. Avis du 25 mai 2021 relatif à la prise en charge des personnes transgenres dans les lieux de privation de liberté. *Journal officiël de la République française*, texte 6/11.

CPT. 2012. *Report to the Government of Greece on the Visit to Greece Carried Out by the European Committee for the Prevention of Torture and Inhuman or Degrading Treatment or Punishment (CPT) from 19 to 27 January 2011*. CPT/Inf (2012) 1. Strasbourg: Council of Europe.

CPT. 2017. *Report to the Italian Government on the Visit to Italy Carried Out by the European Committee for the Prevention of Torture and Inhuman or Degrading Treatment or Punishment (CPT) from 8 to 21 April 2016*. CPT/Inf (2017) 23. Strasbourg: Council of Europe.

CPT. 2018. *Factsheet: Women in Prisons*. CPT/Inf(2018)5. Strasbourg: Council of Europe. https://rm.coe.int/168077ff14

Crenshaw, K.W. 1989. Demarginalizing the Intersection of Race and Sex: A Black Feminist Critique of Antidiscrimination Doctrine. *University of Chicago Legal Forum* 1: 139–168.

Crenshaw, K.W. 1991. Mapping the Margins: Intersectionality, Identity Politics, and Violence Against Women of Color. *Stanford Law Review* 43 (6): 1241–1299.

Crewe, B., S. Hulley, and S. Wright. 2017. The Gendered Pains of Life Imprisonment. *Britisch Journal of Criminology* 57: 1359–1378.

Davis, A.Y. 2003. *Are Prisons Obsolete?* New York: Seven Stories Press.

Davis, A.Y. 2005. *Abolition Democracy: Beyond Empire, Prisons and Torture*. New York: Seven Stories Press.

Douglas, N., E. Plugge, and R. Fitzpatrick. 2009. The Impact of Imprisonment on Health: What Do Women Prisoners Say? *Journal of Epidemiology and Community Health* 63 (9): 749–754.

Elias, N. 1994. *The Civilizing Process*. Oxford: Blackwell.

Enggist, S., L. Møller, G. Galea, and C. Udesen. 2014. *Prisons and Health*. Copenhagen: World Health Organization, Regional Office for Europe.

Federale Ombudsman. 2019. *Naaktfouilleringen - Het evenwicht tussen de veiligheid in gevangenissen en de waardigheid van de gevangenen*. Brussels: Federale Ombudsman.

George, A. 1993. Sexual Assault by the State. *Alternative Law Journal* 18 (1): 31–33.

Ghosh, A., and S. Bourothu. 2021. *Existing Beyond Constitutional Rights: Transgender Persons in Indian Prisons*. Available at: http://dspace.jgu.edu.in:8080/jspui/handle/10739/4494.

Goldblatt, B., and L. Steele. 2019. Bloody Unfair: Inequality Related to Menstruation—Considering the Role of Discrimination Law. *Sydney Law Review* 41 (3): 293–326.

Gordon, B.G. 2020. Vulnerability in Research: Basic Ethical Concepts and General Approach to Review. *Ochsner Journal* 20: 34–38.

Gorden, C., C. Hughes, D. Roberts, E. Asbury-Ward, and S. Dubberley. 2017. A Literature Review of Transgender People in Prison: An 'Invisible' Population in England and Wales. *Prison Service Journal* 233: 11–22.

Harner, H.L., and S. Riley. 2013. The Impact of Incarceration on Women's Mental Health. *Qualitative Health Research* 23 (1): 26–42.

Herdt, G. 1996. *Third Sex, Third Gender: Beyond Sexual Dimorphism in Culture and History*. New York: Zone Books.

HMPPS Diversity and Inclusion Team. 2020. *The Care and Management of Individuals Who Are Transgender: Operational Guidance*. London: Her Majesty's Prison & Probation Service.

Human Rights Watch. 2004. *In a Time of Torture. The Assault on Justice in Egypt's Crackdown on Homosexual Conduct.* New York: Human Rights Watch.

Hutchison, J. 2019. "Bend Over and Spread Your Butt Cheeks": Access to Justice for Women Strip Searched in Prison. *The Annual Review of Interdisciplinary Justice Research* 8: 65–90.

Hutchison, J. 2020. "It's Sexual Assault. It's Barbaric": Strip Searching in Women's Prisons as State-Inflicted Sexual Assault. *Affilia: Feminist Inquiry in Social Work* 35(2): 160–176.

James, S.E., J.L. Herman, S. Rankin, M. Keisling, L. Mottet, and M.a. Anafi. 2016. *The Report of the 2015 U.S. Transgender Survey.* Washington, DC: National Center for Transgender Equality.

Jenness, V., L. Sexton, and J. Sumner. 2019. Sexual Victimization Against Transgender Womenin Prison: Consent and Coercion in Context. *Criminology* 57 (4): 603–631.

Kirkup, K. 2009. Indocile Bodies: Gender Identity and Strip Searches in Canadian Criminal Law. *Canadian Journal of Law & Society / La Revue Canadienne Droit et Sociétè* 24 (1): 107–125.

Lamble, S. 2012. Rethinking Gendered Prison Policies: Impacts on Transgender Prisoners. *The Howard League for Penal Reform: Early Career Academics Network Bulletin* 16: 7–12.

Lamble, S. 2019. Why Context Matters in the Trans Prisoner Policy Debates. *Critical Legal Thinking*. https://criticallegalthinking.com/2019/10/08/why-context-matters-in-the-trans-prisoner-policy-debates/.

Lehtmets, A., and J. Pont. 2014. *Prison Health Care and Medical Ethics: A Manual for Health-Care Workers and Other Prison Staff with Responsibility for Prisoners' Well-Being*. Strasbourg: Council of Europe.

Liamputtong, P. 2007. *Researching the Vulnerable: A Guide to Sensitive Research Methods*. London: Sage.

Maras, D., J. Motmas, and F. Vander Laenen. 2021. Gender-binaire tralies: Een kwalitatief-exploratief onderzoek naar de ervaringen en uitdagingen van transgender personen in detentie. *Fatik* 172: 14–28.

Marcoux Rouleau, A. 2021. Reform to Abolish: A Pragmatic Analysis of Prison Labor & Strip Searches in Quebec Correctional Law. *Lex Electronica* 26 (2): 302–332.

Matsuno, E., and S.L. Budge. 2017. Non-binary/Genderqueer Identities: A Critical Review of the Literature. *Current Sexual Health Reports* 9 (3): 116–120.

Maycock, M. 2020. The Transgender Pains of Imprisonment. *European Journal of Criminology*: 1–21.

McCulloch, J., and A. George. 2008. Naked Power: Strip Searching in Women's Prisons. In *The Violence of Incarceration*, ed. P. Scraton and J. McCulloch, 117–133. London: Routledge.

Meyer, I.H., A.R. Flores, L. Stemple, A.P. Romero, B.D.M. Wilson, and J.L. Herman. 2017. Incarceration Rates and Traits of Sexual Minorities in the United States: National Inmate Survey, 2011–2012. *American Journal of Public Health* 107 (2): 267–273.

Moore, L., and P. Scraton. 2014. *The Incarceration of Women: Punishing Bodies, Breaking Spirits.* Basingstoke: Palgrave Macmillan.

Murray, K., and Hunter Blackburn, L. 2019. Losing Sight of Women's Rights: The Unregulated Introduction of Gender Self-identification as a Case Study of Policy Capture in Scotland. *Scottish Affairs* 28 (3): 262–289. https://doi.org/10.3366/scot.2019.0284

National Center for Transgender Equality [NCTE]. 2018. *LGBTQ People Behind Bars: A Guide to Understanding the Issues Facing Transgender Prisoners and Their Legal Rights.* https://transequality.org/sites/default/files/docs/resources/TransgenderPeopleBehindBars.pdf.

Observatoire International des Prisons—Section Française [OIP-SF]. 2021. 'Femmes trans en prison, ostracisées et discriminées', *Dedans-Dehors,* 112.

Pemberton, S. 2013. Enforcing Gender: The Constitution of Sex and Genderin Prison Regimes, *Signs: Journal of Women in Culture and Society* 39 (1): 151–175.

Penal Reform International [PRI]. 2003. *Penal Reform International—Training Manual n°1. Human Rights and Vulnerable Prisoners.* Paris: Penal Reform International.

Penal Reform International [PRI], and Association for the Prevention of Torture [APT]. 2015. *LGBTI Persons Deprived of Their Liberty: A Framework for Preventive Monitoring*. London: Penal Reform International.

Poulantzas, N. 1978. *State, Power, Socialism.* London: Verso.

Psutka, M., and E. Sheehy. 2016. Strip-Searching of Women in Canada: Wrongs and Rights. *Canadian Bar Review* 94 (2): 241–280.

Reyes, H. 2006. Fouilles corporelles. In *Médecine, Santé et Prison,* ed. D. Bertrand and G. Niveau, 397–418. Geneva: Editions Médecine et Hygiène.

Richards, C., and M.J. Barker. 2013. *Sexuality and Gender for Mental Health Professionals: A Practical Guide*. London: Sage.

Richards, C., W.P. Bouman, L. Seal, M.J. Barker, T.O. Nieder, and G. T'Sjoen. 2016. Non-binary or Genderqueer Genders. *International Review of Psychiatry* 28 (1): 95–102.

Ricordeau, G. 2004. Enquêter sur l'homosexualité et les violences sexuelles en détention. *Déviance et Société* 28 (2): 233–253.

Ricordeau, G. 2008. *Les détenus et leurs proches: Solidarités et sentiments à l'ombre des murs*. Paris: Autrement.

Robinson, R. 2011. Masculinity as Prison: Sexual Identity, Race, and Incarceration. *California Law Review* 99: 1309–1408.

Routh, D., G. Abess, D. Makin, M.K. Stohr, C. Hemmens, and J. Yoo. 2017. Transgender Inmates in Prisons: A Review of Applicable Statutes and Policies. *International Journal of Offender Therapy and Comparative Criminology* 61 (6): 645–666.

Sauer, A.T., and A. Podhara. 2013. Sexual Orientation and Gender Identity in Human Rights Impact Assessment. *Impact Assessment and Project Appraisal* 31 (2): 135–145.

Schilt, K., and L. Westbrook. 2009. Doing Gender, Doing Heteronormativity: "Gender Normals", Transgender People, and the Social Maintenance of Heterosexuality. *Gender & Society* 23 (4): 440–464.

Scraton, P., and L. Moore. 2005. Degradation, Harm and Survival in a Women's Prison. *Social Policy & Society* 5 (1): 67–78.

Scraton, P., and L. Moore. 2007. *The Prison Within: The Imprisonment of Women at Hydebank Wood 2004-06*. Belfast: Northern Ireland Human Rights Commission.

Sevelius, J.M., and V. Jenness. 2017. Challenges and Opportunities for Gender-Affirming Healthcare for Transgender Women in Prison. *International Journal of Prison Health* 13 (1): 32–40.

Shalev, S. 2021. *First, Do No Harm. Segregation, Restraint, and Pepper Spray Use in Women's Prisons in New Zealand*. Auckland: New Zealand Human Rights Commission.

Stanley, E.A., and N. Smith. 2011. *Captive Genders: Trans Embodiment and the Prison Industrial Complex*. Oakland, CA: AK Press.

Stohr, M.K. 2015. The Hundred Years' War: The Etiology and Status of Assaults on Transgender Women in Men's Prisons. *Women & Criminal Justice* 25 (1–2): 120–129.

Stryker, S. 2017. *Transgender History: The Roots of Today's Revolution*, 2nd ed. New York: Seal Press.

Sumner, J.M., and V. Jenness. 2014. Gender Integration in Sex-Segregated U.S. Prisons: The Paradox of Transgender Correctional Policy. In *Handbook of LGBT Communities, Crime, and Justice*, ed. D. Peterson and V.R. Panfil, 229–259. New York: Springer.

Sykes, G. 1958. *The Society of Captives: A Study of a Maximum Security Prison*. Princeton: Princeton University Press.

Tschanz, A. 2016. Le nouveau BOSS en prison: Une alternative technologique à la pratique de la fouille? *Déviance Et Société* 40 (4): 457–475.

United Nations Development Programme [UNDP]. 2020. *Mapping of Good Practices for the Management of Transgender Prisoners*. Bangkok: UNDP.

UNODC. 2009. *Handbook on Prisoners with Special Needs*. Vienna: United Nations Office on Drugs and Crime.

Wacquant, L. 1999. *Les prisons de la misère*. Paris: Raisons d'agir.

Wahidin, A. 2016. The 'Norms of Our Conflict': The Use of Strip Searching as Gendered Punishment. In *Ex-Combatants, Gender and Peace in Northern Ireland. Women, Political Protest and the Prison Experience*, ed. A. Wahidin, 169–196. London: Palgrave Macmillan.

Westbrook, Laurel, and Kristen, Schilt. 2014. Doing Gender, Determining Gender: Transgender People, Gender Panics, and the Maintenance of the Sex/Gender/Sexuality System. *Gender & Society* 28 (1): 32–57. https://doi.org/10.1177/0891243213503203.

Body Searches in Belgian Prisons: Dignity, Security and Denial

Tom Daems

1 Introduction

Over the past two decades, strip searches have been at the centre of controversy and debate in Belgium. In 2005 Belgian parliament adopted its first law on prisoners' rights. The objective of the new law was to regulate and reduce the use of strip searches. Because of their intrusive nature, strip searches were meant to be exceptional measures: according to the prison law they can only take place following an individual assessment and decision by the prison governor.

In this chapter, we will return to the original intentions of the Belgian Prison Act of 12 January 2005 and we will demonstrate how these intentions and the procedures that were designed, aligned with prevailing European norms on regulating strip searches (Sect. 2). We will then

T. Daems (✉)
Faculty of Law and Criminology, KU Leuven, Leuven, Belgium
e-mail: tom.daems@kuleuven.be

T. Daems (ed.), *Body Searches and Imprisonment*, Palgrave Studies in Prisons and Penology, https://doi.org/10.1007/978-3-031-20451-7_7

reconstruct the many ways in which those original intentions were challenged and how procedures were bent through various interventions, both from the prison administration and the legislator, in order to circumvent the new rules that were perceived to be an obstacle to prison security (Sect. 3). However, notwithstanding heated debate, sharp critique and prisoners' litigation, striking a balance between dignity and security still proves to be difficult. We will illustrate this by discussing some of the findings of a research project that was executed by De Federale Ombudsman and that was published at the end of 2019 on the one hand (Sect. 4), and the recent experiences with prisoners' complaints about strip search practices which are now being dealt with by the newly created Complaint Commissions, which have become operational since 1 October 2020 in the Belgian prison system on the other hand (Sect. 5).

2 The Ambitions of the Prison Act: Reducing the Use of Strip Searches, Protecting the Dignity of Prisoners

In 2005 Belgian parliament adopted its first law on prisoners' rights, which is still in place today. A major part of the Prison Act of 12 January 2005 deals with disciplinary and control measures.[1] Article 108 introduced a clear distinction between the (more superficial) search of an inmate's clothes (a rub-down or frisk search) on the one hand, and the (substantially more intrusive) measure of searching the inmate's body (a strip search) on the other hand. The searching of the clothes has as its objective to verify that the prisoner does not have any objects or substances in his possession which are forbidden or potentially dangerous. When such a search is judged to be insufficient, the prison governor can, by means of an individual decision, order for a search of the body. This includes, if necessary, stripping an inmate of his clothes and inspecting his naked body, including the openings and cavities of the body, without touching it. The governor will notify the prisoner in

[1] Sections 2 and 3 of this chapter draw upon, revise and update the history of strip searches in Belgian prisons, as previously discussed in Daems (2014).

writing no later than 24 hours after the strip search has taken place. The main difference between these two measures is therefore that the latter involves forcing prisoners to strip naked. Because of their intrinsic intrusiveness, such strip searches are meant to be exceptional measures: they should only take place following an individual assessment and decision by the prison governor. It was explicitly stated that such searches should never be executed in a routine way:

> The search of the body is ... a much more intrusive measure which is in itself an encroachment of the feeling of honour. Such a search may certainly never be executed in a routine way and is only justified when given specific circumstances or suspicions a search of the prisoner's clothes is not sufficient. (House of Representatives 2001: 179)

Moreover, it was emphasized that there is an important, gradual difference between the search of a prisoner's clothes and the search of the body. Searching one's clothes could therefore never include the obligation to fully undress:

> The search of a prisoner's clothes means that the clothes are touched and searched in order to verify that the prisoner does not have any objects or substances in or underneath his clothes that are forbidden or dangerous. In this respect, one can request a prisoner to take of his outer clothes, but one cannot force him to fully undress. The search of the body is a measure that goes much further. This measure not only gives prison staff the permission to force a prisoner to fully undress but even to inspect the cavities of his body externally without touching the body. (House of Representatives 2001: 250)

Next to setting out rules with respect to the decision-making, the Prison Act also regulates some aspects of the execution of that decision. A strip search can only take place in a closed space, in the absence of other prisoners and it needs to be executed by a minimum of two prison officers who are of the same sex as the prisoner (Article 108, §2). The Prison Act also stresses that searches of the clothes and strip searches cannot be humiliating and should be executed with respect for the dignity of the prisoner (Article 108, §3).

With these procedures the Belgian legislator aimed to restrict the use of strip searches and to make them more fair, humane and legitimate in the eyes of the prisoners. Moreover, these new rules did not come out of the blue: they are in line with the European regulation of prison life. Indeed, in line with other aspects of prison and penal policy (van Zyl Smit and Snacken 2009; Daems et al. 2013; Daems and Robert 2017), the Council of Europe has also come to focus on regulating strip searches. Rule 54 of the European Prison Rules, an important recommendation of the Committee of Ministers of 2006 which was recently revised,[2] is devoted to search practices in prisons. With respect to strip searches it stipulates *inter alia* that "…situations in which searches are necessary and their nature shall be defined by national law" (Rule 54.2); that staff shall be trained to "…to carry out these searches in such a way as to detect and prevent any attempt to escape or to hide contraband, while at the same time respecting the dignity of those being searched and their personal possessions" (Rule 54.3); that persons being searched "…shall not be humiliated by the searching process" (Rule 54.4); that persons shall only be searched "…by staff of the same gender" (Rule 54.5); that there shall be no "…internal physical searches of prisoners' bodies by prison staff" (Rule 54.6) and that "…an intimate examination related to a search may be conducted by a medical practitioner only" (Rule 54.7).

On the occasion of a visit to the Netherlands (10 to 21 October 2011) the European Committee for the Prevention of Torture (CPT), a body that currently visits places of detention in the 46 member states of the Council of Europe,[3] offered the following observations and instructions on prison searches:

---

[2] Recommendation Rec(2006)2-rev of the Committee of Ministers to Member States on the European Prison Rules (Adopted by the Committee of Ministers on 11 January 2006, at the 952nd meeting of the Ministers' Deputies and revised and amended by the Committee of Ministers on 1 July 2020 at the 1380th meeting of the Ministers' Deputies).

[3] Because of the invasion of Ukraine Russia, which had been a member of the Council of Europe since 1996, ceased to be a member as from 16 March 2022. Resolution CM/Res(2022)2 on the cessation of the membership of the Russian Federation to the Council of Europe (Adopted by the Committee of Ministers on 16 March 2022 at the 1428ter meeting of the Ministers' Deputies).

> A strip search is a very invasive – and potentially degrading – measure. Therefore, resort to strip searches should be based on an individual risk assessment and subject to rigorous criteria and supervision. Every reasonable effort should be made to minimise embarrassment; detained persons who are searched should not normally be required to remove all their clothes at the same time, e.g. a person should be allowed to remove clothing above the waist and to get dressed before removing further clothing. In addition, more than one officer should, as a rule, be present during any strip search as a protection to detained persons and staff alike. Further, inmates should not be required to undress in the presence of custodial staff of the opposite sex. (CPT 2012: 19)

After a visit to Slovakia the CPT added the following: "Moreover, prisoners should never be required to strip naked in front of other inmates or a large group of persons" (CPT 2014: 25).

Also the European Court of Human Rights has on several occasions dealt with strip searches in its case-law (for earlier discussions, see e.g. van Zyl Smit and Snacken 2009: 285–290; Claes 2017: 126–127). In a recent case *Roth vs. Germany* a prisoner complained *inter alia* about repeated random strip searches in prison.[4] Here the European Court repeats and applies the principles it has come to formulate on strip searches. The Court highlights that strip searches "...may be necessary on occasion to ensure prison security or to prevent disorder or crime". However, so the Court adds, such strip searches "...should be carried out in an appropriate manner with due respect for human dignity and for a legitimate purpose" (para 65). The Court further reiterates that "...in respect of a person who is deprived of his liberty, or, more generally, is confronted with law-enforcement officers, any recourse to physical force which has not been made strictly necessary by his own conduct diminishes human dignity and is, in principle, an infringement of the right set forth in Article 3" (para 66). The Court also recalls how debasing elements, which significantly aggravate the inevitable humiliation, such as being obliged to strip in the presence of a female officer, having his

[4] *Roth v Germany*, App. No 6780/18 and 30776/18, 20 October 2020. For a more extensive discussion of the case law of the European Court of Human Rights, see the chapter by Mavronicola and Webster in this volume.

sexual organs and food touched with bare hands or being searched before four guards who deride and verbally abused a prisoner, violate Art. 3 (para 68). The same may apply when there is no established connection with the preservation of prison security and the prevention of crime or disorder (para 69). In *Roth vs. Germany* the Court observed that the applicant had been subjected to eleven random searches, which included an inspection of the anus, without any concrete security concerns (all searches were related to visits or meetings with public officials). It therefore concluded that

> ...owing to the absence of a legitimate purpose for these repeated and generalised searches, the feeling of arbitrariness and the feelings of inferiority and anxiety often associated with them, as well as the feeling of a serious affront to dignity indisputably prompted by the obligation to undress in front of another person and submit to inspection of the anus, resulted in a degree of humiliation exceeding the – unavoidable and hence tolerable – level that strip-searches of prisoners inevitably involve. (para 72)

3 Bending the New Rules

What happened with the new procedures for strip searches that were introduced by the Prison Act of 2005? In this section we will reconstruct the recent history of strip searches in Belgium. In doing so, we will demonstrate how the original intentions of the legislator in 2005, that is, to restrict the use of strip searches and, in line with European prison norms, to strike a balance between dignity and security, were challenged, first by new rules that were introduced by the prison administration (Sect. 3.1) and, later, by an attempt to amend the Prison Act in order to make strip searches an automatic and standard procedure in three different occasions (Sect. 3.2). These automatic routine strip searches were then successfully challenged in front of the Constitutional Court and further criticized by the UN Committee Against Torture (CAT) (Sect. 3.3). Eventually, after the decision of the Constitutional Court to repeal the automatic strip search procedure, the prison administration introduced yet another set of rules aimed at making it easier to strip search prisoners (Sect. 3.4).

3.1 The Prison Administration Introduces a New Set of Rules

On 15 January 2007 Article 108 of the Prison Act came into force but it rapidly became the object of serious controversy. Indeed, notwithstanding the law's rationale to restrict the use of strip searches prisoners were still forced to strip naked as a standard procedure. On 19 February 2007 the prison administration sent a Collective Letter (n° 86) to all Belgian prisons in order to explain and clarify the new framework for executing strip searches. This Collective Letter introduced a distinction between three different searches of a prisoner's clothes: a summary search, a thorough search and a full search of the clothes. In the last case, that is, the full search of a prisoner's clothes, prisoners were instructed to fully undress and to hand over their clothes to a prison officer. The prison officer, then, verified—by looking briefly at the naked body of the detainee—whether the prisoner had handed over all his clothes and subsequently inspected his clothes. According to the prison administration, there was no individual decision of the prison governor required for such a procedure since it was, in its opinion, a search of the clothes and not a search of the body (Prison Administration 2007).

This interpretation, however, provoked critical responses. A number of prisoners openly disagreed with these new procedures and objected that they violated Article 108. Because some prisoners were sanctioned by local prison governors for lack of cooperation with the safety procedures, they filed formal complaints with the Council of State in order to nullify such sanctions arguing that a legal basis was absent because the evidence that led to the disciplinary sanctions was obtained by means of searches that violated Article 108. Between 2007 and 2013 a substantial number of disciplinary sanctions were nullified by the Council of State. In line with the argumentation of the prisoners and their lawyers, the Council of State argued in a large number of cases that the prison administration's so-called 'full search of a prisoner's clothes' was, in fact, a search of the body which required an individualized decision of the prison governor. This interpretation was also supported in a number of commentaries on judicial decisions by Belgian legal scholars (see, e.g., Hanoulle and Verbruggen 2009; De Hert 2011).

3.2 The Government Introduces a New Bill to Make Strip Searches a Standard Procedure

In April 2012 the Minister of Justice declared in the House of Representatives that she planned to revise the whole policy of strip searches. In the wake of a number of violent incidents in prisons and various strikes of prison officers throughout the country, she promised to change the Prison Act of 12 January 2005 in order to make it possible for prison officers to strip search inmates without prior order from the prison governor. In February 2013 the Council of Ministers approved a draft law that would make the necessary adaptations to Article 108. In May 2013 the House of Representatives approved the new rules. On 16 September 2013 the law of 1 July 2013, which introduced a number of important changes to the policy of searches, came into force.

The new Article 108 no longer formulated the search of the inmate's body as an exceptional control measure that was only permitted after an individualized order by the prison governor. Rather, the search of the prisoner's body became standard procedure in three cases: upon entrance into the prison; prior to being detained in a safety or disciplinary cell and after a visit at a table in the visiting room or after a conjugal visit. In these cases a separate order from the prison governor was no longer required. In a new Collective Letter (n° 125) of 6 September 2013 the prison administration explained that searches of the prisoner's body were permitted without an order from the governor when an inmate had been in contact with persons that were not to be considered as prison staff (Prison Administration 2013). It was hoped that this legal change would discourage inmates to challenge the strip searches before the Council of State since they were deprived of their ammunition to contest the now legalized practice of standard strip searches. Moreover, the government added an additional justification for making searches of the prisoner's body a standard procedure: it was not only necessary for security reasons but it also helps protect vulnerable prisoners since they are often put under pressure to smuggle forbidden goods and substances into the prison.

3.3 The Constitutional Court and the Committee Against Torture Intervene

Nonetheless, this legal reform aimed at rewinding the clock proved to be quite controversial. In its advice of 14 March 2013 the Council of State had already formulated serious objections to the draft Bill. In particular the standardization of the search of the prisoner's body, with no possibility to abstain from such a procedure when there is no threat for security, could possibly violate Article 3 of the European Convention of Human Rights, so the Council of State warned. Moreover, the Council of State was very critical about the paucity of justification for the planned changes to the procedures: the government restricted its explanation to some vague notions about 'multiple problems' and the 'inefficiency' of existing procedures but failed to clarify clearly why the substantial changes were necessary. In addition, some Members of Parliament had objected that the new procedures would be detrimental to the philosophical foundations of the Prison Act and raised doubts about whether it would pass the test of Strasbourg (Daems 2013). Expressions of concern about the changes were also heard in other corners of Belgian society: in August 2013 a major Flemish newspaper published a critical article about the standardized strip searches on its cover page (Van Hecke 2013) and, one month later, the Belgian section of the *Observatoire International des Prisons* criticized the law of 1 July 2013 and warned, again, that the new policy would violate Article 3 of the European Convention of Human Rights (Observatoire International des Prisons 2013: 56–57).

Against the background of the earlier post-2007 phase of prisoners' litigation against the rules as introduced by the prison administration (see Sect. 3.1), it was to be expected that inmates and their lawyers would also challenge this new policy. And, indeed, on 12 September 2013, less than a week after the publication of the law of 1 July 2013 in the Belgian Official Journal, and just a couple of days before these rules entered into force, a former prisoner who was at risk of being reincarcerated, filed a complaint with the Constitutional Court, arguing *inter alia* that the new policy violated Article 3 of the European Convention of European Rights. With its judgement of 30 October 2013 the Constitutional Court suspended the new rules relating to strip searches: it found that the automatic strip searches in the three cases mentioned in the reformulated Article 108, were not sufficiently justified on the basis of the behaviour of the detainee and, therefore, went beyond what is strictly necessary.[5]

Shortly thereafter also the UN Committee Against Torture (CAT) joined the debate. Under the heading 'Full body searches' the CAT adopted the following concluding observations at its 1201st meeting, held on 18 November 2013, when it considered the third periodic report of Belgium:

> The Committee is concerned about the amendments made to the Principles Act by the Act of 1 July 2013, which authorizes routine full body searches when a detainee has been in contact with the outside world. Although the Constitutional Court has ruled that the application of these measures should be suspended, the Committee is still concerned that they have not yet been repealed and could be implemented in the future... The Committee urges the State party to repeal the provisions of the Act of 1 July 2013 which authorize systematic body searches. The State party should ensure that body searches are conducted only in exceptional cases and by the least intrusive means possible, with full respect for the dignity of the person. The State party should take steps to adopt precise and strict instructions to restrict the use of body searches. (CAT 2014: 5)

On 29 January 2014 the Constitutional Court, which had earlier provisionally suspended the new rules related to strip searches, repealed the relevant passages of Article 108, based on its earlier reasoning, that is,

[5] Constitutional Court, decision No. 143/2013, 30 October 2013, para B.9.

that systematic strip searches which are not being justified precisely with reference to a prisoner's behaviour, are excessive measures of control.[6]

3.4 The Prison Administration Introduces (Again) a New Set of Rules

The repeal of the relevant passages of Article 108 may, at first sight, seem like a victory for those prisoners (and their lawyers) who have fought a long battle over the admissibility of strip searches in Belgian prisons. However, the story does not end here. The day after the decision of the Constitutional Court the prison administration issued a new Collective Letter (n° 126) which intended to clarify the new rules on strip searches. In this Letter the prison administration introduced a new distinction, that is, between the so-called 'one-off search of the prisoner's body' on the one hand, and the 'recurrent search of the prisoner's body' on the other. In the latter case, the prison governor could decide that an inmate's body had to be searched systematically, over a fixed period of time, on a number of occasions, as mentioned in the governor's decision approving the strip search (Prison Administration 2014).

But, unsurprisingly, also these rules came to be challenged. In the end, three years later, a new Collective Letter (n° 141) of 30 January 2017 was issued which abolished the distinction between one-off and recurrent searches of the prisoner's body (Prison Administration 2017). The Central Prison Monitoring Board ('Centrale Toezichtsraad voor het Gevangeniswezen') welcomed the new Collective Letter in one of its commentaries (16 June 2017) with the telling title: "Prison administration finally accepts the prohibition of systematic strip searches" (Centrale Toezichtsraad voor het Gevangeniswezen 2017). Three years after the Constitutional Court's 2014 judgement on the incompatibility of systematic strip searches with the requirements of Article 3 of the European Convention of Human Rights it seemed as if the instructions of the prison administration were finally in line with the intentions of the Belgian legislator and European human rights norms.

---

[6] Constitutional Court, Decision No. 20/2014, 29 January 2014, para B13.

However, that does not mean that the story is over: the rules may have been clarified, but what with prison practice? In the remainder of this chapter we will first look at an important report from the federal Ombudsman, so far the only large-scale empirical study on strip searches in Belgium (Sect. 4). Data collection for that project started before the changes introduced by Collective Letter N° 141 of 30 January 2017 so the study did not take into account if these changes had any impact in practice. However, as we will see in Sect. 5, where we will discuss the first experiences of the Complaint Commissions with strip searches, many of the observations still seem to hold and problems tend to persist.

4 The Report on Strip Searches of the Federal Ombudsman

The federal Ombudsman has as its task to contribute to the protection of the rights of persons in their relation with the federal government. In that capacity the federal Ombudsman can investigate complaints concerning dysfunctions of the federal public services and can undertake research to work towards a responsible, integer and just government. In November 2019 the federal Ombudsman published the findings of a large-scale project on strip searches in Belgian prisons in a report with as title: *Naaktfouilleringen: het evenwicht tussen de veiligheid in gevangenissen en de waardigheid van de gedetineerden* ('Strip searches: the balance between safety in prisons and dignity of prisoners'). The research was initiated because the federal Ombudsman had, over the years (in 2015 and 2016), received a number of complaints from prisoners, their families as well as several prisons monitoring bodies about strip searches in Belgian prisons. The objective was to explore to what extent strip searches respect the balance between security in prisons and the dignity of prisoners. The research team of the federal Ombudsman focused on both the decision-making with respect to strip searches (whether the decision-making process respected the rules, as set out in the Prison Act) and the way these were executed.

Based on an analysis of the existing regulations, relevant case-law (ECtHR, Constitutional Court, Council of State), international recommendations (such as the European Prison Rules and the Mandela Rules) and the standards of the federal Ombudsman itself a number of indicators were formulated that were subsequently used to evaluate strip search practices in Belgian prisons (De Federale Ombudsman 2019a: 37). For the evaluation of the decision-making process four indicators were being formulated: (1) are decisions taken by the competent authority?; (2) are decisions taken before the execution of the strip search and are these afterwards communicated to the prisoners?; (3) are the strip searches restricted to what is strictly necessary and are they used as a last resort measure? and (4) are decisions sufficiently motivated? In order to study the execution of strip searches six indicators were used: (1) are strip searches taking place in an appropriate space?; (2) are strip searches being executed by prison officers of the same sex as the prisoner and is the number of staff present at the strip search reasonable?; (3) is the attitude of the prison officers conducive to a smooth execution of the strip search?; (4) in cases of lack of cooperation, is physical force being used in a thoughtful manner?; (5) are prison officers capable of applying the methods and instructions in a correct manner? and (6) are the methods adapted to the most vulnerable prisoners?

The research combined desk research and questionnaires that were sent to all prisons and the local prison monitoring bodies, field work in twelve prisons (2 to 3 day visits to each prison), interviews with prisoners ($N = 212$), prison officers ($N = 146$), prison governors and members of staff from different departments of the prison administration, as well as an analysis of a sample of decisions (1187 in total) and the local instructions for executing strip searches ("fouilleringsplannen"). Data collection started in January 2016. A first draft of the report was sent to the prison administration for feedback and comments.

In the report the federal Ombudsman observes that the rules were not always followed. Four practices were highlighted, as these could possibly affect the dignity of the prisoners (see De Federale Ombudsman 2019b: 5–6, 8–9). First, all prisons included in the study were executing strip searches in a systematic way. These practices violated Art. 108 of the Prison Act. Indeed, in such cases there was no individual assessment of the need for such a search. The research team was able to document such unacceptable practices, for example, prisoners moving to and returning from the workplace, who had to endure a strip search several times per day. Second, many strip searches took place without a preceding decision by the prison governor. The Ombudsman stresses that this implies that, in these cases, prison governors did not make an individual assessment whether in that specific case a strip search was necessary and whether it was proportional in view of the safety risk. Such practices are against the law and increase the risk of abuse. The federal Ombudsman notes that, in practice, it is not always possible to have a preceding decision from the governor and advices, therefore, to make it possible to delegate such decisions to certain other members of staff in the prison. Third, the vast majority of the decisions for a strip search were written in a stereotypical way and did not mention any concrete facts (this applied to 81% of the decisions in the sample, see De Federale Ombudsman 2019a: 85). Prisoners did not always know what the exact grounds were to justify a strip search. Fourth, when prisoners changed clothes or when they were subjected to a urine test, they often had to fully undress. In practice this procedure is similar to a strip search. However, prisons did not perceive this as a strip search which implied that, in their view, no individual decision was needed.

What with the execution of strip searches? Here six problems were identified that can lead to situations that are humiliating for prisoners. First, in general, strip searches are not executed in the correct way. Some prisons still use methods that have been abolished in the meantime and members of staff have insufficient training. Second, the search procedures do not take into account the special needs of certain prisoners, such as persons with a disability, transgenders and persons with a psychic vulnerability. Third, when prisoners refuse to be subjected to a strip search, then prisons make ample use of physical pressure, which is not always necessary. The Ombudsman recalls that a refusal to cooperate can be legitimate, particularly when the strip search is illegal because it takes place in a systematic way or when it recalls traumatic experiences from the past. In such cases it can be particularly humiliating to undergo a strip search. Fourth, the attitude of members of staff towards prisoners during a strip search differs strongly from prison to prison and even from prison officer to prison officer. The Ombudsman observed that in one prison members of staff dealt with prisoners in a very respectful manner. Elsewhere prisoners complained about inappropriate and at times provocative and even violent behaviour from some prison officers. Fifth, strip searches should be executed by members of staff of the same sex as the prisoner. That is required by the Prison Act and prisons respect this. However, sometimes other members of staff are present without any justification for their presence. The Ombudsman stresses that strip searches can be humiliating for the prisoner when too many people are present. Sixth, even though strip searches were not always taking place in a closed space, most spaces did respect the privacy of the prisoners. However, the research team observed how some strip searches happened in spaces that are not adapted because they made it possible for others to watch the procedure.

At the time of publication (November 2019) Guido Herman, who was then one of the two federal Ombudsmen, stressed in particular: "We ask that all prisons immediately stop systematic strip searches. Prisons should consider, before any strip search takes place, whether it is necessary, taking into account the prisoner's profile. Putting a person naked for an inspection should be absolutely exceptional" (De Coninck 2019). The head of the prison administration had received a draft of the report prior to its publication. In a letter of 15 September 2019 (which is included in the report, see De Federale Ombudsman 2019a: 154–155) he writes that the findings of the report emphasize the need to find a better balance between safety and dignity of the prisoners. At the central level of the prison administration the follow-up of this topic was spread over too many entities, so he added, and this may be one of the explanations for the differing practices in the prisons. In the future a new entity on 'integral safety' ('Directie Integrale Veiligheid') will be responsible for the follow-up. This entity will be responsible for *inter alia* the implementation of processes, procedures and safety techniques. Practical fiches will be developed and distributed in the prisons and in the future this new entity will monitor the application of these fiches.

5 Strip Searches and the New Complaint Commissions

Since 1 October 2020 prisoners in Belgium can file complaints with the Complaint Commissions with respect to decisions taken by or on behalf of the prison governor. This is a separate mechanism, next to the existing judicial avenues. The introduction of this right of complaint in Belgian prisons has been a far-reaching reform which took a long time to implement: it took more than fifteen years before the relevant articles of the Prison Act (Articles 147–166) entered into force. Nowadays there are 33 local Complaint Commissions (every prison has its Complaint Commission) and two Appeal Commissions (Daems and Tulkens 2021a, b). The right of complaint is a special mechanism, tailored to the special context of detention. It has been described as:

> ... a type of low-threshold right of complaint, specifically oriented to situations of detention, for an independent body that is particularly familiar with penitentiary praxis, and which has the power to defend both the prisoner's legitimate claims to respecting his rights and freedoms as well as effectively implementing his legitimate expectations that the decisions taken against him meet the requirements of reasonableness and fairness. (House of Representatives 2001: 96–97)

In practice, the Complaint Commissions, which consist of three members and are chaired by a lawyer, deal with prisoners' complaints. Appeals can be made to the Dutch- or French-speaking Appeal Commissions, which have been set up under the auspices of the Central Prison Monitoring Board.

These new Complaint and Appeal Commissions can also receive complaints with respect to strip searches. For that reason it is interesting to see what kind of issues prisoners have complained about since its implementation on 1 October 2020, and how these new Commissions have dealt with such complaints.

A first issue to note is that, at the time of writing, Complaint Commissions seem to have different opinions on what they can—and what they cannot—decide on (Daems 2021). The Complaint Commission of the prison of Antwerp, for example, received a complaint from a prisoner about the execution of a strip search.[7] The prisoner complained about the fact that he was not being given a towel during the strip search. Other prisoners in Antwerp had similar experiences, so the prisoner added. During the hearing of the Complaint Commission the prison governor confirmed that such a towel forms part of the procedure that prison officers should follow. The Complaint Commission of the prison of Antwerp concluded, however, that it could not further investigate the complaint: according to Article 148 of the Prison Act the Complaint Commission is only competent to deal with complaints about decisions taken by or on behalf of the prison governor. As the complaint was not about the prison governor's decision but rather about how it was executed by the prison officers involved, the Complaint Commission came to the conclusion that the prisoner's complaint was inadmissible.[8]

However, the Complaint Commission of the prison of Leuven Centraal sees this differently.[9] A prisoner had complained about a strip search which was being executed in the presence of another prisoner. According to the prisoner they could see each other's naked bodies. The prison governor explained that because of the "urgency of the situation" the strip search was being executed in the cell of another prisoner. According to the governor both prisoners were being searched in different corners of the cell. Nonetheless, during the hearing the prison governor acknowledged that the strip search had been executed in the wrong way. Interestingly, the Complaint Commission of Leuven Centraal did conclude that the complaint was admissible because the execution was directly and immediately related to the decision taken by the prison governor. And, indeed, in this case, it was decided that the complaint was justified. Interestingly, this way of reasoning seems to be in line with how the Complaint Commissions in the Netherlands tend

[7] Complaint Commission Antwerp, Decision No. KC02/21-0002, 19 January 2021.

[8] The Complaint Commission of Antwerp is not alone in its opinion, see eg Complaint Commission Merksplas, Decision No. KC21/21-0020, 22 April 2021; Complaint Commission Hasselt, Decision No. KC10/21-0018, 2 June 2021, Complaint Commission Merksplas, Decision No. KC21/21-0022, 20 May 2021, Complaint Commission Merksplas, Decision No. KC21/21-0023, 20 May 2021.

[9] Complaint Commission Leuven Centraal, Decision No. KC16/21-0033 and 0034, 27 April 2021.

to interpret this: in the recent past the Dutch Appeal Commission has declared complaints on the execution of strip searches admissible, e.g. when strip searches were being executed in the presence of one[10] or two female members of staff,[11] or when the search was being executed in a cell with an open door.[12] The Belgian Complaint Commissions, unfortunately, tend to adopt a more restrictive interpretation. Indeed, in its decision of 25 February 2022 the Dutch-speaking Appeals Commission rejected the line of reasoning of the Complaint Commission of Leuven Centraal (and, therefore, implicitly also the reasoning of the Appeal Commission in the Netherlands) and restricted the scope of the right to complain to the governor's decision. In doing so, the Dutch-speaking Appeals Commission deprived prisoners in Belgium of an effective means to complain about the execution of strip searches (Daems 2022).

Apart from these procedural issues, what do prisoners complain about? For our purpose here, it is interesting to observe that some of the strip search practices that have been challenged before the courts or that have been criticized in the report of the federal Ombudsman, have also returned before the Complaint Commissions: prisoners have complained about strip searches taking place in the presence of a large number of prison staff (five or more in one case,[13] about ten, in other cases[14]) or in the presence of another prisoner[15]; about strip searches that were executed each time by the same prison officer, which can give the prisoner the impression that he is being targeted[16]; about strip searches that were executed without being offered a towel, even when a prisoner asked for it[17]; about searches that have been executed with the obligation to

[10] RSJ 05/2112/GA, 21 November 2005, appeal.

[11] RSJ 14/0023/GA, 30 April 2014, appeal.

[12] RSJ 17/0322/GA, 14 April 2017, appeal.

[13] Complaint Commission Merksplas, Decision No. KC21/21-0023, 20 May 2021.

[14] Complaint Commission Merksplas, Decision No. KC21/21-0020, 22 April 2021; Complaint Commission Hasselt, Decision No. KC10/21-0018, 2 June 2021; Complaint Commission Merksplas, Decision No. KC21/21-0022, 20 May 2021.

[15] Complaint Commission Leuven Centraal, Decision No. KC16/21-0033 and 0034, 27 April 2021.

[16] Complaint Commission Antwerp, Decision No. KC02/21-0007, 3 February 2021.

[17] Complaint Commission Beveren, Decision No. KC04/21-0017, 9 April 2021.

squat.[18] Further research is needed but such complaints, as received by the Complaint Commissions, at least indicate that some of the problems that have been identified over the past fifteen years still persist. The Central Prison Monitoring Board seems to confirm this in its 2021 annual report:

> Multiple local monitoring boards report recurring complaints about problematic practices during strip searches and the non-compliance with procedures in certain circumstances. Those complaints include the following elements: lack of a towel to cover the intimacy of the prisoner, bare-hand search by the prison officer, search in a room where many people pass through, prisoners who are asked to squat. The use of these practices probably explains why the detainees often regard the strip search as humiliating. In addition, questions arise about the systematic nature of the searches in certain establishments. Especially when one is placed in a disciplinary cell or when someone returns from leave, then searches are often carried out without individual indications and/or without a decision from the prison governor. (Centrale Toezichtsraad voor het Gevangeniswezen 2021: 50)

6 Conclusion: Body Searches and Denial

In an earlier discussion of strip searches in Belgian prisons we argued that the Belgian prison administration had, since 2007, when Article 108 came into force, engaged in strategies of interpretive denial (Cohen 2001; see Daems 2014): the objective of Collective Letter n° 86 of 19 February 2007 was to neutralize the new approach towards strip searches and to prevent restricting its use. The introduction of a new kind of search (the so-called 'full search of a prisoner's clothes'), which was neither mentioned in Article 108 nor in the Parliamentary preparatory documents, enabled the prison administration to jump the barriers that the legislator had erected. Indeed, it re-named and re-classified what it was doing and continued to force prisoners to strip naked.

[18] Complaint Commission Beveren, Decision No. KC04/21-0036, 27 April 2021.

The persistent problems with strip searches, which have been documented in the report of the federal Ombudsman and the complaints received by the Complaint Commissions, demonstrate that even today, fifteen years after the introduction of the new body search regime in Belgium, there is still a large gap between law in the books and law in action. The discussion in this chapter—but also in other chapters in this book[19]—therefore also shows the limits of legal reform and top-down (European) regulation of strip searches. The fact that body searches are regulated by law and that unlawful practices can be challenged before the courts, is a sign of progress, but unfortunately, it is no guarantee for practices to change or disappear.

References

Centrale Toezichtsraad voor het Gevangeniswezen. 2017. *Verbod op systematische naaktfouilles eindelijk aanvaard door de penitentiaire administratie.* Advies 2017-07 van 16 juni 2017. Brussels: Centrale Toezichtsraad voor het Gevangeniswezen.

Centrale Toezichtsraad voor het Gevangeniswezen. 2021. *Jaarverslag 2020.* Brussels: Centrale Toezichtsraad voor het Gevangeniswezen.

Claes, L. 2017. Het EHRM en de strafuitvoering. De onmenselijke en vernederende behandeling van gedetineerden. *Nullum Crimen*: 98–129.

Cohen, S. 2001. *States of Denial. Knowing About Atrocities and Suffering.* Cambridge: Polity.

CAT. 2014. *Concluding Observations on the Third Period Report of Belgium.* CAT/C/BEL/CO/3. January 3. Retrieved from http://daccess-dds-ny.un.org/doc/UNDOC/GEN/G14/400/46/PDF/G1440046.pdf?OpenElement.

CPT. 2012. *Report to the Government of the Netherlands on the Visit to the Netherlands Carried Out by the European Committee for the Prevention of Torture and Inhuman or Degrading Treatment or Punishment (CPT) from 10 to 21 October 2011.* CPT/Inf (2012) 21. Strasbourg: Council of Europe.

CPT. 2014. *Report to the Government of the Slovak Republic on the Visit to the Slovak Republic Carried Out by the European Committee for the Prevention of*

[19] See in particular the chapters by Falxa (on France) and Güerri (on Spain) in this volume.

Torture and Inhuman or Degrading Treatment or Punishment (CPT) from 24 September to 3 October 2013. CPT/Inf (2014) 29. Strasbourg: Council of Europe.

Daems, T. 2013. De geest is uit de fles: Wijzigingen titels V, VI en VII van de basiswet gevangeniswezen en rechtspositie van gedetineerden. *Panopticon* 34 (6): 513–522.

Daems, T. 2014. 'Ceci n'est pas une fouille à corps': The denial of strip searches in Belgian prisons. In *Punishment and Incarceration: A Global Perspective*, ed. M. Deflem, 75–94. Bingley: Emerald Group Publishing.

Daems, T. 2015. Between Human Standards and Institutional Efficiency: The Regulation and Deregulation of Strip-Searches in Belgium. *Prison Service Journal* 222 (November): 40–46.

Daems, T. 2021. Het klachtenrecht en de rechtmatigheid van naaktfouilles in de gevangenissen. *Tijdschrift voor Strafrecht* 22 (5): 289–293.

Daems, T. 2022. Nederlandstalige beroepscommissie zet gedetineerden in hun blootje. 6 April (blog post). https://tomdaems.com/2022/04/06/nederlandstalige-beroepscommissie-zet-gedetineerden-in-hun-blootje/.

Daems, T., and L. Robert, eds. 2017. *Europe in Prisons.* London: Palgrave Macmillan.

Daems, T., and F. Tulkens. 2021a. Het klachtenrecht voor gedetineerden. *Tijdschrift voor Strafrecht* 22 (5): 259–279.

Daems, T., and F. Tulkens. 2021b. Actualité du droit de plainte des détenus. *Revue de Jurisprudence de Liège, Mons et Bruxelles* 36: 1612–1630.

Daems, T., D. van Zyl Smit, and S. Snacken, eds. 2013. *European Penology?* Oxford: Hart.

De Coninck, J. 2019. Federale Ombudsman vraagt stopzetting systematische naaktfouilleringen in gevangenissen. *VRTNWS*, 25 November. https://www.vrt.be/vrtnws/nl/2019/11/25/federale-ombudsman-vraagt-stopzetting-systematische-naaktfouille/

De Federale Ombudsman. 2019a. *Naaktfouilleringen. Het evenwicht tussen de veiligheid in gevangenissen en de waardigheid van de gedetineerden.* Brussels: De Federale Ombudsman.

De Federale Ombudsman. 2019b. *Samenvatting: Naaktfouilleringen. Het evenwicht tussen de veiligheid in gevangenissen en de waardigheid van de gedetineerden.* Brussels: De Federale Ombudsman.

De Hert, P. 2011. Onderzoek van gevangeniskledij of fouillering op het lichaam? *Tijdschrift voor Strafrecht*: 80–83.

Hanoulle, K., and F. Verbruggen. 2009. 'Fouille'-arrest? Foei, arrest! Het schaamteloos uitkleden van (de rechten van) gedetineerden. *Nullum Crimen*: 208–211.
House of Representatives. 2001. Final Report of the Commission 'Principles Act on the Prison System and the Legal Position of Detainees'. Parliamentary Documents of the House of Representatives. DOC 50 1076/001.
Observatoire International des Prisons. 2013. *Notice de l'état du système carcéral belge*. Brussels: OIP – section belge.
Prison Administration. 2007. *Collective Letter n° 86 of 19 February 2007*. Brussels: FOD Justitie.
Prison Administration. 2013. *Collective Letter n° 125 of 6 September 2013*. Brussels: FOD Justitie.
Prison Administration. 2014. *Collective Letter n° 126 of 30 January 2014*. Brussels: FOD Justitie.
Prison Administration. 2017. *Collective Letter n° 141 of 30 January 2017*. Brussels: FOD Justitie.
Van Hecke, N. 2013. Harde kritiek op naaktfouilles. *De Standaard*, 12 August.
Van Zyl Smit, D., and S. Snacken. 2009. *Principles of European Prison Law and Policy: Penology and Human Rights*. Oxford: Oxford University Press.

Body Searches in French Prisons: Dignity and Security on a Roller Coaster

Joana Falxa

1 Introduction

Body searches are a means of control to ensure security and prevent misconduct or offences within prisons. However, such measures can invade the private sphere of the prisoners (e.g. when these involve body touching or nudity) and are likely to violate human dignity when they are carried out arbitrarily or improperly. These concerns led to a necessary change in France when the Prison Act was adopted in 2009, which provided for strict supervision in view of the violation of prisoners' privacy and the risk of injury to dignity (Sect. 2). However, in recent years the legislative framework has undergone considerable changes, leading to more flexible regulations in this area, including the possibility

J. Falxa (✉)
Université de Pau et des Pays de L'Adour, Pau, France
e-mail: joana.falxa@univ-pau.fr

T. Daems (ed.), *Body Searches and Imprisonment*, Palgrave Studies in Prisons and Penology, https://doi.org/10.1007/978-3-031-20451-7_8

of systematic searches (Sect. 3). Although the current regulation specifically regulates the use of searching techniques, it entails a serious risk of violation of the dignity of the inmates (Sect. 4), which is why it is widely contested (Sect. 5).

2 The Influence of Dignity on the Original French Prison Act

Current regulation of body searches in French prisons is directly related to various internal and European courts decisions condemning the breach of inmates' right to dignity by the use of indiscriminate body searches (Sect. 2.1). The regulation was first introduced under the French Prison Act (*Loi pénitentiaire*, 24 November 2009) and provided the three principles that are supposed to guide all body searches in prison: necessity, proportionality, and subsidiarity (Sect. 2.2).

2.1 Decisions of the Courts as a Deciding Factor

The conduct of body searches has been the subject of several decisions, both in European jurisprudence (Sect. 2.1.1) and in national courts (Sect. 2.1.2).

2.1.1 Jurisprudence of the ECtHR

The European Court of Human Rights (ECtHR) is vigilant about body searches in prison because of the particularly vulnerable situation in which prisoners are. Although it does not consider searches as measures that directly violate human dignity when they are carried out in an appropriate manner,[1] the Court has argued that, under certain circumstances, the use of this practice by the prison administration exceeds the threshold of inhuman or degrading treatment.

[1] E.g. *Wainwright v. United Kingdom*, App. No. 12350/04, 26 September 2006.

This was the case in several decisions condemning France.[2] These were cases concerning inmates falling under the category of 'DPS' (which stands for 'Détenu Particulièrement Signalé', these are high-security prisoners) and, as such, they were subject to a special security regime, including many changes of location (so-called 'security rotations'), prolonged solitary confinement and systematic body searches. In each of these cases, the finding of a violation of Article 3 of the European Convention on Human Rights was based on a combination of factors including (but not limited to) the use of a regime of systematic searches, i.e. without any requirement of necessity or proportionality. Thus, in *Khider v. France* the ECtHR held that '...the applicant's conditions of detention, his classification as a high-security prisoner, his repeated transfer from prison to prison, his lengthy solitary confinement and the frequent full body searches he was subjected to all added up to inhuman and degrading treatment within the meaning of Article 3.'[3] In *El Shennawy v. France,* the ECtHR considered that '...although the searches had taken place over a short period of time, they had been liable to arouse in the applicant feelings of arbitrariness, inferiority and anxiety characteristic of a degree of humiliation going beyond the level which the strip-searching of prisoners inevitably entailed.'[4] Recently, the ECtHR strengthened its position by condemning Germany for the use of repeated and random strip searches against an inmate without a legitimate aim.[5] It thus prohibited systematic search regimes that are not based on any balanced justification (Portier 2019).

2.1.2 Jurisprudence of French Administrative Courts

French administrative courts, which have jurisdiction over penitentiary matters, have taken a position that has long kept France behind in the area of the protection of dignity in the context of prison searches. At

[2] See e.g. *Frérot v. France*, App. No. 70204/01, 12 June 2007; *Khider v. France*, App. No. 39364/05, 9 July 2009; *El Shennawy v. France*, App. No. 51246/08, 20 January 2011.

[3] *Khider v. France*, App. No. 39364/05, 9 July 2009, para 133.

[4] *El Shennawy v. France*, App. No. 51246/08, 20 January 2011, para 46.

[5] *Roth v. Germany*, App. No. 6780/18, 22 October 2020.

that time, which is before the adoption of the Prison Act of 2009, body searches were regulated not by law but rather by rules issued by the government or administration.[6] Thus, Article D275 of the Code of Criminal Procedure (hereinafter referred to as CCP) provided:

> Prisoners shall be searched frequently and as often as the director deems it necessary. They shall be searched in particular when they enter the institution and whenever they are removed from it and returned to it for whatever reason. They must also be searched before and after any visit[7]

This version of the text was based on Decree No. 98-1099 of 8 December 1998, reinforcing the previous regime, which, since 1985, provided for a purely optional procedure for searches before and after passing to the visiting room. The modification introduced in 1998 thus implemented a systematic and mandatory search regime. This provision was also repeated in an article providing for the possibility of use of 'control measures' on visitors (Article D406 of the CCP: 'Access to the visiting room involves, in addition to the search of prisoners before and after the visit, the control measures deemed necessary in respect of visitors for security reasons'[8]). The administrative courts thus validated the systematic use of searches at the exit of the visiting rooms, these being expressly stated in the texts.[9]

However, the Conseil d'État (i.e., the highest French administrative court, hereinafter referred to as 'CE') reversed its position by the ruling of 14 November 2008, *El Shennawy*, whereby it affirmed that any search operation carried out by the prison administration must be justified by necessity and proportionality.[10] What do these conditions mean?

- *Necessity*: Any body search of a prisoner must be specifically justified with regard to the particular risks he or she may pose in view of his

---

[6] For a detailed review, see Herzog-Evans (s.d.) and Herzog-Evans (2019).

[7] Translation: JF.

[8] Translation: JF.

[9] CE, *Mouesca*, No. 176389, 8 December 2000; CE, No. 237437, 12 March 2003.

[10] CE, *El Shennawy*, No. 315622, 14 November 2008.

or her personality.[11] The personality of the inmate includes his/her criminal and prison profiles;

- *Proportionality*: The principle of proportionality (in conjunction with the principle of subsidiarity, *infra*) requires the gradual adjustment of the means of searching that are used. The choice of the type of search to be carried out (palpation or full search) and the frequency of the search shall be made by taking into account not only the aim pursued (prevention of an offence, personal security or good order enforcement) but also the personality of the inmate;
- *Subsidiarity*: full body searches should only be carried out in a subsidiary way to electronic detection and palpation searches. In view of its subsidiary nature, a full search may only be carried out when other means of control prove to be insufficient.

French administrative jurisprudence, in the wake of European jurisprudence in this field, has therefore imposed on the prison administration a reasoned and limited use of searches. These incentives were instrumental in the drafting of the provisions on searches in the Prison Act of 24 November 2009.

2.2 The Original Rule on Body Searches: Necessity, Proportionality, and Subsidiarity

The entry into force of the Prison Act provided an opportunity to establish a strict framework for a practice that had previously been largely left to the discretion of the prison administration and that was regulated only by sub-legal regulations. The use of full body searches, the most intrusive of all searches available to the prison service, was strictly regulated by Article 57 of the Prison Act, which in its initial version stated that:

> The search must be based on the presumption of an offence or on the risk to the security of the person and to the good order in prison as a result of the behaviour of the prisoners. The nature and frequency of the

[11] CE, *Section française de l'Observatoire international des prisons* (OIP), No. 368816, 6 June 2013.

> searches are strictly adapted to these needs and to the personality of the inmates.
>
> Full body searches are only possible if the searches by palpation or the use of electronic means of detection are insufficient.
>
> Internal bodily examinations are prohibited, unless a specifically motivated need exists. They may then be carried out only by a doctor who does not practice in the same prison and is required for that purpose by the judicial authority[12]

Since the entry into force of the Prison Act, body searches have been subject to increased scrutiny by administrative courts, who have argued that certain practices are contrary to human dignity. The law requires to comply with the principles of necessity, proportionality, and subsidiarity of full body search measures. On 1st May 2022, a new Prison Code came into force, with the aim of integrating all relevant texts (legislative and administrative rules) relating to penitentiary law in a single volume, including the Prison Act of 2009. There has been no substantive change in the content of the texts, only their arrangement and numbering have been modified (see Bonis 2022; Falxa 2022).

Article R225-1 of the Prison Code (previously Article R57-7-79 of the CCP) states that any search measure must be carried out by the decision of the director. The decision to search an inmate shall be made in writing, except in urgent cases, when it may be made orally. In such cases, it shall be subsequently transcribed in writing, in order to ensure traceability.

The search decision must contain the following information:

- the date or period of implementation of the measure in the case of an overriding regime;
- the identity of the prisoner (surname, first name and prisoner's record number) and the area concerned;
- the type of search: palpation or full body search;
- the identity of the authority which decided to carry out the search;
- the legal and factual reasons.

[12] Translation: JF.

The legal reasoning consists of listing the legal grounds for the decision (e.g. Article 57 of the Prison Act of 24 November 2009 and Articles R57-7-79 et seq. of the CCP, now, respectively, Articles L2225-1 to L2225-3 and Articles R225-1 et seq. of the Prison Code). The factual reasoning consists of referring to the factual elements that characterize the existence of a risk justifying the search. The reasoning must make it possible to understand the decision on its reading alone. However, it is not necessary to give an exhaustive account of all the factors upon which the decision is based. There is no adversarial procedure.

Inmates may only be searched by officers of their own sex and under conditions that, while ensuring effective supervision, preserve respect for the inherent dignity of the human person (Article R57-7-81 of the CCP, now Article R225-3 of the Prison Code). The use of individual cameras is thus prohibited (law of 3 August 2018). A specially equipped room must be reserved for searches or, if this is not possible, a visual separation must be provided to ensure that the inmate is not exposed to the sight of others. Searches carried out must be recorded, either on GENESIS—a software for prisoners' data processing—or on another register.

According to Article R225-2 of the Prison Code (before R57-7-80 of the CCP), prisoners are searched '...whenever there is reason to suspect a risk of escape, the entry, exit or circulation in the detention area of objects or substances prohibited or dangerous for the security of persons or the good order of the prison institution'.[13]

The systematic conduct of searches of any inmate placed in the same situation without ascertaining whether the search is necessary in the light of the existing legal criteria and without adapting the nature and frequency of the search to the prisoner's personality was therefore prohibited under Article 57 of the original version of the Act. The *Conseil d'État* has thus recalled on several occasions that '...the measures of searches cannot have a systematic nature.'[14]

---

[13] Translation: JF.

[14] CE, *Section française de l'Observatoire international des prisons*, No. 347146, 11 July 2012; CE, *M. T.*, No. 359479, 26 September 2012; CE, *Section française de l'Observatoire international des prisons*, No. 368816, 6 June 2013; CE, *M.E.*, No. 368875, 6 June 2013. On this, see Slama (2013).

The need to ensure security and order within the prison could, for example, justify the use of searches when the structure of the visiting room area could not accommodate electronic detection equipment. However, the administration was still required to adapt the procedures for using searches not only to the security objectives they pursued but also to the personality of the prisoners. In this regard, the director had to take into account the behaviour of each inmate, his or her previous actions and the frequency of visits to the visiting rooms in order to adapt the nature of the search (by palpation or full body search) to be carried out and its frequency. The full body search should remain the exception.

Even so, some establishments continued to operate systematic search regimes under this initial regulation, and objections were therefore made on a case-by-case basis, e.g. with regard to searches carried out at the exits of visiting rooms, the fact that these latter constitute a risk area, due to the possibility of introducing therein prohibited or dangerous objects or substances, did not in itself justify that, at the end of the visit, all prisoners without distinction were being subjected to a full body search.[15]

The fact that all prisoners accessing the visiting room at the same time[16] were subjected to a full body search (a so-called 'random search' system) was also deemed to be contrary to Article 57 of the Prison Act.[17]

Administrative courts have therefore been confronted with notes drawn up by various directors providing sometimes for a general system of searches before and after visiting hours, sometimes for a specific period. It follows from this jurisprudence that such notes are not per se unlawful provided that, on the one hand, they are temporary and, on the other, the prison administration is able to prove that, in each prison, the immediately preceding period was characterized by particular security problems (e.g. large-scale entry of drugs or mobile phones). Furthermore, even if they create forms of temporary security operations

---

[15] CE, *M. D.*, No. 352372, 9 September 2011.

[16] In French prisons visits take place at definite hours, and there can be more than one rotation of visit during this period.

[17] CE, *M. T.*, No. 359479, 26 September 2012.

in visiting rooms, these searches must maintain a certain level of individuality and not lead to the systematic search of all prisoners, namely, as far as the integral search is concerned.

3 The Weight of Security on the Most Recent Legal Evolutions

Despite a decidedly favourable start for the protection of the dignity of prisoners, the wording of Article 57 of the Prison Act did not stand up to the security demands of staff. Faced with a text designed to provide a precise framework for the practice of searches and to avoid recourse to searches that are not strictly motivated by security considerations that take into account the personality of the prisoners concerned, considerable resistance quickly emerged from the prison administration, as part of a growing demand for security (Sect. 3.1). This pressure led to the reintroduction of the law of the possibility of systematic and indiscriminate searches (Sect. 3.2).

3.1 A General Context in Awes of Security

The entry into force of Article 57 in its original wording was immediately hampered by various forms of resistance from the prison administration against such a strict framework and the subsequent de facto limiting of the possibility of carrying out full body searches. The reports are unanimous in this respect: as early as 2011, the reports of the *Contrôleur général des lieux de privation de liberté* ('CGLPL', the French Prison Ombudsman) and the *Défenseur des droits* (General Ombudsman) mention the persistence of systematic searches in many prisons, in particular, at the exit from visiting rooms, but also after appointments with lawyers or after transfers, even though the prisoner would have remained under the supervision of staff or law enforcement officers.[18] The findings

[18] See e.g. the letter sent by the Prison Ombudsman (CGLPL) to the joint committee of the French parliament, 3 May 2016, about the proposed legislative changes.

of both ombudsmen were then repeated year after year, prison visit after prison visit.

From the outset, the prison staff unions strongly protested against the new legal provision, demanding its repeal, and even affirming their intention not to apply it. For example, the powerful SNP-FO union delivered a press release addressed to the Minister of Justice in May 2013, saying that '...the repeal of Article 57 of the Prison Act is not an option, rather a duty towards constituents who trust you with their security', and describing its refusal to respond favourably to their demand as 'shameful' and 'scandalous' (Observatoire international des prisons, Section française 2018: 6).

For its part, the UFAP-UNSA Justice, another important union within the prison administration, had stressed '...the urgency of repealing or modifying Article 57 of the Prison Act', stating that it had '...never approved such permissive law!'. Adamant in their position and refusing to change their practices by invoking the impossibility of properly selecting on a daily basis those who constitute an actual risk, given the risks that the new regime entails for their safety, the unions were strongly calling for the reinstatement of systematic searches during certain critical movements (visiting rooms and transfers in particular). Faced with a possible escalation of the conflict, the central administration allowed the practices concerned to continue (Observatoire international des prisons, Section française 2018: 6).

The Senate information report on the application of the Prison Act, published by Jean-René Lecerf and Nicole Borvo Cohen-Seat on 4 July 2012, confirmed the above when it highlighted the almost general persistence of systematic search regimes in French prisons, in violation of the law, and the 'major source of tension' that this represented for prison staff (Lecerf and Borvo Cohen-Seat 2012: 43).

Although, following insistent referrals from the NGO *Observatoire international des prisons* (OIP), the administrative courts have tried to curb the process, the outcry caused by some of these decisions among the unions of prison guards and prison directors is proof of the massive rejection of the initial wording of Article 57 of the Prison Act within the prison administration. Some prison directors, whose internal notes introducing systematic full body searches had been censured by the administrative judge, refused to comply with the magistrates' injunctions. This circumstance prompted the *Défenseur des Droits* to recommend, in a decision of 23 February 2017, that disciplinary proceedings be taken against one of them, the director of Fresnes prison.[19]

3.2 Towards the Reintroduction of Systematic and Indiscriminate Searches

Considering such resistance, the jurisprudential and then legislative deviations from the original spirit of the text have accumulated, eventually allowing the reintroduction of systematic full body searches. First the judge and then the legislator have intervened on the strict framework regulating the use of full body search measures.

To begin with, and as an exception, the administrative courts decided that systematic search regimes could be established for certain prisoners identified as presenting particular risks. The needs of public order and the constraints of the public prison service could legitimize the application of a systematic search regime to an inmate, including full body searches.[20] Such an exorbitant regime was validly implemented if it met the legal criteria of necessity and proportionality. It had to be justified by the existence of suspicions based on the inmate's behaviour, his or her previous actions or the circumstances of his or her contacts with third parties. The *Conseil d'État* thus accepted that an exorbitant system of systematic thorough searches could be set up against a prisoner in view of the nature of the events leading to his conviction (participation in a criminal conspiracy aimed at preparing a terrorist act), and his overall behaviour during detention, which could explain why he is under special supervision.[21] Although such an approach was exceptional, it went against the regime as foreseen in Article 57 and can therefore be

[19] Défenseur des Droits, Decision 2017-046 of 23 February 2017 on the practice of systematic full body searches on the exit of the visiting room at the Fresnes detention centre.

[20] CE, *M. G.*, No. 339259, 20 May 2010; CE, *M. E.*, No. 368875, 6 June 2013.

[21] CE, *M. E.*, No 368 875, 6 June 2013.

seen as the first crack in the legal framework. it opened a breach in the legal system.

Under pressure from the prison staff lobby, the legislator finally gave in and amended Article 57 of the Prison Act twice, allowing the legalisation of full body search practices in prisons, which was yet questionable from the point of view of guaranteeing the prisoners' right to dignity.

At that time, France was under terrorist threat, and the general climate was very tense. Demands on security were growing. The law of 3 June 2016 strengthening the fight against organised crime, terrorism and its financing first supported the position of the prison administration (Poncela 2016: 565). Article 111 of the law specified that searches may be systematically carried out in certain places and for a specific period of time, provided the existence of serious reasons to suspect that prohibited objects or substances or substances that pose a threat to the security of persons and property have been brought into the establishment. This a priori restrictive condition is in practice totally illusory since, in a penitentiary context, such suspicions are permanent. Searches can therefore now be carried out without regard to the personality of inmates (i.e. indiscriminately), and are decided by the director, who must transmit his or her specially reasoned decision to the public prosecutor and to the prison administration. These searches must also be the subject of a detailed report. Despite the intended framework, the law adopted during the state of emergency has effectively brought back systematic and indiscriminate searches regardless of the personality of the persons searched.

This first move was then reinforced by the new wording of Article 57 of the Prison Act resulting from the law of 23 March 2019. In addition to the possibility of one-off full searches justified '...by the presumption of an offence or by the risks that inmates' behaviour poses to the safety of individuals and the maintenance of good order in the establishment', this new wording provides two new systematic search regimes:

- One inspired by the exorbitant regime admitted by the *Conseil d'État* in its aforementioned judgement of 6 June 2013, authorizing the

implementation of a systematic search regime under the same conditions as these ad hoc searches but only '...when the necessities of public order and the constraints of the public prison service so require';
- The other, formulated in the same way, applies when '...prisoners enter the prison without having remained under the constant surveillance of the prison administration or the police or gendarmerie', i.e. after any movement outside (leave, medical appointment, sentence adjustment).

It is therefore a real return to the possibilities of systematic searches, as under the previous regime.

4 The Use of Body Searches in Prison Practice

The practice of searching prisoners can take different forms, each of which is based on a specific technique (Sect. 4.1). The use of full body searches, the most intrusive of the searches available to the prison administration, poses actual risks in terms of violation of inmates' dignity (Sect. 4.2).

4.1 Searching Techniques

The purpose of a body search is to look for prohibited or dangerous substances or objects that the prisoner might have. Three types of searches exist for this purpose:

- *Search by palpation*: it consists of palpating the prisoners' clothed body. There is a second type of search by palpation, which is also used in prisons: a stronger kind of search in the event of a threat to the integrity of officers following a serious incident in detention. In the latter case, the person may be handcuffed, must stand with his/her hands on the wall and legs apart, and the officer must lean on the prisoner's knees and wrist in order to impede any movement as he or she performs the search. In other words, in some circumstances, this type of search can be perceived as invasive as a full search;

- *Full body search*: also known as 'body search', this involves stripping the prisoner naked to ensure that he or she is not concealing any object or substance that could escape detection by technical equipment (walk-throughs, hand-held detectors) or by a pat-down search;
- *Internal search*: also known as internal body investigations, these are only possible if there is a specially motivated need (Article 57 of the Prison Act, now on Articles L225-3 of the Prison Code). Very exceptional, they consist of an examination carried out by a doctor practicing outside the establishment on the instructions of the judicial authority (X-rays or checks of the oral, anal or vaginal cavities).

Only the first two of these can be carried out by the prison authorities. In practice, it is the full search that raises the most difficulties from the point of view of respect for human dignity. The technical steps for executing such a full search are outlined in a Circular of 15 July 2020 on searches of prisoners in application of Article 57 of the Prison Act of 24 November 2009:

- The main purpose of a full search is to look for prohibited or dangerous items or substances that may escape technical detection or pat-down. The full search prohibits any physical contact between the prisoner and the officer: the officer asks the prisoner to undress alone and to place his or her clothing on a special rack to prevent it from lying on the floor;
- After removing the prisoner's clothing, the officer asks him/her to run his/her hand through his/her hair and to show his/her ears to check that nothing is hidden; if necessary, the officer asks the prisoner to remove his/her hearing aid;
- Depending on the prisoner's profile or the situation, the officer may ask the prisoner to open his or her mouth and lift his or her tongue and remove any dental prosthesis (for example, if the prisoner has a habit of hiding razor blades in his or her mouth, or has just hidden something in his or her mouth);

- The officer then carries out the armpit check by having the prisoner raise and lower his/her arms, before inspecting his/her hands by asking him/her to spread his/her fingers;
- He asks the prisoner to spread his/her legs slightly: under no circumstances, the prisoner is asked to bend over;
- The prisoner's feet are then examined, in particular, the arch of the foot and the toes;
- Before handing over to the prisoner, the officer finally proceeds to the control of the clothing, paying attention to check the seams, hems, linings, as well as shoes, making sure that they do not contain any hidden covers;
- Stocks of disposable gloves are made available to the officers in charge of searches, which the officers make sure to wear. A water point must be provided near the place of search, or any other device enabling the officer to wash his/her hands if necessary.

4.2 Practical Consequences for the Inmates

The consequences of systematic and indiscriminate search regimes are serious and manifold for prisoners subjected to them.

The first consequence is obviously the risk of infringing on the dignity and privacy of the prisoner. The search itself inevitably gives rise to a feeling of embarrassment or even humiliation for the person subjected to it: nudity, sometimes coldness, the gaze of the persons carrying out the search ... All this contributes to a situation which, in itself, implies an intrusion into the privacy and dignity of the person, although such searches are generally considered not to reach the threshold of a violation of Article 3 of the European Convention on Human Rights. Nonetheless, a violation happens indeed when searches are carried out in a systematic manner, without reasons relating to the personality or background of the prisoner, as they may be according to the new wording of Article 57 of the Prisons Act (now Articles L225-1 to L225-3 of the Prison Code).

Some searches (i.e., searches that were executed by the Regional Intervention and Security Teams [ERIS], a prison administration corps which travels to various prisons to carry out security missions) have been filmed for a while. But after the ECtHR condemned France in the *Frérot* and *El Shennawy* cases which included these practices in the assessment of the respect of the threshold of Article 3 of the European Convention on Human Rights, a note from the Prison Administration of 18 May 2008 entitled 'Video recordings made by the Regional Intervention and Security Teams (ERIS) during full searches' stated that full searches should no longer be subject to video recordings as this '…could, quite rightly, be interpreted as a violation of human dignity.[22] However, the note recommended that ERIS interventions in the event of opposition or rebellion by the inmates being searched, and in particular 'forced full searches', be filmed. In such cases, it recommended '…framing the shots by filming only the upper body', 'as far as possible'. Nevertheless, there was no legal basis for this practice. It should also be noted that, apart from the interventions of the ERIS, the general circular of 14 April 2011 on the means of controlling detainees does not at any time provide for the recording of body searches.

It should also be noted that some full body searches, particularly those carried out on women, may be perceived as sexual assault (Georges 1993; McCulloch and Georges 2009), especially considering that many women in detention have already been sexually assaulted. However, the judge does not allow these acts to be classified as a criminal offence because of the absence of the moral element (no intention on the part of staff to commit an act of a sexual nature[23]). Still, the problem remains, and practices perceived as sexual assault or even rape by a person in custody (forcibly spreading the buttocks, inserting a finger into the vagina) have been recently denounced in front of the courts (Petitot 2022), echoing a recent report by the CGLPL pointing out the difficulties related to searches in the women's prison of Fleury-Mérogis (CGLPL 2019: 57–60).

With regard to the effectiveness of these systematic body searches, as they are practiced, now somewhat outdated data show that systematic full body searches did not reveal many objects or products (Observatoire

---

[22] Translation: JF.

[23] Court of Cassation, Criminal Division, No. 08-83.148, 10 December 2008,

international des prisons, Section française 2018: 14). Nonetheless, such results might be attributed precisely to their systematic nature.

Conversely, these systematic searches discouraged more than one prisoner from having visits. Indeed, some inmates would rather renounce to visits than having to undergo regular full-scale searches. Such a situation might affect family ties, which are essential for future reintegration. While some authors argue for a 'cultural revolution' in the prison service, inviting it to '...move from security measures imposed indiscriminately on all prisoners to a discernment and a culture of intelligence' (Herzog-Evans s.d.) (translation: JF), the illusion did not last, and it was indeed the 'might is right principle' that eventually prevailed.

If a search is refused, the prisoner may be subjected to a forced search and disciplinary proceedings. When the prisoner refuses to undress or comply with orders given, and after having called in a supervisory member of staff, force may, if necessary, be used to remove the prisoner's clothing.[24] The use of force during a full body search shall be the subject of a professional report which shall specify, inter alia, the context, the persons involved in the search, and the role of each of them. In addition, three types of disciplinary faults may be found against a prisoner who refuses to submit to a control measure:

- If the prisoner has shown inertia to the orders given, without any real physical resistance, it is a second-degree disciplinary offence of '...refusal to submit to a security measure defined by a law or regulation, by the internal regulations of the penitentiary institution or by any other service instruction' (Article R232-5, 1st of the Prison Code, previously Article R57-7-2, 1st of the CCP);
- If the prisoner has violently resisted the instructions of the staff, this constitutes a case of rebellion on the basis of a first-degree disciplinary offence (Article R232-4, 3° of the Prison Code, previously R57-7-1 3° of the CCP);

[24] Article R227-1 of the Prison Code (previously, Article R57-7-83 of the CCP) states that "...prison administration staff shall only use force against detainees in cases of self-defence, attempted escape, violent resistance or physical inertia to orders given, provided that such use is proportionate and strictly necessary to prevent escape or to restore order".

- If the prisoner commits or attempts to commit physical violence against a member of the prison staff, it is a matter of '…exercising or attempting to exercise physical violence against a member of the staff or a person on mission or visiting the prison', first-degree disciplinary offence (Article R232-4, 1st of the Prison Code, previously article Article R57-7-1, 1st of the CCP).

The prisoner may be placed, as a preventive measure, in confinement in an ordinary individual cell or in a disciplinary cell, if this measure is the only way to put an end to the misconduct or to preserve order within the prison, in accordance with Article R234-19 of the Prison Code (previously R. 57-7-18 of the CCP).

When asked whether the refusal to submit to a search that could potentially infringe human dignity could be justified (and thus possibly preclude the risk of disciplinary proceedings), the administrative judge considered that '…apart from the sole hypothesis that the injunction addressed to a prisoner by a member of the staff of the penitentiary establishment would be manifestly of such a nature as to infringe human dignity, any order from the penitentiary staff must be carried out by the inmates'.[25] In this case, the debate concerns the possibility of an infringement of the prisoner's dignity: the existence of such an infringement has been admitted a posteriori in a number of cases by courts, which seems to indicate a problem of a priori assessment of the reality of the infringement on dignity by the agents or the administration. A judgement of the ECtHR[26] raised a question in this regard, without directly condemning the imposition of a disciplinary sanction for refusing to submit to a search that violates the prisoner's right to privacy. A French administrative court later recognized the disproportionality of a full body search and the violation of the prisoner's dignity by this measure, leading to the annulment of the disciplinary sanction imposed because of the prisoner's refusal to submit to the body search measure.[27]

[25] CE, *Letona Biteri*, No. 326084, 20 May 2011.

[26] *Milka v. Poland*, App. No. 14322/12, 15 September 2015.

[27] CAA Douai, No. 16DA00715, 7 December 2017. On this, see Costa (2018).

5 The Risks of the Current Regulation

The current French regulation on body searches therefore raises some questions and criticisms. Article 57 of the Prisons Act, as amended twice and now included on article L225-1 to L225-3 of the Prison code, seems to present some risks from the point of view of the prisoner's right to dignity.

5.1 Criticisms

Under its latest version, Article 57 of the Prison Act marked a significant step backwards in terms of protecting prisoners' dignity by considerably broadening the scope for full-scale searches without regard to the prisoner's personality, thus undermining the requirement of proportionality of these measures. There are now four search regimes. They are described in detail in Circular NOR: JUSK2 017 670C of 15 July 2020 on searches of prisoners. The annexes to the circular, which contain a summary table of all the procedures applicable to searches of prisoners, reveal the distance that the prison administration takes from the principles laid down in European human rights law.

Two situations are particularly noteworthy. Firstly, the systematic searches regime for prisoners entering the prison without having remained under the constant supervision of the prison administration or law enforcement officers: the table annexed to the circular indicates that only the principle of subsidiarity applies to such searches, thus effectively excluding the principles of necessity and proportionality. Secondly, the regime of systematic, non-individualized searches ordered in specific places and for a specified period (particularly searches at the exit of visiting rooms), the application of which, although apparently subject to the aforementioned principles of necessity, proportionality and subsidiarity, does not take into account the personality of the prisoner in order to carry out this proportionality balance.

In this context, criticism of systematic search regimes is increasing, coming both from the Council of Europe's Committee for the Prevention of Torture (CPT) in its 2017 and 2021 reports on France, and from the CGLPL. In its reports, the CPT regrets the legislative changes that occurred in 2016 and 2019 with regard to searches, highlighting the return of systematic and non-individualised strip searches, which are contrary to its own recommendations on the matter (CPT 2017: 51–52; CPT 2021: 62–63). For its part, the CGLPL has repeatedly pointed out abuses of systematic searches permitted at certain places and for certain periods of time in some prisons, which automatically renew the periods for systematic searches, thus establishing a permanent regime of systematic searches (particularly at the exit of the visiting room) where the law does not provide for such searches (see CGLPL 2016: 89–90).

Some of these criticisms are also echoed in an information report by MPs Xavier Breton and Dimitri Houbon (2018) on the prison searches regime (Dufourq 2018). As we have seen, far from having been abolished, the system of systematic searches has emerged strengthened by the latest legislative changes in this area, as the most authoritative doctrine in this area has not failed to point out (Poncela 2016: 565; Herzog-Evans 2019: 699).

5.2 New Sentences Awaiting

The current regime marks a return to the situation prior to that intended by the 2009 Prison Act. In the current state of positive law, the risk of non-conformity with the requirements of the ECHR and thus of violation of its Article 3 by the practice of systematic searches seems to be very likely, as demonstrated by the recent decision of the ECtHR in *Roth v. Germany*.

The French administrative courts could also condemn the current regime under the European Convention on Human Rights, as they can check the regime in terms of conformity with the treaties. Some courts of the first instance did not hesitate to do so, considering that the implementation of systematic search regimes at the exit of visiting rooms, decided under the previous law (before the reforms of 2016 and 2019), was contrary to the requirements of Article 3 of the European Convention on Human Rights. It would not be incongruous for them to apply the same logic to the new legal framework.

6 Conclusion

Although searches, as introduced in French domestic law, are subject to certain conditions of prior control and can only be decided by authorities designated as competent, they present a real risk of being in contradiction both with the provisions of the European Convention on Human Rights, the relevant case-law of the ECtHR, and with the recommendations made by independent supervisory bodies in recent years (such as the CPT and the CGLPL). The risk of a prison administration becoming entangled in practices that restrict rights and violate human dignity in the name of security is often highlighted by these bodies. This situation cannot persist, and the day when France will be condemned again for the practice of indiscriminate and non-individualized searches may not be far off.

Criticisms concerning the reduced effectiveness of these practices in terms of the objective of combating trafficking of all kinds and the sometimes counterproductive nature of these mass searches in view of the distrust they create in the prison administration are, however, still too often dismissed in the face of both the power of the prison officers' union lobby and the growing demands for the security of the administration.

References

Bonis, E. 2022. Le code pénitentiaire est entré en vigueur. *La Semaine Juridique Ed. Générale* 19: 970–971.

Breton, X., and D. Houbron. 2018. *Rapport parlementaire en conclusion des travaux d'une mission d'information relative au régime des fouilles en détention.* 8 Octobre. https://www.assemblee-nationale.fr/dyn/15/rapports/cion_lois/l15b1295_rapport-information

CGLPL. 2016. *Rapport de visite: 28 novembre – 9 décembre 2016 – 2ème visite Centre pénitentiaire d'Aix-Luynes (Bouches-du-Rhône).* Paris: CGLPL. http://www.cglpl.fr/wp-content/uploads/2018/04/Rapport-de-la-deuxi%C3%A8me-visite-du-centre-p%C3%A9nitentiaire-dAix-Luynes-Bouches-du-Rh%C3%B4ne.pdf

CGLPL. 2019. *Rapport définitif: 11 au 15 février 2019 – 3ème visite Maison d'arrêt des femmes de Fleury-Mérogis (Essonne)*. Paris: CGLPL. https://www.cglpl.fr/wp-content/uploads/2020/12/Rapport-de-la-troisi%C3%A8me-visite-de-la-maison-darr%C3%AAt-des-femmes-de-Fleury-M%C3%A9rogis-Essonne.pdf

Costa, D. 2018. Désobéir légalement en prison au nom de la dignité. *Actualité Juridique De Droit Administratif (AJDA)* 18: 1041.

CPT. 2017. *Rapport au Gouvernement de la République française relatif à la visite effectuée en France par le Comité européen pour la prévention de la torture et des peines ou traitements inhumains ou dégradants (CPT) du 15 au 27 novembre 2015*. CPT/Inf (2017) 7. Strasbourg : Council of Europe.

CPT. 2021. *Rapport au Gouvernement de la République française relatif à la visite effectuée en France par le Comité européen pour la prévention de la torture et des peines ou traitements inhumains ou dégradants (CPT) du 4 au 18 décembre 2019*. CPT/Inf (2021) 14. Strasbourg : Council of Europe.

Dufourq, P. 2018. Fouilles en détention: un rapport appelle à la clarification du régime et à une hausse des moyens, *Dalloz Actualité*, 11 Octobre (online).

Falxa, J. 2022. Le code pénitentiaire: une codification à "droit inconstant". *AJ Pénal*: 295.

George, A. 1993. Strip-searches: Sexual Assault by the State. *Alternative Law Journal* 18 (1): 31–33.

Herzog-Evans, M. 2019. *Droit pénitentiaire 2020–2021*, 3ème édition. Dalloz Action.

Herzog-Evans, M., s.d. Fouilles corporelles. In: *Répertoire de droit pénal et de procédure pénale*, Dalloz (online).

Lecerf, J.-R., and N. Borvo Cohen-Seat. 2012. *Rapport d'information fait au nom de la commission des lois et de la commission pour le contrôle de l'application des lois n° 629 (2011–2012)*, 4 July. https://www.senat.fr/rap/r11-629/r11-6291.pdf

McCulloch, J., and A. George. 2009. Naked Power. Strip Searching in Women's Prisons. In *The Violence of Incarceration*, ed. P. Scraton and J. McCulloch, 107–123. London: Routledge.

Observatoire international des prisons, Section française. 2018. *Les fouilles intégrales en détention, Cadre juridique et pratique*, Note à l'attention de la mission d'information de la Commission des lois de l'Assemblée Nationale sur le régime des fouilles en détention, 31 May. https://oip.org/wp-content/uploads/2018/06/oip-note-fouilles-31052018.pdf

Petitot, P. 2022. À Fleury-Mérogis, une détenue porte plainte pour viol contre une surveillante, *Lettre de l'OIP*, 16 March 2022.

Poncela, P. 2016. Peines et prisons: La régression. À propos des lois du 3 juin et du 21 juillet 2016. *Revue De Sciences Criminelles Et De Droit Comparé* 3: 565–576.

Portier, J. 2019. L'acquis jurisprudentiel de la CEDH en matière de fouilles à corps en milieu carcéral. Douze ans après l'arrêt Frérot. *Actualité Juridique De Droit Administratif (AJDA)* 30: 1738–1743.

Slama, S. 2013. Encadrement jurisprudentiel du rapport d'humiliation intégral des fouilles à nu systématiques. Lettre "Actualités Droits-Libertés" du CREDOF, 20 June. https://revdh.wordpress.com/2013/06/20/encadrement-jurisprudentiel-du-rapport-dhumiliation-integral-des-fouilles-a-nu-systematiques/

Stripping the Self Away: Security, Control, and Punishment in the Practice of Strip Searches in Spanish Prisons

Cristina Güerri

1 Introduction[1]

In *Asylums*, Erving Goffman (1961) argues that, upon entering a total institution, individuals experience a "mortification of the self", that is, they suffer from a series of degradations and humiliations that, through

The original version of this chapter was revised: Incorrect abstract has been updated. The correction to this chapter is available at https://doi.org/10.1007/978-3-031-20451-7_13

[1] This research is part of the project "Mecanismos de Petición y Queja: Participación, Calidad de Vida y Legitimidad en Prisión", Grant PID2019-105042RB-I00/AEI/10.13039/501100011033. I have been able to carry out this research thanks to a Juan de la Cierva-Formación Fellowship, Grant FJC2019-039,426-I. I must thank Mireia Bes, from the Catalan Prison Administration, for her patience in providing me with the requested data; Maria Contreras, Pau González, David Cuaresma and Òscar for their help to interpret the categories used in the datasets; and Elena Larrauri for her pertinent questions and helpful comments. All translations from Spanish to English in this chapter are mine.

C. Güerri (✉)
Instituto Andaluz Interuniversitario de Criminología, Universidad de Málaga, Málaga, Spain
e-mail: cristina.guerri@uma.es

T. Daems (ed.), *Body Searches and Imprisonment*, Palgrave Studies in Prisons and Penology, https://doi.org/10.1007/978-3-031-20451-7_9

their continued action, strip the person from their old self and force them into becoming an inmate. Prison searches are one such mortifications.

Prison searches penetrate the private sphere of the individual, whether it is their cell or their body, and violate the person's self (e.g. HRLC 2017: 12). The fact that such an invasion of privacy is permitted by law transmits the message that they are no longer the person they were on the outside, but rather an inmate subjected to the power of the institution. The following extract from an interview by Crawley (2004: 178) with an English Senior Officer clearly illustrates that:

> I mean the minute somebody's got their knickers round their ankles, their dignity disappears. Erm, and certainly in *their* eyes, you've got so much *power* over them [...] they're there with their dangly bits flopping in the breeze. They're vulnerable. Erm, it brings home to them the fact that they're in prison that you can do that.

This message is conveyed since the admission process. As it will be explained (see Sect. 2), Spanish Prison Rules determine that inmates must be searched upon admission in prison, and Prison Orders by both the Spanish and Catalan prison administration[2] specify that this search should be a strip search. Afterward, body searches will be carried out routinely in the cases provided by prison regulations and discretionally when prison staff deems it necessary according to the criteria set by the law, continuing the mortification of inmates' selves.

Among all the degradations that contribute to the mortification of the self, body searches are particularly harmful because they invade the private sphere of the individual through forced interpersonal contact, as it is the case for frisks (see Warr, this volume); or may involve humiliating situations such as being completely naked in front of a prison officer or being requested to do push-ups during a strip search (Tschanz, this volume). For example, a research report about Belgian prisons observed that strip searches are described as one of the most demeaning aspects of prison life by both inmates and prison officers (Snacken et al. 2000,

[2] Although the Prison Law applies for the whole of Spain, Catalonia has its own prison administration.

cited in van Zyl Smit and Snacken 2009). This is also true in the Spanish context, where some inmates referred to strip searches and cell searches[3] when asked if they had received humiliating treatment in prison (Rodríguez et al. 2018). Furthermore, the extent of physical contamination that strip searches imply is evinced by the substantial amount of literature and testimonies that equate strip searches to sexual assault (e.g. Pereira 2001; HRLC 2017: 14; Hutchison 2020).

Another issue highlighted by previous literature is that the degraded status of the inmate as an individual subjected to the power of the prison administration is transferred to their family members and close friends (e.g. Melo 2021: 101). Regarding body searches, those who visit an inmate may not only be frisked but also strip searched if provided by the law, as the European Court of Human Rights has admitted.[4] Moreover, in the Spanish case, the visitors' consent is needed for a body searching them, but if the visitor denies consent, they will not be permitted to do the intimate or family visit. Under such a threat, it is difficult to think that visitors' consent is not coerced.[5]

Given the impact of strip searching on prisoners and their families we need to take into consideration the rationale that is employed in prison systems to justify these assaults upon the self. Regarding prisons, "security" tends to be the official rationale,[6] as it is the case with strip searches in Spain (see Sect. 2), Europe (van Zyl Smit and Snacken 2009), and other jurisdictions such as Canada or Australia (e.g. HRLC 2017; Balfour 2018). However, Goffman (1961) argues that, very often, the rationale of security is a mere rationalization generated by the efforts to manage the daily activity of a large number of inmates within the closed

---

[3] Some prisoners described cell searches as humiliating because prison officers would throw all their things to the floor after examining them or make mocking comments about the pictures of their families. It is telling that prison officers use the expression "to burst the cell" ("reventar la celda") to talk about cell searches (Güerri 2020: 160–161).

[4] See *Wainwright v. United Kingdom*, App. No. 12350/04, 26 September 2006. Here the European Court of Human Rights argued that prison visitors can be strip-searched when the law stipulates so and there is a "legitimate aim" to carry out the search.

[5] See Intxarube et al. (2017: 19–21) for a testimony regarding the families of ETA prisoners.

[6] Goffman (1961) also contemplates that, in some prison systems, degrading or humiliating acts may be arranged mainly for their mortifying power, although this is more typically a rationale of concentration camps.

space of the prison which lacks sufficient resources. In this sense, criminological research has demonstrated that routine strip searches are not effective (HRLC 2017) and that the rationale of security often conceals a disciplinary practice of power (Balfour 2018) that heightens the level of control and adds to the punitive character of prison life (Drake 2012).

In Spain strip searches have only been analyzed from a legal perspective (see e.g. Vicente 2009; Guillén 2016: 165–209), and very few data exist regarding their practice (Ríos Martín and Cabrera 2002; Gallego et al. 2010). The research discussed in this chapter aims to fill this gap in Spanish criminological literature and to add to the discussion on the functions of strip searches in penitentiary institutions by studying the practice of strip searches in Spanish prisons.

This chapter is structured as follows. First, the legal regulation of body searches in Spain will be detailed. Second, I will build on original data from the Catalan Prison Administration and reports by prison supervision mechanisms to analyze the practice of strip searches in Spanish prisons. Third, it will be discussed whether it can be argued that strip searches are really justified in terms of security or if, on the contrary, they serve a different purpose within the prison. Lastly, I conclude by reflecting on the meaning and the implications of the current practice of strip searches in Spanish prisons.

2 Legal Regulation of Body Searches in Spain

The Prison Law of 1979 (hereafter, LOGP)[7] establishes that inmates, their cells, and belongings may be searched according to the periodicity and legal guarantees determined in the prison regulations and must always respect the prisoner's dignity (Art. 23).

The Prison Rules of 1996 (hereafter, RP)[8] include body searches on the list of security measures that can be implemented to prevent incidents in prison, together with others such as observing inmates, head counts,

[7] Ley Orgánica 1/1979, de 26 de septiembre, General Penitenciaria.

[8] Real Decreto 190/1996, de 9 de febrero, por el que se aprueba el Reglamento Penitenciario.

or cell searches (Art. 65 RP). As with all security measures, body searches must follow the criteria of necessity and proportionality, prioritize electronic means, and respect inmates' dignity and other fundamental rights (most notably, privacy[9]) of prisoners (Art. 71 RP).[10]

Three kinds of body searches can be distinguished (Art. 68.1 RP): superficial searches (over the clothes, by frisking or with a security wand), strip searches (involving nudity), and radiographies for security reasons.[11] In the following subsections, the regulation of these body searches will be outlined, putting special emphasis on the regulation of strip searches.

2.1 Superficial Searches

As previously mentioned, prison legislation establishes that prisoners must be searched prior to their admission to prison (Art. 15.bis.2 LOGP and 18 RP) and daily if they are classified in high-security regime (Art. 93.1.2ª RP). In addition, there are other cases where inmates will be searched superficially, as established in Instructions by the Spanish Prison Administration (Secretaría General de Instituciones Penitenciarias, hereafter, SGIP)[12]:

---

[9] The Constitutional Court states that this fundamental right, which stems from the right to dignity from Article 10.1 of the Spanish Constitution, may be compromised during strip searches (Sentencia del Tribunal Constitucional 171/2013, of 7 October).

[10] The old Prison Rules of 1981 only determined that every new inmate had to be searched prior to their admission (Art. 29) and that inmates in high-security regime had to be searched daily (Art. 47). However, no further detail was given regarding how the searches should be carried out and prison officers enjoyed broad discretion in terms of when to search inmates (Art. 303, 308, 310, 315 and 332 stated that one of the tasks of prison officers is to perform searches "when deemed necessary"). Therefore, the new regulation established in the Prison Rules of 1996 was welcomed by the doctrine.

[11] Cavity searches are not allowed in Spanish prisons.

[12] Currently, there are three prison administrations in Spain. The Spanish Prison Administration (SGIP) is responsible for all Spanish prisons except those in Catalonia and the Basque Country. All prison administrations are regulated by the same Prison Law (LOGP) and Prison Rules (RP), but they have competence to regulate certain aspects of organization and management through Instructions and Prison Orders. In this chapter, we will focus on the regulation of the Spanish Prison Administration (SGIP) because it is the one affecting most Spanish prisons, and the Catalan Prison Administration (SMPRAV) as it is the one that has provided us with quantitative and qualitative data on the practice of searches in prison.

- Inmates who are transferred from one prison to another will be searched prior to leaving the prison (Instruction 3/2021 SGIP);
- Inmates who work outside their wing will be searched with a metal detector or security wand before entering and leaving the premises. Moreover, prisoners who work at certain premises (e.g., loading bay or parcel service) will be frisked twice a day to prevent the entry of mobile phones (Instruction 3/2010 SGIP);
- Inmates who return from a prison leave or have been transferred from a different prison will be searched upon admission (Instruction 3/2010 SGIP);
- Inmates who have overdosed will be searched in order to ensure that they do not have more narcotic substances with them (Instruction 10/2014 SGIP).

Moreover, Instruction 3/2011 of the Spanish Prison Administration, defining the General Intervention Plan in relation to Drugs inside Prisons, identifies family and intimate visits and prison leaves as the main ways to introduce drugs inside prisons, and establishes the "…increase in the frequency of searches of inmates and their visitors" (Instruction 3/2011 SGIP: 45–46).[13]

To carry out these searches, metal detectors and security wands should be prioritized over frisks when their efficacy is expected to be the same (Art. 71 RP). In fact, Instruction 3/2010 states that metal detectors "…are *more effective to detect weapons and other objects* that may be dangerous for the security of the prison, as well as for officers and inmates" (Instruction 3/2010 SGIP: 29, emphasis in the original). Similarly, in the Catalan Prison Administration (Secretaria de Mesures Penals, Reinserció i Atenció a la Víctima, hereafter, SMPRAV), Circular 1/2008 SMPRAV considers that usually superficial searches and metal detectors will be enough to determine if an inmate is in possession of prohibited or dangerous substances or objects (Circular 1/2008 SMPRAV: 2). When these kinds of searches are not deemed sufficient, strip searches can be used.

[13] For a detailed analysis of this Instruction, see Rodríguez Yagüe (2016).

2.2 Strip Searches

Strip searches can be carried out when there is reasoned suspicion that a certain inmate is hiding prohibited substances or dangerous objects in their clothes or their body, and less detrimental security measures are not deemed sufficient to seize them. According to the Prison Rules (Art. 68.2), this security measure requires the authorization of the Senior Manager (*Jefe de Servicios*) and must be motivated by adducing *specific* reasons (i.e., generic statements such as 'for security reasons' or 'visits are the usual means for introducing drugs in prison' are not allowed).[14]

More concretely, the Constitutional Court stated that the specific reasons to justify a strip search must refer to the "...circumstances of the penitentiary centre" (e.g., there has been a shiv fight, but the weapon has not been found) or "previous behaviour of the inmate" (e.g., the inmate was caught dealing drugs, so prison officers will strip search him/her after an intimate visit of their partner).[15] It must be noted that no other justifications besides *individualized* and *verified* security risks are admitted. In this sense, Prison Surveillance Judges (*Jueces de Vigilancia Penitenciaria*, hereafter, JVP) have stated that strip searches cannot be practiced randomly as a means of control or for deterrence.[16]

Despite the abovementioned requirements, the Spanish Prison Administration has defined certain cases in which strip searches will be carried out routinely. In particular, strip searches should be carried out when inmates enter prison from the outside (upon admission, return from a prison leave, or transfer from a different prison)[17] and prior to

---

[14] The requirements for strip searches in high-security regime are written slightly different: "When there is a *well-founded suspicion* that the inmate is in possession of prohibited objects and there is *need to act immediately*, strip searches could be ordered by the Security Manager, giving notice to the prison Director. This strip search will be carried out according to Article 68" (Art. 93.1.2ª, emphasis added).

[15] Sentencia Tribunal Constitucional 57/1994, of February 28th. Legal Grounds § 6.

[16] See, for example, JVP A Coruña Decree of 3 January 1995 and JVP Granada Decree of 31 July 1995.

[17] In 2011, SGIP sent a Notice to the Director of every prison amending this Instruction, as Prison Rules state clearly that every strip search must be individually justified for specific reasons and, therefore, these general cases were contravening the law. However, this is a "*rather irregular*" procedure (González Vinuesa 2021): usually, Instructions are amended by publishing a new Instruction that partially revokes the previous one. As Instruction 3/2010 has remained

the application of physical restraint measures (Instruction 3/2010 SGIP). This is different in Catalonia, where "ordinary" (routine) strip searches are only required upon admission and when inmates are placed in temporary confinement or transferred from an ordinary wing to a high-security unit. In Catalan prisons, when inmates return from a prison leave or from an intimate or family visit strip searches should always be motivated following the established protocol (Circular 1/2008 SMPRAV).

In order to preserve inmates' privacy, the Prison Rules determine that strip searches must be carried out in a closed room, by prison officers of the same gender as the inmate,[18] and without the presence of other prisoners (Art. 68.3). Further detail is given in the protocols by both prison administrations, where it is stated that the visual inspection of the inmates' body must be as brief as possible, and that inmates should be given a robe to cover their body while their clothes are being examined (Prison Order of 9 March 2005 by SGIP and Circular 1/2008 SMPRAV). Moreover, the Catalan protocol forbids that inmates are asked to squat while naked (Circular 1/2008 SMPRAV). In the Spanish administration, however, squatting will be tolerated in certain circumstances depending on the Prison Surveillance Judge that is assigned to the prison (Vicente 2009).[19]

Lastly, to increase accountability, the Prison Rules provide that every strip search must be reported to the Senior Manager, detailing information such as the name of the inmate, the reasons adduced to carry out the strip search, which prison officers did the search, the followed procedure and its result (Art. 68.5). Moreover, in 2004, Prison Surveillance Judges recommended the prison administration that a copy of each

the same, it is highly likely that, in many prisons, prison officers are carrying out strip searches every time an inmate enters the penitentiary centre.

[18] Transexual inmates must be asked about the preferred gender of the person that will be strip searching them (Instruction 7/2006 SGIP and Instruction 1/2019 SMPRAV).

[19] For example, JVP Malaga Decree of 13 January 1994 found that squatting during a strip search is always degrading but JVP Ciudad Real Decree of 20 May 1995 judged that squatting could be justified under certain circumstances. Regarding this matter, the Constitutional Court found that squats during strip searches are humiliating but not intrinsically degrading, although they could become degrading if inmates were asked to squat repeatedly or during excessive time (Sentencia Tribunal Constitucional 57/1994, of February 28th).

report had to be sent to them (Bueno Arús 2004), and this suggestion was included in the protocols issued by the prison administration. However, the recommendation was reiterated in 2018, suggesting that some prisons do not yet account to Prison Surveillance Judges for the strip searches that they carry out (González Vinuesa 2021).

2.3 Radiographies for Security Reasons

If the outcome of a strip search has been negative but the prison staff has good reasons to believe that the inmate is carrying contraband, the Director can request to the Prison Surveillance Judge to use additional measures, such as a radiography or an echography of an inmate (Art. 68.4 RP). The positive or negative result of such explorations must be reported quarterly to the Prison Administration (Instruction 3/2011 SGIP and Circular 1/2008 SMPRAV).

3 Strip Searches of Inmates in Spain

As previously explained, according to Spanish law, strip searches are a security measure that affects inmates' privacy and may result degrading if not carried out properly. Therefore, certain requirements—of necessity and proportionality—and standards—of good treatment—have been set to protect inmates' dignity and their fundamental right to privacy. In this section, I examine whether these requirements and standards are met in the practice of strip searches in Catalan prisons. More specifically, I explore the following questions:

1. *To what extent are inmates strip searched? What is the outcome of such searches?*

To answer these questions, I will rely on three datasets about the strip searches carried out in the Catalan Prison Administration, which were obtained through different Requests of Access to Public Information of the Catalan Government ('Sol·licitud d'Accés a la Informació Pública,

Generalitat de Catalunya').[20] These datasets, which are built with the information that prison officers introduce in the Catalan Prison Information System (*Sistema d'Informació Penitenciari Català*, SIPC),[21] vary on the kind of data they contain:

Dataset 1: This dataset includes aggregated information from 2011 to 2019 on the number of strip searches, the type (ordinary or extraordinary),[22] the number of inmates that were strip-searched and the result of the strip search (positive or negative).

Dataset 2: This dataset contains 89,955 entries regarding all the strip searches carried out in Catalan prisons from 2016 to 2019.[23] The following information is provided for every strip search: an anonymized ID, date of the strip search, sex and nationality of the person searched, wing/department and prison where the strip search was carried out, and result of the strip search (positive or negative, and type of result when positive).[24]

Dataset 3: This dataset includes every Statement of Facts ('*Comunicat de fets*') issued by prison officers or Senior Managers of Catalan

[20] The same request was made to the Spanish Prison Administration, but it was denied alleging that SGIP does not have the requested information in their databases. A subsequent request was made to the Ministry of Justice to inquiry if Prison Supervision Courts could provide the data, but the Open Data portal remitted the request to SGIP and, therefore, it was denied once again. A final request was made directly to the General Council of the Judiciary and the result was the same.

[21] The cases in which and how searches have to be recorded is detailed in the Prison Order 1/2016 on the approval of the Program for the management of incidents, implementation of coercive measures and searches in the prisons of Catalonia.

[22] See footnote 28.

[23] It needs to be noted that there are certain inconsistencies between Dataset 1 and Dataset 2. Dataset 2 reports a higher number of strip searches (around 3,000 additional strip searches in 2016, 2018 and 2019, and almost 4,000 in 2017). However, the number of positive strip searches is always the same, suggesting that both sources of data are reliable regarding positive results. This means that, in total, Dataset 2 includes 13,000 negative strip searches more than Dataset 1. With the aim of not overestimating the number of strip searches or underestimating the positivity rate, Dataset 2 will be used only to analyze the information that Dataset 1 cannot provide.

[24] The dataset also includes information regarding the occurrence of an incident during the strip search (e.g., if the prison officer was assaulted by the strip-searched inmate) or if coercive measures (e.g., temporary isolation or mechanical restraints) were used.

prisons in 2018 (13,020 entries).[25] Every entry comprises: type of report (informative or security-related), who issued the report (Prison Officer/Senior officer or Senior Manager), written statement of facts, additional information written by the Senior Manager when transmitting the information to the Director of the prison ('*Comunicat d'elevació*'), prison and date. The dataset contains 155 statements of facts that include written information on strip searches, which provides relevant qualitative information on the motivation and implementation of body searches.

2. *To what extent do strip searches respect inmates' dignity and privacy? How do inmates experience these searches?*

In order to assess if Spanish prisons meet the standards of good treatment set by the law in relation to strip searches, I will draw on the Annual Reports (2010–2020) by the National Prevention Mechanism (hereafter, NPM) of Spain,[26] decrees by Prison Supervision Judges and previous research.

The results of our analysis are detailed below.

3.1 The Extent of the Use and the Outcome of Strip Searches

If the criteria set by the law are followed and strip searches are used only when there are *specific*, *individualized*, and *verified* security reasons that justify the measure, we could expect that: (a) there is a limited number of strip searches, (b) the outcome is mostly positive, and (c) the objects and substances found during the search are a considerable threat to inmates' integrity or prison order.

---

[25] Statements of facts are a specific kind of report used by Prison Officers, Senior Officers and Senior Managers to leave a record of an incident (regimental report) or something they think that their superior should know (informational reports).

[26] The Spanish NPM was created by the Ley Orgánica 1/2009, de 3 de noviembre, after Spain ratified the Optional Protocol to the Convention Against Torture (OPCAT) in 2006.

Table 1 Strip searches in Catalan prisons (2011–2019), by type of search

Year	Strip searches	Ordinary		Extraordinary	
		N	%	*N*	%
2011	14,646	10,299	70.3	4,347	29.7
2012	15,738	10,639	67.6	5,099	32.4
2013	18,058	12,680	70.2	5,378	29.8
2014	16,903	11,599	68.6	5,304	31.4
2015	16,748	11,464	68.4	5,284	31.6
2016	16,865	11,667	69.2	5,198	30.8
2017	19,608	14,898	76.0	4,710	24.0
2018	20,832	16,128	77.4	4,704	22.6
2019	19,687	15,917	80.9	3,770	19.1
Mean	**17,676**	**12,810**	**72.5**	**4,866**	**27.5**

Source Catalan Prison Administration (SMPRAV), via an Open Data request. Dataset 1

According to the data provided by the SMPRAV, between 2011 and 2019, Catalan prisons, which have a capacity of 9,934 inmates,[27] reported a mean of 17,676 strip searches per year. Of these, 12,810 (72,5%) were reported as *ordinary* strip searches—routine searches carried out in cases predefined by the Prison Administration—and the remaining 4,866 (27,5%) as *extraordinary* strip searches—targeted searches decided or approved by the Senior Manager due to the characteristics of the inmate or the circumstances of the prison (see Table 1).[28]

This means that almost 3 out of 4 strip searches are deemed to be routine searches by the prison officers who report them. Considering that, according to the Prison Rules, strip searches should only be carried out when there are *specific* security reasons to search an inmate, the fact that there is such a high proportion of "ordinary" strip searches results surprising.

[27] SPACE I [Custody] Council of Europe Annual Penal Statistics. Prison stock on 1st January 2019.

[28] This distinction between 'ordinary' (routine searches predefined by the Prison Rules and specific instructions) and 'extraordinary' (targeted searches based on individual assessment) does not appear in any official document and I had to consult prison workers to understand the meaning of these categories. It needs to be noted that one prison officer warned me that, precisely because there is no prison order making this distinction explicit, it may happen that prison officers are registering as 'ordinary' strip searches that should be tagged as 'extraordinary'.

As we discussed earlier, the Catalan prison administration prescribes that inmates are strip searched upon admission (Circular 1/2008 SMPRAV). This may explain the figures in part as there were on average 6,227 admissions per year in Catalan prisons.[29] The other situation in which strip searches are prescribed is when inmates are transferred to a high-security wing, but we do not have data in this regard. However, we should not rule out the possibility that prison officers are classifying as "ordinary" strip searches that should be reported as "extraordinary" (see footnote 28).

Another way to assess the extension of strip searches is to analyze *how many inmates* have been subjected to this security measure (see Table 2). The figures suggest that strip searches are not focused on a reduced group of inmates, but rather affect a high proportion of the imprisoned population. More specifically, the ratio of strip searches per inmate searched is of 2.12—which means that these inmates are strip-searched twice a year on average—and the 54.6%[30] of all the inmates that have been imprisoned in Catalonia in a given year are subjected to a strip search. This result is quite consistent with the data provided by Gallego et al. (2010: 140) for Spanish prisons. In the referred study, the authors report that up to 60% of 1,271 surveyed inmates affirmed that they had been subjected to a strip search at least once.

However, the annual ratio of strip searches per inmate hides the fact that some prisoners are subjected to strip searches on *repeated occasions*. Our second dataset allows us to recount the number of times that different inmates are searched during a year, showing that dozens of prisoners are strip-searched more than 15 times per year, a few of them being strip-searched more than 50 times (see Table 3). If we locate the wing in

[29] This would represent, on average, 35.2% of the total number of strip searches and 48.6% of ordinary strip searches carried out from 2011 to 2019. The mean has been calculated for the studied years (2011–2019) using data from the Catalan Prison Statistics website (*Descriptors Estadístics Serveis Penitenciaris*).

[30] This figure is probably underestimated, as the data used to do the calculation also include inmates imprisoned in open prisons, and Prison Law establishes that one of the principles of the open regime is "the attenuation of control measures" (Art. 83.2.a RP). In this regard, between 2016 and 2019 (Dataset 2), the average number of strip searches carried out per year in the open prisons of Catalonia was only 32. Considering a mean population of 790 inmates in open prisons (2016–2019), this implies that only 4,1% of prisoners in open prisons were strip searched.

Table 2 Strip searches to different inmates in Catalan prisons (2011–2019)

Year	Strip-searched inmates	Strip searches	Strip searches per inmate	Different inmates in Catalan prisons[a]	% inmates that were searched
2011	8,033	14,646	1.82	17,876	44.9
2012	7,930	15,738	1.98	17,575	45.1
2013	8,259	18,058	2.19	16,755	49.3
2014	8,023	16,903	2.11	15,961	50.3
2015	7,615	16,748	2.20	14,798	51.5
2016	7,549	16,865	2.23	14,137	53.4
2017	9,125	19,608	2.15	13,868	65.8
2018	9,170	20,832	2.27	13,912	65.9
2019	9,101	19,687	2.16	14,015	64.9
Mean	**8,312**	**17,676**	**2.12**	**15,433**	**54.6**

[a]Number of different inmates that spent at least a day in Catalan prisons
Sources Catalan Prison Statistics (Descriptors Estadístics de Serveis Penitenciaris); Catalan Prison Administration (SMPRAV), via an Open Data request. Dataset 1

Table 3 Number of times the same inmate has been searched in a year (2016–2019)

	2016	2017	2018	2019
Strip-searched 1 time	3,578	4,354	4,483	4,560
Between 2 and 5 times	3,172	3,857	3,790	3,704
Between 6 and 10 times	627	724	643	625
Between 11 and 15 times	122	129	160	145
Between 16 and 20 times	34	32	55	39
More than 20 times	16	27	37	15
Max	**64**	**49**	**62**	**124**

Source Catalan Prison Administration (SMPRAV), via an Open Data request. Dataset 2

which most of these inmates are strip searched with so much frequency, it can be observed that a majority of them were placed in high-security units (‘*Departament Especial*’ or ‘*Departament Especial de Règim Tancat*’) (see Table 8 in the Annex), a matter to which we will return later (see Sect. 4.3).

After examining the number of strip searches and prisoners subjected to such control measures, we proceed to assess the result of such searches, which is important to determine if the invasion of inmates’ privacy

Table 4 Strip searches in Catalan prisons (2011–2019), by result

Year	Strip searches	Positive		Negative	
		N	%	*N*	%
2011	14,646	747	5.1	13,899	94.9
2012	15,738	793	5.0	14,945	95.0
2013	18,058	804	4.5	17,254	95.5
2014	16,903	748	4.4	16,155	95.6
2015	16,748	792	4.7	15,956	95.3
2016	16,865	785	4.7	16,080	95.3
2017	19,608	714	3.6	18,894	96.4
2018	20,832	771	3.7	20,061	96.3
2019	19,687	750	3.8	18,937	96.2
Mean	**17,676**	**767**	**4.4**	**16,909**	**95.6**

Source Catalan Prison Administration (SMPRAV), via an Open Data request. Dataset 1

was *needed* for security reasons and *proportional* to the threat that was prevented and, therefore, justifiable. Or, as the Spanish NPM puts it: "It is to be recommended that the results of such searches are periodically analysed in order to assess the justifiability of their practice, as this measure is particularly invasive and restricts inmates' rights".[31]

The results of this analysis indicate that, in most cases, the strip searches carried out in Catalan prisons were not justifiable in terms of security, as only 4.4% of strip searches found prohibited objects or substances (see Table 4). If we compare the proportion of positive results in body searches with less invasive kinds of searches, it is observed that a positive result is more often found in strip searches than in superficial searches (2.1%), but cell searches present better results than strip searches (7.9%).[32]

The low positivity rate for strip searches may be explained by the extensive use of ordinary strip searches: if strip searches are carried out in

[31] Annual Report NPM 2019 § 153. See also Annual Report NPM 2014 § 191; Annual Report NPM 2018 § 127. Annual Reports by the National Prevention Mechanism, retrieved from: https://www.defensordelpueblo.es/informes/resultados-busqueda-informes/?tipo_documento=informe_mnp.

[32] Means for 2011–2019. The percentage in the case of radiographies for regimental reasons is 17.3%. Source: Catalan Prison Administration (SMPRAV), via an Open Data request. Dataset 1.

fixed cases such as new admissions or transfers to high-security regime (ordinary searches, which represent a 72.5% of the total), instead of when there are specific, individualized and verified security reasons to do so (extraordinary searches, which represent a 27.5%), it is to be expected that the positivity rate is lower.[33] However, this explanation does not change the fact that, according to these data, 95,6% of strip searches have a negative result and, thus, it cannot be argued that they are preventing real threats to prison order.

A further issue is whether, in those cases in which the result was positive, the potential harm of seized objects and substances was proportional to the invasion of inmates' privacy caused by the strip search. The kinds of prohibited objects and substances that were seized in strip searches from 2016 to 2019 in Catalan prisons are presented in Table 5.

Prohibited substances are found, on average, in 65.3% of reported positive searches between 2016 and 2019, the most common seized substance being hashish (38.4%), followed by pills (9.3%), packages of unreported content (8.4%) and marijuana (5.6%). On most occasions the drugs found in strip searches are small pieces, but sometimes several packages are seized, as it can be seen in the following examples extracted from our Dataset 3:

> Around 11:37 the inmate [name] is admitted in temporary isolation, coming from the residential module number 1 (MR-1). During the ordinary strip search [...] we find a piece of a brownish substance glued to his lighter, another one inside his underwear [...], and finally he had a white pill in the right pocket of his trousers.
>
> After being confidentially informed of the fact that the inmate [name] would take advantage of a family visit to introduce prohibited substances, I order a strip search of the inmate, seizing 10 packages ('bellotas') of hashish and a little jar with marijuana.

[33] The data provided by the Catalan Prison Administration do not allow to determine the positivity rate for ordinary and extraordinary strip searches separately. However, our second dataset allows us to calculate the positivity rate depending on the wing where inmates were searched. For example, in 2018, 7,095 strip searches were carried out in the Admissions department, of which only 37 resulted in finding prohibited objects and/or substances. In other words, the positivity rate of the Admissions departments was 0,5% in 2018. In comparison, the positivity rate of Residential wings was 5% (477 positives out of 8,963 strip searches).

Table 5 Positive strip searches in Catalan prisons (2016–2019), by type of result

Type of result	2016		2017		2018		2019		2016–2019	
	N	%	*N*	%	*N*	%	*N*	%	Mean	%
Prohibited substances	**517**	**65.9**	**470**	**65.8**	**523**	**67.8**	**462**	**61.6**	**493**	**65.3**
Hashish	316	40.3	288	40.3	289	37.5	267	35.6	290	38.4
Pills	78	9.9	58	8.1	72	9.3	72	9.6	70	9.3
Packages of drugs	61	7.8	58	8.1	85	11.0	51	6.8	64	8.4
Marijuana	37	4.7	42	5.9	42	5.4	49	6.5	43	5.6
Powders	18	2.3	19	2.7	24	3.1	18	2.4	20	2.6
Joints	6	0.8	4	0.6	5	0.6	4	0.5	5	0.6
Crafted alcohol	1	0.1	1	0.1	6	0.8	1	0.1	2	0.3
Dangerous objects	**53**	**6.8**	**59**	**8.3**	**64**	**8.3**	**71**	**9.5**	**62**	**8.2**
Sharp object	23	2.9	30	4.2	27	3.5	37	4.9	29	3.9
Pointed object	22	2.8	17	2.4	28	3.6	23	3.1	23	3.0
Syringe	8	1.0	9	1.3	7	0.9	8	1.1	8	1.1
Blunt object	0	0.0	3	0.4	2	0.3	3	0.4	2	0.3
Prohibited objects	**189**	**24.1**	**162**	**22.7**	**165**	**21.4**	**185**	**24.7**	**175**	**23.2**
Mobile phones	75	9.6	74	10.4	72	9.3	101	13.5	81	10.7
Electronic devices and accs	27	3.4	19	2.7	29	3.8	30	4.0	26	3.5
Cigarettes, paper, lighter	21	2.7	22	3.1	16	2.1	19	2.5	20	2.6

(continued)

Table 5 (continued)

	2016		2017		2018		2019		2016–2019	
Type of result	*N*	%	*N*	%	*N*	%	*N*	%	Mean	%
Handwritten notes	18	2.3	13	1.8	12	1.6	9	1.2	13	1.7
Money, jewelry, make-up	13	1.7	8	1.1	11	1.4	14	1.9	12	1.5
Other proh. objects	35	4.5	26	3.6	25	3.2	12	1.6	25	3.2
Other results[a]	**26**	**3.3**	**23**	**3.2**	**19**	**2.5**	**32**	**4.3**	**25**	**3.3**
Total	**785**	**100**	**714**	**100**	**771**	**100**	**750**	**100**	**755**	**100**

[a]This category includes the cases reporting that during the strip search it was observed that inmates had superficial injuries (1,55%) and those cases where objects belonging to very different categories are reported (e.g., drugs and mobile phone) or in which the type of result is not described (1,75%)

Source Catalan Prison Administration (SMPRAV), via an Open Data request. Dataset 2

The finding of dangerous objects (generally shivs) is reported in 8.2% of positive strip searches:

> At approximately 11:05, while inmates were exiting to the yard, the metal detector ringed when the inmate [name] was passing through. [...] We use the security wand and it keeps ringing around his waist. We proceed to frisk him and around his waist we find a metal plate of about 21 cm long and 4,5 width, with a sharpened end as a kind of shiv. We seize it and notify the Senior Manager, who comes immediately to the wing and orders a strip search in case he hid more prohibited objects.

Finally, prohibited objects represent 23,2% of positive strip searches. Among these, we can find mobile phones (10,7%); electronic devices and accessories (e.g., pen drives and memory cards, SIM cards, Mp3, USB cables or earphones with microphone) (3,5%); cigarette packs, cigarette paper, and lighters (2,6%); handwritten notes (e.g., bank account numbers) (1,7%); money, jewelry, and make-up (1,5%). Other prohibited objects mentioned include items as diverse as a pencil sharpener or two pairs of socks received during a family visit.[34]

> By order of the Security Manager, the inmate [name] was strip searched after an intimate visit with his partner. The search is performed according to Circular 1/2008. The inmate is offered a robe, but he rejects it.[35] During the search he is asked if he possesses any prohibited object or substance. He answers affirmatively and immediately pulls out of his buttocks a transparent plastic bag containing two mobile phones. We report the result of the search to the Security Manager, who orders

[34] The category 'Other prohibited objects' did not contain disaggregated data. It has been recoded manually using the annotations where prison officers specified what they found.

[35] During my visits to a Catalan prison in 2016, I read several documents hung in the board of the prison officers' office of one wing, one of which was a model of how to fill in properly a strip search report. In this model, the phrase "The inmate was offered a robe, but it was rejected" was included as a predefined sentence, which made me question whether prison officers were indeed offering the robe. However, in a recent communication with a former Senior Manager, he explained that robes are always offered by prison officers, but that inmates usually reject them because it is their way of showing that they have nothing to hide. Moreover, he adds that when an inmate asks for the robe, prison officers become suspicious and "put more effort" into the search. More about the offer of robes during strip searches in Sect. 3.2.

> that the inmate is transferred to the high-security wing ('*Departament Especial*').
>
> We inform that the inmate [name] has been found in possession of prohibited objects upon return of a prison leave. When the inmate was passing through the metal detector of the Admissions department, it has rung. The inmate has been asked to pass through the metal detector several times, and every time it was detecting a metal object. When we use the security wand, it also rang around his inner tights. After reporting the situation to the Security Manager, he orders that we strip search the inmate. During the search, the inmate hands over to the prison officer a pair of earphones with micro function and a USB cable that he had hidden inside his underwear.

As it can be observed, these "Prohibited objects", although forbidden by prison rules, do not apparently pose a serious threat to inmates' safety or to prison security, which questions the judgment of necessity and proportionality to carry out the strip search in these cases. This is even more debatable in the instances where electronic devices are found, as it could be argued that they should not be prohibited in the first place because they do not represent a threat to prison order and, in addition, their unavailability hinders inmates' rehabilitation (Mapelli 2013; McDougall et al. 2017; Güerri et al. 2021).

3.2 "Making a Man Strip off and Putting Him Through Such a Humiliation Is Just Too Much": The Practice of Strip Searches

The second question I wanted to explore is how inmates experience strip searches and to what extent such searches respect their dignity and privacy.

In order to protect inmates' fundamental rights, the Prison Rules determine that strip searches must be carried out in a closed room, by prison officers of the same gender as the inmate, and without the presence of other prisoners (Art. 68.3). More concretely, the protocol establishes that, after inmates take their clothes off, prison officers must do a visual inspection of the inmates' body, which must be as brief as possible. Then, prison officers must offer a robe to the inmate so they can cover their body while their clothes are being searched.[36] However, reports by prison supervision bodies and previous research suggest that these standards are not always followed.

The standard that is most frequently infringed is the one that obliges prison officers to offer a robe to inmates in order to avoid their prolonged nudity. In their research, Gallego et al. (2010) already denounced that 79.2% of surveyed inmates reported that they were never offered a robe when they were strip-searched, 14.9% were offered the robe at least on one occasion, and only 5.9% every time they had been strip searched. Similarly, the National Prevention Mechanism (NPM) has detected this problem in many of the prisons it has visited.[37] Thus, it would seem that there is a general disregard of protecting inmates' privacy during strip searches, even though the importance of preventing that inmates are completely naked during these searches has been reiterated on many occasions by different prison supervision bodies.[38]

Although not as generalized, prison supervision mechanisms have also detected signs of "potentially degrading treatment" to some inmates during strip searches (CPT 2017: 53). Concretely, the Committee for the Prevention of Torture (CPT), during its 2016 visit, reported that at CP León, CP Puerto III and CP Sevilla II inmates complained that "...they had to perform push-ups while naked, and had to lift up their testicles and retract the foreskin of their penis in front of prison officers" (CPT 2017: 53). The reports by the NPM also include complaints about having been strip-searched in a hallway in front of other inmates (3 complaints) and degrading treatment during the strip search (11

---

[36] Prison Order of 9th March 2005 by SGIP and Circular 1/2008 SMPRAV.

[37] More concretely, the prisons that were not offering robes or towels to inmates were: CP Castellón (Annual Report 2011 NPM); CP Puerto I (Cádiz) (Annual Report 2012 NPM); CP Álava, CP Dueñas, CP León, CP Tenerife II (Annual Report 2016 NPM); CP Quatre Camins (Catalonia), CP Brians 2 (Catalonia) (Annual Report 2018 NPM); and CP Madrid VII (Annual Report 2019 NPM). Annual Reports by the National Prevention Mechanism, retrieved from: https://www.defensordelpueblo.es/informes/resultados-busqueda-informes/?tipo_documento=informe_mnp.

[38] E.g., JVP Madrid nº3 Decree, of 21st January 1994; Annual Report 2014 NPM § 191; and CPT (2017: 53).

complaints).[39] Moreover, in CP Las Palmas II women and transgender individuals complained about unrespectful treatment during searches.[40]

To summarize, reports by prison supervision bodies mention a general disregard for inmates' privacy during strip searches and occasional degrading treatment. However, it is important to acknowledge that even those strip searches that abide by the law may affect prisoners negatively.

In this respect, inmates interviewed by the Spanish NPM explained that strip searches are always humiliating moments that make them feel bad even days after the search. One inmate expressed it in the following terms: "Making a man strip off and putting him through such a humiliation is just too much".[41]

In conclusion, the evidence presented in this section shows that strip searches are extensively used in Catalan prisons—17,676 searches affecting 54.6% of inmates—and that, on too many occasions, inmates are not offered a robe or a towel to cover their naked body, making the experience of strip searches more humiliating. In the following section, I move on to discuss if this extensive use may be justified on security terms.

[39] 1 complaint in Annual Report 2010 NPM, 2 complaints in Annual Report 2011 NPM, 5 complaints in Annual Report 2015 NPM, 2 complaints in Annual Report 2016 NPM, 2 complaints in Annual Report 2017 NPM, and 2 complaints in Annual Report 2020 NPM. Annual Reports by the National Prevention Mechanism, retrieved from: https://www.defensordelpueblo.es/informes/resultados-busqueda-informes/?tipo_documento=informe_mnp.

[40] Annual Report 2019 NPM § 355.

[41] Annual Report 2011 NPM § 136. Some prison officers are aware of the emotions that strip searching generates in prisoners. In this sense, Crawley (2004: 178) found that some English prison officers relied on banter to reduce the potential for embarrassment or conflict. This is something that I also observed during my fieldwork in Spanish prisons (Güerri 2020): "If you get on well with them, I mean, when I do a search… if I usually deal with them, I tell them: 'You know: you put drugs here, shivs go there…' and they laugh. You banter to make it seem like it's not a big deal, it's just a search" (Prison officer, GSA-02, quote from field notes, unpublished).

4 In the Name of Security: What Is the Rationale of Strip Searches in Catalan Prisons?

As previously explained, according to the Prison Law, strip searches are a security measure to prevent inmates' possession of prohibited substances and dangerous objects. This rationale is accepted and reproduced by both inmates and prison officers. For example, inmates interviewed by the NPM stated that body searches are uncomfortable and often humiliating, but that they understand that this measure is needed for prison security.[42] Similarly, one Spanish officer said to me:

> They [inmates] assume it is our job, that doing a search is for their security, for ours too. As we say, no one wants a shiv in the yard. Thus, inmates understand that searches must be done. It does not generate frictions because they know it's part of our job, that it's for everybody's security. (Senior Officer, Interview GSA-01, quote from field notes, unpublished)

However, the data presented in the previous section question the effectiveness of such searches. Strip searches are extensively used in Catalan prisons but, on most occasions, they are not preventing any breach of security—as we have seen, only 4.4% yield positive results and 60% of these are for drugs. Therefore, in this section we will delve into our data to discuss whether it can really be argued that strip searches in Catalan prisons are justified in terms of specific threats to prison security or if, on the contrary, they serve a different purpose within the penitentiary institution. With this aim in mind, we will analyze ordinary and extraordinary strip searches separately.

[42] Annual Report 2010 NPM § 136.

4.1 Ordinary Strip Searches

As previously explained, strip searches can only be carried out when there is a reasoned suspicion that indicates that an inmate is hiding prohibited substances or dangerous objects in their clothes or their bodies (Art. 68.2 RP), and the Constitutional Court has required these searches to be motivated alleging individualized and verified security reasons.[43]

However, both the Spanish and Catalan prison administrations have defined certain cases in which strip searches will be carried out ordinarily.[44] This is questionable, in the first place, because it implies that an administrative body is determining cases in which fundamental rights will be affected without needing any motivation to do so.[45] This becomes more worrying if we take into consideration that these unmotivated searches represent 72,5% of the strip searches carried out in Catalonia between 2011 and 2019 (Table 1). Furthermore, if we analyze in more detail the practice of these ordinary strip searches in Catalan prisons, it can also be questioned that these searches are preventing specific security risks.

The Catalan Prison Administration (SMPRAV) stipulates that strip searches should always take place *upon admission of a new inmate*, and when inmates are *transferred to a high-security unit*.

Regarding the former, we consider that the provision ordering strip searches upon admission lacks justification and, moreover, our data shows that it is not effective. First, the SMPRAV prescribes these searches alleging that Article 18.1 of the Prison Rules establishes so. However, this is a misinterpretation, as the abovementioned article only states that "Upon admission (…) inmates will be searched", but the type of search

[43] Sentencia Tribunal Constitucional 57/1994, of February 28th.

[44] As previously noted, Instruction 3/2010 SGIP states that strip searches will be carried out ordinarily upon admission, when the inmate returns from a prison leave and when the inmate has been transferred from a different prison, but this Instruction was amended by a "rather irregular" procedure, and thus it is not clear which regulation is being implemented in practice (González Vinuesa 2021).

[45] According to the Spanish Constitutional Court, the motivation is not an elemental courtesy, but a rigorous requirement of the act of sacrificing rights (Sentencia Tribunal Constitucional 26/1981), which becomes unavoidable in the case of measures that limit fundamental rights (e.g., Sentencia Tribunal Constitucional 27/1989) (Ríos Martín and Cabrera 2002: 94).

is not defined. This means that the SMPRAV is doing an extensive interpretation of Article 18.1, which is improper considering the implications that it has for the fundamental rights of every person that enters the prison.[46]

Secondly, our data show that in 2018 29,7% of all strip searches were carried out in the Admissions department, but the positivity rate was only 0,5%.[47] The lack of justification for these searches and their limited effectiveness make this measure hardly defendable in security terms, as the risk prevented is not proportional to the inflicted harm. Moreover, we could question why it is reasonable to strip search systematically newly admitted inmates, but strip searches of inmates returning from a prison leave need to be motivated (Circular 1/2008 SMPRAV) when they all come from outside the prison. In our view, by subjecting every person that is admitted into prison to a strip search, the penitentiary institution is sending new inmates the message that they are no longer free citizens, which is the first step in the creation of the "inmate" as a subject under the power and control of the prison administration.

With respect to strip searches carried out when inmates are transferred to high-security wings, the Catalan prison administration argues that inmates must be strip searched because "...the transfer to a high-security unit implies the existence of an exceptional situation of risk to people, prison security, and good order in prison. In these cases, strip searches will be justified by the concurrent motives [that motivated the transfer to the high-security unit]" (Circular 1/2008 SMPRAV: 3). Even if we considered—as the Catalan prison administration does—that a strip search is necessary to prevent that inmates harm themselves after they are locked up in the high-security unit, we need to acknowledge that such a rule is increasing the punitive character of being transferred to a high-security unit. Therefore, it would be better if the individual circumstances of each case were considered—as in extraordinary strip searches—instead of prescribing a strip search in every transfer to the high-security unit.

---

[46] "...in matters of fundamental rights, interpretations must always be restrictive" (JVP Madrid nº1, 29th April 1994, cited by Ríos Martín and Cabrera 2002: 94).

[47] See Tables 6 and 7 in the Annex.

4.2 Extraordinary Strip Searches

Our data put into question that extraordinary strip searches are carried out only when there is *reasoned* suspicion that a certain inmate is hiding prohibited substances or dangerous objects in their clothes or their body. Even if we would assume that every positive strip search (767) had been an extraordinary strip search (4.866), positive strip searches would only represent 15,7%. This figure seems excessively low considering that strip searches should be carried out only when *individualized* and *verified* security risks have been identified. This suggests that strip searches are carried out routinely in certain cases or as a means of enhancing control and minimizing risks.

Our Dataset 3 on informative and regimental reports provides several examples of the reasons used to justify strip searches. In this regard, some strip searches are reasonably ordered after finding that the inmate has infringed the rules (e.g., a prohibited object has been found during a superficial search, so a strip search is ordered to see if they are hiding more objects; the inmate is found in the toilet smoking a hookah; or an inmate enters a cell which is not theirs) or because "suspicious movements" have been observed (i.e. the inmate seems to have hidden something). However, there are also several examples that support the hypothesis that strip searches are *regularly used* in predefined situations:

> I inform that the inmate [name] has been transferred from the Department of External Services to the Department of Admissions at 16:35 hours, after a special communication (family visit). *Due to the suspicion that he could be trying to introduce into the prison prohibited or narcotic substances in his clothes or his body, according to confidential information that we received*, by order and with presence of the Security Manager, we have strip searched the inmate, with a negative result. [Emphasis added]

> I inform that the inmate [name] from MR-6 should have returned from a leave the 23rd of August at 8:00 hours but he returned on the 24th of August at 15:30 hours. When asked about the reason for the delay, he answers "the day slipped my mind, I thought today was the 23rd, and when I realized I called to inform that I would be late". We informed the Senior Manager, who came to the department and authorized a strip

search *to rule out the possible introduction of prohibited objects or substances* (the report of the strip search is attached). [Emphasis added]

At 20:35 hours, when inmates go to their cells, we heard shouts. When prison officers arrive upstairs, they see the inmate [name] dancing and agitating the other inmates, who shouted around him. We take the inmate [name] to our office to scold him and, after asking for permission to the Security Manager, we strip-search him *because he seems to have consumed narcotic substances*. The inmate, visibly annoyed, resisted the strip search throwing his clothes at the officers and afterwards he resisted his transfer. [Emphasis added. The triangulation of the report with Database 2 shows that the result of this strip search was negative.]

In the latter examples, we find different kinds of situations in which strip searches have been used, such as after a family visit, when returning from a prison leave or because an inmate seemed to have consumed narcotic substances.[48] Although these situations are mentioned in prison orders as cases in which *searches* could be appropriate, none of the examples provide specific security reasons to justify the *strip* search.

In this regard, the most recent ruling on strip searches by the Constitutional Court, as we mentioned, has stated that generic motivations such as "...due to suspicion that he could be hiding some prohibited object or substance in his body after the intimate communication" or "suspicion that he could introduce in the prison objects or substances that can entail a risk to the security of the prison or its workers" cannot be admitted (Sentencia Tribunal Constitucional 171/2013, Legal Grounds § 2–4). The National High Court (*Audiencia Nacional*) is more categorical in its Decree 875/2014 of 6 November 2014, when it states that "Saying that the control over the body of the inmate by means of a strip search is justified by the suspicion of possessing prohibited substance or objects, in terms of fundamental rights, equals to not saying anything" (Legal Grounds § 4).

---

48 Similarly, the inmates surveyed by Gallego et al. (2010: 141) also reported that prison searches were carried out routinely in situations such as "when I return from a prison leave", "when you are transferred", "when you are placed in temporary isolation" or "when I have an intimate visit".

However, it needs to be noted that, on some occasions, these generic arguments are not contested by the courts. For example, in 2011, the National High Court stated:

> in the present case no fundamental right has been affected because the action of the administration is based on by the Prison Law and the Prison Rules that restrict inmates' rights. (…) In other words, intimate visits have as counterpart the subsequent strip search, so that only when that search is done inappropriately, offensively or with abuse or deviation of power will the action of the administration be culpable, but not just because of the execution of the body search itself. (Auto Audiencia Nacional 23/2011, Legal Grounds § 1)

Sustaining such an argument has three important implications that need to be addressed. First, the court assumed that a strip search will only violate inmates' fundamental rights if it is degrading "…because the action of the administration is based on the Prison Law and the Prison Rules that restrict inmates' rights". This affirmation stems from the "principle of special subjection" (*principio de sujeción especial*), which implies that inmates' fundamental rights may be restricted by prison legislation for reasons of security and order in prison and, therefore, this provides a legal basis to justify the "mortifications of the self" (Goffman 1961) imposed on inmates.[49] However, as previously stated, the legitimate use of strip searches to protect prison security and prison order needs to be balanced with prisoners' constitutional rights (Sentencia Tribunal Constitucional 57/1994, Legal Grounds § 6). By not taking this into account, the National High Court is disregarding inmates' right to privacy.

Second, perceiving strip searches "as counterpart" to the exercise of certain rights, such as intimate visits, is dangerous because it could act as a disincentive and coerce the free exercise of such rights (e.g., HRLC 2017: 15). Finally, by not analyzing whether the reasons for carrying out the strip search were individualized and verified, the National High

[49] For an explanation of this principle in relation to strip searches and a discussion on the different positions defended by the doctrine, see Guillén (2016: 165–170).

Court was accepting that strip searches may be used as a regular means of control and deterrence, instead of as a specific security measure.

To sum up, both our quantitative—low positivity rate—and qualitative data—use of generic expressions to motivate strip searches that are occasionally legitimized by the courts—suggest that strip searches may have been more often used as a regular means of general prevention and control in given situations (e.g., after an intimate or family visit) than in specific, individualized cases,[50] which can lead to a systematic breach of inmates' right to privacy.

4.3 The Targeting of Certain Prisoners

A further issue that needs to be analyzed is the observation that certain inmates are repeatedly strip searched, as it was shown in Table 3. A possible explanation could be the (unjustified) routine use of strip searches to control inmates who are returning from a prison leave. However, a detailed analysis of all the cases in 2018 in which inmates were strip searched more than 20 times shows that, on most occasions, these searches happened in the high-security unit (Table 8 in the Annex), where no prison leave is allowed.

Prison law stipulates that the intensity of security measures will be adjusted to the dangerousness of the inmates to whom such measures are applied, especially regarding those who are in a high-security regime because they are "extremely dangerous" and those who belong to terrorist or organized crime groups (Art. 65.2 RP).

In the case of a high-security regime, where inmates spend 21 or 22 hours per day locked up in their cell, the prison law establishes that inmates' cells and bodies must be searched once a day and allows the use of strip searches only when there are well founded suspicions that the inmate is in the possession of prohibited objects (Art. 93.1 RP). However, the available data suggest an excessive use of strip searches in high-security units.

---

[50] However, an in-depth study of the motivations expressed in post-search reports is needed to fully support our tentative conclusion, as Dataset 3 is not a representative sample of all post-search reports.

For instance, in their study in Spanish prisons, Ríos Martín and Cabrera (2002) found that out of the 190 high-security prisoners they surveyed, 186 affirmed that they had been strip-searched at least once. Regarding Catalan prisons, our data show that, in 2018, 16.3% of strip searches were carried out in high-security wings,[51] although high-security prisoners only represented 1.96% of the penitentiary population,[52] showing the disproportional use of this security measure in a high-security regime. Moreover, as discussed before, inmates who are repeatedly strip searched in Catalan prisons tend to be housed in high-security units.

The question of high-security prisoners being repeatedly strip searched has been addressed by the National High Court.[53] In the examined case, an inmate in the high-security regime had been systematically searched after family and intimate visits: over a period of two years, he was strip searched 17 times. The court determined that these searches were "arbitrary" due to their lack of justification and for constituting a "systematic practice of control" over an inmate who was already subjected to strict surveillance and control in the high-security regime (Auto Audiencia Nacional 874/2014, 6th November 2014, Legal Grounds § 4).[54] Ríos Martín and Cabrera (2002: 91) agree with this reasoning: they even question the need for carrying out superficial searches on a daily basis and suggest that the ultimate goal of such practices appears to be an increase of the punitiveness that characterizes the isolation in high-security units.

---

[51] This figure excludes strip searches that were carried out concurrently to temporary confinement measures, as they are done ordinarily when the inmate enters the high-security unit and including them would have overestimated the weight of 'extraordinary' strip searches carried out on high-security prisoners over the total of strip searches (see Table 7 in the Annex).

[52] Source: Estadística Penitenciaria. SGIP. Prison population on 31st December 2018.

[53] Auto Audiencia Nacional 874/2014, 6th November 2014.

[54] At the European level, the European Court of Human Rights found that the routine searching of prisoners in a particularly strict regime of high-security prisons in the Netherlands was a critical factor in determining that such regime contravened Article 3 of the European Convention of Human Rights (Van Zyl Smit and Snacken 2009). For example, in the case *van der Ven v. The Netherlands* (App. No. 50901/99, 4 February 2003) the court considered that "...in a situation where the applicant was already subjected to a great number of surveillance measures, and in the absence of convincing security needs, the practice of weekly strip searches that was applied to the applicant for a period of approximately three and a half years diminished his human dignity and must have given rise to feelings of anguish and inferiority capable of humiliating and debasing him" (§ 26).

This also seems to be the case in Catalan prisons, where the systematic use of strip searches in high-security units does not seem to be very effective in detecting contraband (see Table 8 in the Annex). Rather than increasing security, the subjection of inmates to such a systematic control and the constant intrusion of their private sphere (not only their bodies, but also their cells) is adding to the punitive character of this specific regime (Drake 2012: 116–117).

In conclusion, the extensive practice of strip searching in Catalan prisons puts into question that strip searches are used as a security measure aimed at addressing concrete security risks. The systematic use of ordinary strip searches upon admission and the seemingly regular use of this security measure without proper justification in cases such as after a family visit or a prison leave, suggests that the argument of security is being used to heighten the level of control over inmates, thus facilitating their daily management and minimizing possible breaches of security (Goffman 1961). Furthermore, the targeting of certain inmates, specifically those in the high-security regime, does not seem justified in security terms and appears to serve the function of increasing the punitiveness of this isolation regime (Ríos Martín and Cabrera 2002; Drake 2012).

5 Conclusion: Security, Control, and Punishment in the Practice of Strip Searches

In Europe, strip searches are considered to be security measures that may be legitimately used to maintain good order in prison (Van Zyl Smit and Snacken 2009), as it is the case in the Spanish context. It has been recognized, however, that these searches could affect the rights to dignity and privacy of those subjected to such measures if not carried out properly and with due justification (Mavronicola and Webster, this volume).

For this reason, Spanish prison regulations and jurisprudence only allow the recourse to strip searches in the face of specific and concrete security threats, and a respectful procedure must be followed while conducting the search. The purpose of this chapter has been to analyze the practice of strip searches in Spanish prisons from a criminological perspective, adding to the discussion of the functions they fulfill within the penitentiary institution.

The first question that has been examined is the extent of the use of strip searches in Catalonia. Our data about Catalan prisons show that strip searches are used extensively—on average 17,676 strip searches per year between 2011 and 2019, within a prison system with a capacity for 9,934 inmates—and affect a considerable proportion of prisoners—on average 54.6% of all the persons who are incarcerated in a given year in Catalonia have been subjected to, at least, one strip search. Moreover, of those strip searched between 2016 and 2019, 10% were strip searched more than five times in a year, and 2.3% more than ten times. These figures are not coherent with a security measure that, according to the law, should only be used to prevent *specific* threats to inmates' safety and prison order. In fact, an examination of the *justification* and the *outcome* of these searches demonstrates that their extensive use is not attributable to specific security risks.

Regarding the grounds on which strip searches are carried out in Catalan prisons, we have shown that, on average, 72.5% are reported as "ordinary", meaning that almost three quarters of the total number of strip searches are *systematic* (in cases predefined by Prison Orders). Moreover, our exploratory analysis of informative and regimental reports suggests that "extraordinary" strip searches, which should be based on individualized and verified security risks, are regularly used in *predefined situations* (e.g., after a family visit or when returning from a prison leave) without proper justification.

As for the outcome of these searches, our data show that, on average, only 4.4% of strip searches have a positive result—of which 65.3% are drugs, 23.2% other prohibited (non-dangerous) objects, and only 8.2% dangerous objects. These figures mean that in 95.6% of the registered cases the strip search was *not needed* and that in a considerable proportion of positive searches (e.g., those finding mobile phones) it could be argued that the threat prevented was *not proportional* to the harm inflicted by affecting inmates' fundamental right to privacy.

Altogether, our data shows that strip searches are used extensively, usually in a routinary, non-individualized manner, and lead to few positive results. Therefore, it is difficult to uphold that, in practice, strip searches in Catalan prisons are a security measure only used to prevent specific security risks. On the contrary, as Drake (2012) suggested in the case of English prisons, they seem to function as a coercive measure of general prevention and control.

Strip searches in the high-security regime deserve a separate comment. On this issue, our data show that strip searches are carried out disproportionately in high-security units, with some inmates being targeted and repeatedly strip searched with virtually no positive results. The systematic strip searching of inmates already subjected to a highly controlling regime raises concerns on the arbitrariness and degrading nature of such a practice, as the Spanish National High Court and the European Court of Human Rights have highlighted. In view of the lack of justification for this way of proceeding, the targeted repetition of strip searches in high-security units can only be interpreted as a deliberate increase in the levels of punishment and mortification inflicted on high-security prisoners (Ríos Martín and Cabrera 2002; Drake 2012).

The second question this chapter has addressed is how strip searches are conducted by prison officers and experienced by inmates. In this regard, the analysis of reports by prison supervision bodies has evinced that, although the procedure is usually respectful to what is stipulated by the law, robes to cover the naked body are hardly offered to inmates. However, in my view, the most important finding is that, due to the invasion of the private sphere that these searches entail, inmates may be negatively affected by strip searches even in those cases when they cannot be considered degrading in the terms of the European Convention of Human Rights.

In sum, Spanish Prison Law tries to reach a balance between respecting inmates' fundamental rights and ensuring prison security in terms of strip searches, but prison practice turns out differently: rather than only targeting specific security threats, strip searches are used extensively as a form of general prevention and control. Moreover, strip searches in high-security units seem to have a punitive character.

Therefore, and given the impact of strip searches on inmates' privacy and wellbeing, I believe that prison regulations prescribing "ordinary" (routine) strip searches should be reconsidered, and that prison supervision bodies need to pay more attention to the cases in which "extraordinary" (targeted) strip searches are being used, especially in high-security units, making sure that they are only used when there are individualized and specific security reasons to do so.

On a final note, besides the intrusions in inmates' private sphere and their self, we also need to consider the *collateral consequences* that the extensive use of strip searches may entail. For example, the regular subjection to strip searches after intimate or family visits may discourage the free exercise of this right (e.g., HRLC 2017: 15), or the perception of arbitrariness brought by heightened levels of control may deteriorate staff-prisoner relationships (Ríos Martín and Cabrera 2002). Therefore, limiting strip searches to the prevention of specific security threats is not only needed to protect inmates' rights to privacy and dignity, but also to preserve other valuable aspects of prison life.

Annex

See Tables 6, 7, and 8.

Table 6 Strip searches in prison by department and result (Catalonia, 2018)

	Negative result		Positive result		Total	
	N	%	*N*	%	*N*	%
Residential wing	8,486	94.7	477	5.3	8,963	100.0
Admissions	7,058	99.5	37	0.5	7,095	100.0
High security	5,999	96.9	192	3.1	6,191	100.0
Inf./Psych./Hosp.	951	96.3	37	3.7	988	100.0
Observation	391	99.7	1	0.3	392	100.0
Open prison	20	57.1	15	42.9	35	100.0
Open regime	197	94.3	12	5.7	209	100.0
Total	**23,102**	**96.8**	**771**	**3.2**	**23,873**	**100.0**

Source Catalan Prison Administration (SMPRAV), via an Open Data request. Dataset 2. The grouping of departments was coded manually

Table 7 Strip searches in prison by department and concurrency to temporary confinement measures (Catalonia, 2018)

	Concurrent to temp. confinement		Non-concurrent to temp. Confinement		Total	
	N	%	*N*	%	*N*	%
Residential wing	513	14.7	8,450	41.5	8.963	37.5
Admissions	64	1.8	7,031	34.5	7.095	29.7
High security	2,867	82.0	3,324	16.3	6.191	25.9
Inf./Psych./ Hosp.	47	1.3	941	4.6	988	4.1
Observation	4	0.1	388	1.9	392	1.6
Open regime	2	0.1	207	1.0	209	0.9
Open prison	0	0.0	35	0.2	35	0.1
Total	**3,497**	**100.0**	**20,376**	**100.0**	**23.873**	**100.0**

Source Catalan Prison Administration (SMPRAV), via an Open Data request. Dataset 2. The grouping of departments was coded manually

Table 8 Inmates that have been strip searched more than 20 times in Catalan prisons, by department where the search was carried out (2018)

ID	Admissions	High security	Inf./Psych. /Hosp.	Residential wing	Total	Positive searches
10,818		62			**62**	0
6728	1	33	3	2	**39**	2
4598	1	36			**37**	0
2804	4	28		3	**35**	0
4072	1	23		9	**33**	2
3116		30	2		**32**	0
5404	1	27		2	**30**	0
1139		24	1	5	**30**	1
171	1	17	5	5	**28**	2
4486	7	17	2	1	**27**	1
1140		26		1	**27**	0
6664		26			**26**	0
5834				26	**26**	0
10,984				25	**25**	0
5144	1	23		1	**25**	0
3551	2	23			**25**	1
2609	3	10	5	7	**25**	1
4274		6		18	**24**	0

(continued)

Table 8 (continued)

ID	Admissions	High security	Inf./Psych. /Hosp.	Residential wing	Total	Positive searches
3640	1	17		6	**24**	1
1065	1	10		13	**24**	0
10,449		23			**23**	0
11,485		11		12	**23**	0
4755	3	16		4	**23**	1
11,322	2	16	1	3	**22**	0
10,950	4	11		7	**22**	0
6967		22			**22**	0
3248		19	3		**22**	0
4255		15		7	**22**	1
3181		21		1	**22**	0
98	1	19		2	**22**	0
817		9		13	**22**	2
11,587	1	13	3	4	**21**	0
11,652	1	14	1	5	**21**	1
5382	4	15	1	1	**21**	0
3629	4	13	2	2	**21**	0
1330		20		1	**21**	0

Source Catalan Prison Administration (SMPRAV), via an Open Data request. Dataset 2. The grouping of departments was coded manually

References

Balfour, G. 2018. Searching Prison Cells and Prisoner Bodies: Redacting Carceral Power and Glimpsing Gendered Resistance in Women's Prisons. *Criminology & Criminal Justice* 18 (2): 139–155.

Bueno Arús, F. 2004. Conclusiones encuentro de Vigilancia Penitenciaria. *Revista Del Poder Judicial* 68: 407–473.

CPT. 2017. *Report to the Spanish Government on the Visit to Spain Carried Out by the European Committee for the Prevention of Torture and Inhuman or Degrading Treatment or Punishment (CPT) from 27 September to 10 October 2016.* CPT/Inf (2017) 34. Strasbourg: Council of Europe.

Crawley, E. 2004. *Doing Prison Work: The Public and Private Lives of Prison Officers*. London: Routledge.

Drake, D. 2012. *Prisons, Punishment and the Pursuit of Security*. New York: Springer.

Gallego, M., P.J. Cabrera, J.C. Ríos, and J.L. Segovia. 2010. *Andar 1km en línea recta. La cárcel del siglo XXI que vive el preso.* Comillas: Universidad Pontificia Comillas.

Goffman, E. 1961. *Internados. Ensayos sobre la situación social de los enfermos mentales.* Buenos Aires: Amorrutu.

González Vinuesa, F. 2021. *Legislación penitenciaria básica: Comentarios y referencias prácticas. Versión 16-E.* Retrieved from: https://prisionenpositivo.files.wordpress.com/. Accessed March 2022.

Güerri, C. 2020. *De carceleros y ayudantes. El rol de los funcionarios de interior en los centros penitenciarios españoles.* Barcelona: Atelier.

Güerri, C., M. Martí, and A. Pedrosa. 2021. Abriendo ventanas virtuales en los muros de la prisión. *IDP: revista d'Internet, dret i política* 32: 1–16.

Guillén, V. 2016. *La práctica del cacheo en el sistema constitucional español.* Málaga: Iuris Universal Ediciones.

HRLC. 2017. *Total Control: Ending the Routine Strip Searching for Women in Victoria's Prisons.* Sydney: Human Rights Law Centre.

Hutchison, J. 2020. "It's Sexual Assault. It's Barbaric": Strip Searching in Women's Prisons as State-Inflicted Sexual Assault. *Affilia: Feminist Inquiry in Social Work* 35 (2): 160–176.

Intxarube, J.R., E.J. Ruiz, and G. Urrutia. 2017. *Informe sobre el impacto de la política penitenciaria de alejamiento en las familias de las personas presas.* Bilbao: Secretaría General de Derechos Humanos, Convivencia y Cooperación (Gobierno Vasco).

Mapelli, B. 2013. ¿Pueden los privados de libertad usar móviles para comunicarse? *Anales De Derecho* 31: 1–18.

Melo, M.A. 2021. Requisa en las cárceles y la dignidad humana. Un aporte desde la experiencia brasileña. In *La necesaria reforma penitenciaria*, ed. R.M. Mata y Martín, 95–107. Granada: Editorial Comares.

McDougall, C., D.A. Pearson, D.J. Torgerson, and M. Garcia-Reyes. 2017. The Effect of Digital Technology on Prisoner Behavior and Reoffending: A Natural Stepped-Wedge Design. *Journal of Experimental Criminology* 13 (4): 455–482.

Pereira, C. 2001. Strip Searching as Sexual Assault. *Hecate* 27: 187–196.

Ríos Martín, J.C., and P.J. Cabrera. 2002. *Mirando el abismo. El régimen cerrado.* Comillas: Universidad Pontificia de Comillas.

Rodríguez, J., E. Larrauri, and C. Güerri. 2018. Percepción de la calidad de vida en prisión. La importancia de una buena organización y un trato digno. *Revista Internacional de Sociología* 76 (2): e098.

Rodríguez Yagüe, C. 2016. Droga en prisión: Estrategias penitenciarias en materia de ejecución, tratamiento y seguridad. *Revista General De Derecho Penal* 26: 1–98.

Snacken, S., P. Mary, J. Beghin, P. Bellis, T. Bogaert, P. Janssen, and H. Tubex. 2000. *La problématique de la violence en prison.* Brussels: Vrije Universiteit Brussels.

Van Zyl Smit, D., and S. Snacken. 2009. *Principles of European Prison Law and Policy: Penology and Human Rights.* Oxford: Oxford University Press.

Vicente, R. 2009. Registros y cacheos en el ámbito penitenciario. *Revista De Derecho y Proceso Penal* 22: 31–50.

Gendered Punishment and Protest in a Context of Conflict: Strip Searching in Northern Ireland

Conor Byrne and Linda Moore

1 Introduction

Our focus is on strip searching as gendered penal punishment, explored within a context of prolonged violent conflict in Northern Ireland where, during the period from 1969 onwards known as the Troubles, more than 3,700 people died and over 47,000 were injured (CAIN 2007). Since the multi-party Belfast Agreement in 1998, Northern Ireland has been moving towards an imperfect peace, a transition which has significantly impacted on the prison system.

C. Byrne (✉) · L. Moore
Ulster University, Belfast, UK
e-mail: Byrne-C30@ulster.ac.uk

L. Moore
e-mail: l.moore1@ulster.ac.uk

T. Daems (ed.), *Body Searches and Imprisonment*, Palgrave Studies in Prisons and Penology, https://doi.org/10.1007/978-3-031-20451-7_10

The chapter analyses the ways that gender, conflict and sectarianism have shaped prisoners' experiences of strip searching throughout the Conflict, through to the post-Agreement period. The discussion focuses primarily on the strip searching of politically affiliated prisoners[1] but also considers the experiences of prisoners remanded or sentenced for 'ordinary' (i.e. non-conflict related) offences. Prisoners and those working in prisons have been impacted by the environment of violence in Northern Ireland; the loss of life includes the deaths of 32 prison officers, and they and their families have lived with constant threat from non-state paramilitary organisations.

Kieran McEvoy (2001) identifies consecutive, although sometimes over-lapping, strategies through which the United Kingdom (UK) and local Northern Ireland state attempted to manage the Conflict, using criminal justice processes. Reactive containment from 1969 through to 1975 was based upon: the deployment of the British Army to regain control following civil unrest, internment without trial, emergency legislation, and juryless courts. During this time, internees and politically motivated prisoners were afforded special category status, meaning they did not have to conform to the normal prison regime. From 1976, a strategy of criminalisation was adopted which defined paramilitary violence as 'terrorism' and a problem of 'law and order'; as expressed by Prime Minister Margaret Thatcher in 1981: 'crime is crime is crime, it is not political' (Connolly 2013). Removal of special category status meant that republican and loyalist prisoners were expected to wear a prison uniform and conform to the 'normal' regime, a policy resisted through the Blanket and No Wash protests and hunger strikes. This period saw a 'general deterioration' in prison conditions, along with an increase in 'brutality, violence, and dehumanisation' (Bryson et al. 2021: 83). Following the 1981 republican hunger strike during which ten prisoners died, a strategy based on 'managerialism' involved acknowledgement of political violence as an 'inherent and normalised feature' of society in Northern Ireland, and prison as an environment where such violence could be 'managed but not necessarily defeated' (Bryson

[1] For a discussion on terminology regarding republican and loyalist prisoners in Northern Ireland, see McEvoy et al. (2007). Here we are using the term politically affiliated to indicate association with republican or loyalist groupings.

et al. 2021: 83). The Belfast Agreement (1998) led to the early release of around 400 loyalist and republican prisoners. Despite the suggestion that a more pragmatic approach was emerging, an independent review of the Northern Ireland prison system initiated through the multi-party Hillsborough Agreement (2010) produced two highly critical reports (Prison Review Team 2011a, 2011b) which identified two 'fundamental' problems:

> One is the absence of effective leadership and operational management. The other is culture - both the security-led culture among prison staff, which developed during and has continued since the Troubles, and a culture of denial and compromise within the service as a whole. (Prison Review Team 2011a: 11)

These issues, particularly the overwhelming focus on security and control, impacted significantly on strip searching practices, as acknowledged by an independent panel of enquiry into the treatment of republican prisoners during prison protests from 1976–1981 (Coiste na nIarchimí 2020).

The chapter opens with a discussion of findings from primary research by chapter co-author Conor Byrne (Byrne 2022) on the experiences of republican men during the Blanket protest in the Maze Prison from 1976 to 1981, considering the impact of masculinity, collectivity and solidarity on prisoners' experiences of strip searching. Next, the chapter reviews the history of strip searching of republican women in Armagh prison in the 1980s and, following its closure, a mass strip search of women in Maghaberry Prison. The legacy of Conflict on the treatment of both politically motivated prisoners and those imprisoned for 'ordinary offences' in the period following the Belfast Agreement is then explored, based on findings from research on women's imprisonment conducted by chapter co-author, Linda Moore, and Phil Scraton[2]; initially in Mourne House, Maghaberry and then, following the transfer of women in 2004, in Ash House, Hydebank Wood Women's Prison.[3]

[2] Professor Emeritus, School of Law, Queens University of Belfast.

[3] For his doctoral research Conor Byrne conducted in-depth semi-structured interviews in 2019 with 20 men who participated in the republican Blanket and 'Dirt' protests in the Maze Prison

Based on evidence from these studies, the chapter concludes with an analysis of strip searching as part of the continuum of penal coercion, amounting to sexual violence and abuse.

2 Masculinity, Strip Searching and the Blanket Protest

In Her Majesty's Prison (HMP) Maze, formerly Long Kesh internment camp, sited on a disused military airfield about 10 miles outside of Belfast, internees and sentenced republican and loyalist prisoners were held in compounds or 'cages', each accommodating around 80 men, segregated according to political/paramilitary grouping. Special category status meant that the men had free association within each compound, and communication with the prison authorities was through the respective paramilitary grouping's 'officer in command'. These 'concessions' were removed through criminalisation.

Protesting within the Maze Prison began in September 1976 when republican prisoner Kieran Nugent refused to wear a prison uniform upon reception. With his civilian clothes confiscated, Nugent was stripped naked and taken to a cell; the following day being provided with a blanket, which is where the name of the Protest originated. Most 'Blanketmen' were republican, with a much smaller number of loyalists also refusing the uniform. Although participating in the Blanket protest was an act of defiance, it placed prisoners in a position of exposure and vulnerability. Nakedness became a symbol of non-conformity, a challenge to the legitimacy of not only the prison system but also the wider criminal justice and political institutions. With growing numbers joining

---

between 1976–1981. The research gained ethical approval from Ulster University Research Ethics Committee. Linda Moore, with Prof. Phil Scraton, conducted research on women's imprisonment as part of an investigation by the Northern Ireland Human Rights Commission (NIHCR) (Scraton and Moore 2005, 2007). The research was carried out in Mourne House, Maghaberry Prison and then Ash House, Hydebank Wood Women's Prison, following the transfer of women prisoners in 2004. Interviews were conducted with women prisoners, Northern Ireland Prison Service officers and managers, chaplains, professionals and volunteers, and there were observations of both regimes.

the protest,[4] the prison authorities sought to exercise power to make protestors' nakedness synonymous with feelings of disempowerment and humiliation. Frequent, forcible body searching played a significant part in this strategy.

Numerous accounts refer to protestors being spread-eagled across a table or over a mirror and coercively subjected to intimate and violent body searches (Coiste na nIarchimí 2020). These searches would occur when protestors wished to attend Mass on Sunday or when receiving visits from family members or legal representatives. Despite security concerns being cited to justify the searches, the intensity, frequency and violence associated with such methods were recognised by numerous Blanket protestors as 'nothing less than sexual assault' (Campbell 1994: 50–51). Byrne's research confirmed that men who participated in the Blanket protest perceived the searches as physically and verbally abusive, with some men identifying elements of sexualised harm:

> The mirror search basically was something that everybody went through on every wing move ... you were always going to get some kind of physical assault. Not least that they were screwing your arms up behind your back, kicking your legs from under you and then you went down over the mirror and then they would physically stick their fingers up your anus. One of the worst experiences, for me was when I got back to the cell and discovered that I was bleeding from my ass, so it just gives you an idea about how violently they forced their fingers into me. (Participant Z)

> You were bent over a table or bent over a mirror and the cheeks of your butts being parted; and hands inserted inside you and flashlights shone either on the mirror or whenever you were bent over the table. Up your bum. Sexual assault. That's what it was. (Participant U)

> Well, you see when you are put over the table, and there's certain fingers and rubber gloves put into your anus, there has to be a sexual connotation - why would you do that? (Participant Y)

---

[4] By June 1977 over 120 republican prisoners were participating in the Blanket protest (Phoenix 2007).

The requirement to move about the prison naked, and the manner in which strip searches were conducted had a psychological as well as physical impact:

> It was just like, you're totally naked and then you were searched and moved and that was a big deal for me. That is just some attempt to degrade or humiliate or the power relation asserted or whatever. (Participant S)

> Then they take away all your clothes and you're now naked, just the general humiliation. (Participant F)

From the men's perspectives, the prison authorities aimed to use their bodily vulnerability as a vehicle to further break their spirits and mental resolve; prisoners' nakedness being in stark contrast to officers' heavy, protective clothing and equipment. This feeling of disempowerment was a recurrent theme:

> We were taken in then one at a time, and the same thing, we were all stripped naked and there's probably about a dozen screws [prison officers] all standing around you and a lot of them were a lot bigger in stature to us and as well as that they were in their uniform and boots and batons and regalia and whatnot and everything. (Participant X)

> Certainly, men can feel very vulnerable if they don't have any shoes or a belt and faced with screws [prison officers] who have heavy buckled belts and truncheons and heavy boots fully clothed and always more: two, three, four of them. (Participant E)

> Totally violated, I mean you were just, you just felt totally humiliated, you felt totally powerless and helpless. (Participant F)

At times prison officers exploited protestors' position of nakedness during searches as a means to undermine their sense of masculinity:

> There was nothing ever found [through searching] in the three to four years that I was there, but long story short, they used to humiliate you

> about your privates, like you know a wee 16-year-old, 'Aw look at the size of his [penis]' and you know? (Participant W)

> Even in the early days when they were stripping you naked, there was sexual connotations to all that and on occasions, us prisoners would've been manhandled by individual members of the prison staff. Making fun of their bodies, particularly their private parts, just trying to humiliate and demoralise you. (Participant C)

Prisoners were forced to regularly confront any insecurities regarding their naked bodies, and to find ways of retaining dignity while physically exposed, within such a hostile environment:

> I'll always remember walking down the wing ... you become conscious of your hands, hands feel like lead with weights and ... Should you put them in front of your privates? But then that looks as if you're embarrassed you know, so don't do that – but at the same time so you don't feel like swinging your arms down the path. (Participant B)

> Now, that's one thing that prison did teach me... whatever qualms or self-consciousness about nakedness, that was completely gone. I was always saying, they've seen every part of me, inside and out. (Participant X)

While most men considered the searches, alongside other types of treatment, as involving sexualised violence, five participants outright rejected this proposition. To understand why some were not comfortable with labelling intrusive strip searches as 'sexual assault', it is important to acknowledge the demographic of the group, including the societal, cultural and gender values that were instilled from a young age, such as the conservative perspective to preserve one's sexual integrity. Participant M describes the feeling of shame regarding the process of body searches:

> When you're a naked person you know, you're embarrassed anyway. You are an Irish Catholic, and they were up your... I mean nobody saw your private parts at that time until you were married. Unless your mother, you know that sort of way? So, you know that [embarrassment] was part of it all too. (Participant M)

Blanket protesters experienced the stamp of an overwhelmingly male, protestant environment. Politically motivated prisoners also had the experience of 'paramilitary masculinities' through their association with armed non-state organisations (Ashe 2012). While they did not have to directly deal with the restrictive perceptions surrounding feminine stereotypes (discussed below), being subjected to violent and intrusive bodily searches challenged men's sense of masculinity and required individual and collective responses that would re-establish agency. As described by Rolston and McKeown (2017: 266) 'if power, invulnerability and dominance are key components of masculinity, then prison represents a severe threat to masculinity as it is posited on the lack of power and dominance and the inescapable experience of vulnerability.'

Competing versions of hegemonic masculinity existed within the Northern Ireland prison space. The first, hegemonic masculinity as traditionally understood (Connell 1995) involved a team of highly equipped male prison officers perpetuating coercion, abuse and violence. The second more unorthodox version centred around prisoners' ability not only to challenge the regime through the protest, but also to endure punishments with stoicism. Observing that for most male political prisoners being forcibly strip searched was the closest they would come to the experience of rape, Rolston and McKeown (2017: 271–272) stated that 'alternative hegemonic masculinity' within this context involved 'the ability to take this punishment without succumbing.' Byrne's interviewees echo this, suggesting that although not always a conscious effort, enduring the pains of imprisonment with 'masculine' fortitude was valued as a way of *doing* masculinity, as well as providing a routine coping mechanism:

> You did have this sort of, 'the rough tough Provos sort of attitude to surviving'. (Participant U)

It was important to present an image of fearlessness, not only in front of prison officers but sometimes for the benefit of fellow prisoners. However, this did not necessarily serve as an accurate representation of a man's feelings and the reality was that when naked and required to interact with officers; protestors had to compose themselves, to wear a 'mask' symbolically in order to create a 'macho' image.

> Like I say, you're in a cell and you know a 'screw' is coming, and you're panicking and panicking... once the door opens, you put on a façade if you know what I'm saying? You weren't going to bow down to them, so you put on this, 'I don't care' attitude but on the inside, you were really afraid. Maybe that was a 'macho' thing, you know?... But I was really shitting it - excuse my language. (Participant W)

Sutton (2007: 143) contends that whether clothed or naked, '... most political protest is enacted through the body—from marches, to political theatre, to the chaining of the body to a tree or building. The body is a key vehicle of protest.' During the Blanket protest and the escalations that followed, while the prison attempted to assert control through the use of force, including violent and intimate body searching, protestors refused to allow themselves to be conditioned or reconstructed as 'docile bodies' (Foucault 1977), some smuggling items such as tobacco and written messages deep within their body cavities. Directly fighting back was likely to meet with increased violence:

> You also had the forced baths and the mirror searches, and when we responded by wrecking the cells or busting the windows open that also provided them with the opportunities to come in and be violent and exercise their power and violence over us. (Participant C)

Throughout the process of being searched and moved within the prison, Blanket protestors were subjected to physical, psychological and at times sexual harm which emphasised their vulnerability and lack of autonomy. However, through active participation in the protest and stoicism in the face of violent treatment, protestors attempted to confront power differentials and elevate their status above that of the 'ordinary offender'. Following the end of the hunger strike, although political status was not reinstated, some of the key demands were conceded including the right of prisoners to wear their own clothes, which was experienced as empowering:

> By October 81, once we got our clothes and came out of the cell, you were no longer naked, no longer physically naked, but then spiritually or psychologically you didn't feel naked anymore either. (Participant F)

> The power balance, if you would call it that, changed dramatically the day we put clothes on and walked out of the prison cell. (Participant S)

3 Women's Gendered Experiences: Strip Searching in Armagh and Maghaberry

Her Majesty's Prison (HMP) Armagh was an eighteenth-century jail, initially housing women, 'felons' and debtors, and later becoming a women-only institution. Historically Armagh has been used for the detention of republican women during periods of unrest and war. During the phase of 'reactive containment' (McEvoy 2001), between 1972 and 1975 around 30 republican women were interned there without trial (Corcoran 2006: 5). By 1975 there were around 120 republican women in Armagh, a mixture of internees, the last of whom was released in 1975—together with remanded and sentenced prisoners, mainly republican (Loughran 1986), as well as a small number of loyalists.

The removal of special category status from 1976, met with resistance from republican women in Armagh who refused to conform to the regime. Unlike male prisoners, women were still permitted to wear their own clothes so long as these did not resemble paramilitary uniforms. Because they refused to work, women were only allowed out of their cells for a couple of hours in the evenings. In February 1980 the situation escalated when women were confined to their cells, without access to the toilets, a search having allegedly uncovered 'paramilitary clothing and flags' used by republican women in a parade (Corcoran 2006: 38). Only those who agreed to conform to the regime were given access to toilets and wash facilities. Locked in cells for 23 hours each day, women slopped out bodily waste through the windows and subsequently, after windows were boarded up, smeared faeces and menstrual blood on cell walls in what became known as the no-wash or 'dirt' protest. In December 1980 three women participated in a hunger strike for political status along with men in the Maze Prison. The no-wash protest was called off at the start of the 1981 hunger strike in the Maze, which involved only male prisoners.

Strip searching had been routine in the Northern Ireland prison system since 1949, mainly on reception, and sometimes before or after leaving or re-entering the prison (Corcoran 2006). In Armagh, strip searching increased significantly after the end of the hunger strikes (Loughran 1986); just as the situation for male prisoners in the Maze improved 'the conditions for the women got worse'. From November 1982, a 'regime of strip searching' was introduced: 'You were strip-searched coming out for your court appearance and on coming back you were strip-searched again' (McCann in Brady et al. 2011: 210). Former republican prisoner, Marie Wright (in Brady et al. 2011: 243), described the process in a letter from Armagh in 1984:

> The number of screws present at the time of a strip-search can vary from four to seven. Once in the cubicle, the inhuman and degrading treatment begins. A hostile screw will order me to remove all my clothes. She stands watching me while I under. Each item of clothing has to be passed out to the screws. When I have passed the last item out the screws will then inspect my naked body. I stand there naked trying to control my breathing, my anger and other confused feelings. When the screw has finished inspecting my body she slowly moves round me inspecting every part, she lifts my hair to look at my neck. When she gets to the back she bends down and takes hold of my leg and lifts my foot off the floor, running her hand down the side of my feet. She does the same with my hands. When the inspection is over I still have to stand there naked waiting under my clothes have gone through as each item is individually searched.

Jennifer McCann, former republican prisoner, recalled how officers 'would have put a towel around your head so you could not see who was doing the search and could not identify the screws searching you. They literally spread-eagled you and held you down on the floor and ripped the clothes from our back' (in Brady et al. 2011: 210–211).

All women including pregnant women and those who had given birth or miscarried were stripped (Brady et al. 2011). Jacqueline Moore describes her experience having recently given birth:

> Despite my medical condition I was strip searched. Once naked I attempted to cover my breasts with my arms as I was embarrassed with my breasts leaking with milk. I was ordered to remove my arms to facilitate the warders' inspection of my naked body. (1984, cited Moore and Scraton 2014: 88)

Even the stretch marks of women who had given birth were scrutinised (former republican prisoner Christine Poland, in Brady et al. 2011). Women were required to hand over sanitary towels for inspection:

> You had to ask the screw for a clean sanitary towel and if the screw didn't think that the one you'd handed over was soiled enough it was given back to you. (Poland in Brady et al. 2011: 249).

Armagh prisoner Marie Wright described the psychological impact of having her pants pulled down while menstruating, by a prisoner officer and prison medical officer, 'I was completely shattered by this whole ordeal and felt as if my body had been violated' (in Brady et al. 2011: 241). Similarly, a former republican prisoner interviewed by Wahidin (2016: 178–179) described the searching of body cavities as 'sexual assault', noting the 'shame' attached to the experience; 'you don't want to make it public that someone had been putting their fingers inside your body.' Former republican prisoner Dolores O'Neill recalled that when standing naked, 'I could feel the tears on my cheeks and I put my head down as I did not want them to see me crying' (in Brady et al. 2011: 245). The emotional distress caused by searching contributed to physical harms, for example 'many women's periods stopped for months as it was so traumatising' (former republican prisoner Jennifer McCann in Brady et al. 2011: 211). For Christine Poland, 'I thought it was quite a good thing if your period stopped in that at least that part of the humiliation would be removed. It was years later that I discovered the level of stress your body needed to be under in order for your periods to stop entirely' (in Brady et al. 2011).

Sometimes women fought back physically and verbally, however this produced further violence, as 'B' explained, 'all the while you're struggling and struggling and then you'd end up getting punched and stuff like that' (Wahidin 2016: 120). When women fought back they were placed in isolation punishment cells thus undermining their organisational control of the wing (McLaughlin 2020). Therefore, for strategic reasons, it was decided not to offer further resistance, which required forbearance: 'what was happening to you, I felt like punching one of them' (Patricia Moore in McLaughlin 2020: 684).

Some women attempted to shift the burden of moral responsibility onto prison guards:

> I would try to embarrass them with my nakedness. And they hated it. They hated it because we made them feel more uncomfortable with what they did. (Kathleen, cited in Corcoran 2006: 165)

> You would have been standing there with the [sanitary] pad out. I felt like lifting it and sticking it in her face. *This is your shame, it's not mine.* (Republican former prisoner cited in Wahidin 2016: 170)

Armagh closed in 1986, and women were transferred to Mourne House, Maghaberry, a unit in the new purpose-built, high-security, male prison. The intention was to create a regime based on the integration of 'ordinary' together with politically motivated prisoners. However, this was strongly resisted and following the Steele report (Safety Review Team 2003)[5] republican and loyalist prisoners were separated from each other and from 'ordinary' prisoners.

---

[5] Sir John Steele, former Director of the Northern Ireland Prison Service, was commissioned by the UK Government to head up a review into conditions in Maghaberry Prison in the context of escalating protests against integration, including a no-wash or 'dirty' protest by republican prisoners. On the grounds of safety, the 2003 Steele report recommended there should be a degree of separation for republican and loyalist prisoners, from each other and from the 'ordinary' prisoner population. The recommendation was accepted, and politically affiliated prisoners are still accommodated separately: republican prisoners in Roe House, and loyalists in Bush House.

In March 1992 a mass strip search took place of all of the 21 republican women, and 13 out of 14 'ordinary' women prisoners in Mourne House (Wahidin 2016). The search began at 10.30 in the morning, not ending until 9 pm. Male and female prison guards wore riot clothing, with visors and shields, accompanied by dogs. Karen (in Calamati 2002: 87) described how:

> My arms were twisted so far back that I thought they'd break. I yelled that I was having my period but that didn't stop them. ... They grabbed me by the hips and managed to get the trousers down below my waist and then they yanked them down over my ankles … I couldn't breathe for the pain… they managed to strip me naked. As I lay there on the ground they threw me a blanket and a sanitary napkin. The warder who held me down with her knee wasn't finished… as she was leaving, she landed me a violent kick in the ribs.

She reflected, 'I feel as if I had been raped… I was helpless to do anything to protect myself' (Calamati 2002: 89).

This mass search exposed the regime at Mourne House as being far from 'normal' and demonstrated the legacy of conflict for all prisoners—politically motivated and others. This would be confirmed by investigations by the Northern Ireland Human Rights Commission (2005, 2007), successive inspection reports and later by reports of the Independent Prison Review Team (2011a, 2011b).

4 Human Rights and the Strip Searching of Women in a Transitional Society

As noted above, from March 2004 through to 2005, chapter co-author Linda Moore, together with Professor Phil Scraton, conducted an investigation on behalf of the Northern Ireland Human Rights Commission into the treatment of women in Mourne House women's unit in Maghaberry, a high-security male prison, in particular focussing on compliance with Articles 2 (right to life) and Article 3 (right to be free from torture, inhuman or degrading treatment) of the European

Convention on Human Rights (ECHR). The rationale for the investigation, including the focus on Articles 2 and 3, included a highly critical inspection report in 2002 (HMCIP 2003) and the deaths of two women, Janet Holmes, and 19-year-old Annie Kelly who was found hanged in an isolation cell in a punishment block. In and out of prison since she was 14 years old, Annie had been subjected to forced strip searches with the alleged purpose of detecting objects which might be used to hurt herself or others. In a letter to her sister Annie wrote:

> Then they all held me out in the corridor. I only had the suicide dress on and I was told I could keep my pants cause I'd a s.t. [sanitary towel] on. But when the men were holding me they got a woman screw to pull my pants off. That shouldn't have happened. Then they covered me in celatape [sic] to keep the dress closed and handcuffed me and dragged me off to the male hospital (cited in Scraton and Moore 2005: 99).

The Human Rights Commission investigation found a deteriorated regime in Mourne House, with the women's healthcare centre closed, and restricted education and work opportunities. Despite most women being imprisoned for non-violent offences, all were subjected to an oppressive regime, involving long periods of lock-up, and heavy security measures, supervised mainly by male prison officers. Roseanne Irvine, 34 years of age and a mother, died in Maghaberry while the investigation was taking place. The Commission's report recommended a public inquiry with a remit to include women's deaths in Mourne House, regime and conditions and governance arrangements (Scraton and Moore 2005).

In June 2004 women were transferred from Maghaberry to Ash House, a female unit in the male young offender institution at Hydebank Wood the NIHRC decided to extend its investigation. Hydebank Wood is a Category C facility, (now rebranded as a Secure College for young men), and therefore lower security, which was a key motivation for the transfer. Despite this, the investigation found that women's movements were severely restricted to avoid any contact with young men, and they were escorted everywhere by prison officers, many of whom were male. This did not prevent women being verbally abused by some young men when moving about the site and in the prison transport.

Excessive strip searching formed part of the system of surveillance and control; women were routinely stripped on reception, before and after visits, and when leaving or returning to the prison. The Prison Service referred to this process as 'full body searches' whereby women were given a sheet to cover their bottom half while exposing the top of their body, and then vice versa. All women were searched in this way regardless of whether they were young, menstruating, pregnant, post-natal, or menopausal. Some women refused family visits during menstruation to avoid being stripped. The following testimonies were typical of many:

> They don't allow us to call it a strip search. They call it a full search. They're standing pondering over your body. Yeuch! ... I asked for a wee brown bag to put the sanitary towel in, they asked me to hand it to them. They make you burl around so they can look at you. It's downgrading. (Remand prisoner, Scraton and Moore 2007: 29)

> They were counting the spots and they were touching me when they checked. They had an argument about my binding. They put their fingers in my hair. They were feeling if it was mine. I was only wearing a G-string. I asked why they had to do this. They said they were only doing their job: 'It is the law'. I felt very much humiliated. I was vulnerable and scared'. (Immigration detainee, Scraton and Moore 2007: 51)

> I can see why they have to do them ['full searches'], but I don't know – they just are very degrading, and I know the staff don't really like doing them either but some staff are easier than others. Some of them seem as if they're trying to make you feel smaller. (Sentenced prisoner, Scraton and Moore 2007: 52)

> When you're on your menstrual cycle you still have to strip. It's very degrading. You have to show them the pants and pad with the blood on it. It's disgusting, you're embarrassed. Their attitude is indifferent. It's their job, but it's not a nice thing to do. (Sentenced prisoner, Scraton and Moore 2007: 52)

Being searched on reception was linked to a requirement to have a shower, which was also experienced as demeaning, implying uncleanliness and lack of hygiene:

> You're scared enough without that happening. And you have to go and get a shower as if you're dirty and you need it. (Sentenced prisoner, Scraton and Moore 2007: 51)

Strip searching posed particular human rights concerns in the context of women experiencing mental health issues. Women deemed to be a risk to themselves would be placed in isolation cells, 'for their own safety', and required to change into a 'anti-suicide gown'.

> They made me strip in the punishment cell. … They put me in a blue dress, mattress, blue pillow, one wee thin blanket. It was freezing. I didn't sleep. (Remand prisoner, Scraton and Moore 2007: 31)

> Being in a cell with a camera. There's no privacy or nothing. Your whole dignity's taken away from you. The staff sit and watch you get into your stuff [clothes]. But what if a male staff is looking in the camera? I don't know. (woman aged 18, Scraton and Moore 2007: 31)

Noting the 'traumatic impact', the Commission recommended that strip searching 'should not form part of routine procedures'; and should only take place in exceptional situations where 'risk assessment demonstrates the necessity to protect the woman or others from serious harm' (Scraton and Moore 2007: 130).

The Northern Ireland Human Rights Commission further supported a judicial review taken by a woman prisoner over conditions in Ash House. Karen Carson challenged the lack of in-cell sanitation, exposure to harassment by young male prisoners and the strip searching regime, which according to the Northern Ireland Prison Service (NIPS) had been reduced to a random one in five prisoners being selected for searches after visits. Lord Girvan's judgement (April 2005) noted that strip searching engages Article 3 (freedom from torture, inhuman or degrading treatment) and Article 8 (respect for privacy) of the ECHR, and alternative ways of preventing the smuggling of items must first be considered.[6] He criticised the prison service for its failure to have 'proper and explicit

[6] Judgement of Girvan J in the matter of an application by Karen Carson and in the matter of decisions of the Northern Ireland Prison Service, ref GIRF5249, delivered 20 April 2005.

regard to the relevant convention rights' and concluded that this policy of strip searching had not been demonstrated to be 'proportionate and necessary'. In response, the NIPS committed to review the policy, later reducing random strip searches to one in ten. However, while searching after every visit had been replaced, even the prospect of random searching could provoke anxiety as women were never sure when they might be selected:

> It's all power – we [prison officers] have the power to do this and we will do it if we feel like it. I think that's what it's all about – to show their power. (Long-term prisoner, Scraton and Moore 2007: 64)

Influenced by Baroness Jean Corston's 2007 review of vulnerable women in the criminal justice system in England and Wales, as well as inspectorate and Northern Ireland Human Rights Commission reports, in 2010 the NIPS adopted revised procedures described as part of a 'gender specific approach' (NIPS 2010), acknowledging the 'significant distress' caused through searching, especially when menstruating, as well as the high proportion of women prisoners with mental health issues and who have experienced physical, emotional and sexual abuse. NIPS further conceded that 'full searching' as protection from self-harm tended to have the opposite impact from that intended and had been largely ineffective in preventing the smuggling of substances. Since 2014, the procedure for women is now a 'rub down' search, with 'full' searches requiring 'specific intelligence' and management authorisation (McCracken 2014). Yet a recent inspection found that women in Northern Ireland were 'more negative' about their search than those in English prisons, and the inspectorate asked the prison service to 'explore why some women were so negative about this procedure' (CJINI 2020: 19).

5 Conclusion: The Gendered Harms of Strip Searching in a Context of Conflict

In *Society of Captives*, Gresham Sykes (1958) identified the most painful aspects of incarceration, including the deprivations of liberty, autonomy and security which are of particular relevance to the practice referred to as 'body', 'full' or 'strip' searching. Being stripped, inspected and 'cleansed' form an integral part of the institutional 'Welcome' (Goffman 1961), alerting prisoners that their freedom and individuality have been restricted and they no longer have control of their own lives. When routinely repeated, whether for control, punishment, or 'protection', searching becomes a constant reminder of the loss of bodily autonomy, dignity and personal safety, with damaging physical, psychological and emotional consequences. Strip searching is an inherently violent process, whether overt or implied. Prisoner testimonies demonstrate that this violence is significantly exacerbated within a context of conflict. During the republican Blanket protest particularly brutal methods were used, including internal searches of body orifices (sometimes using implements), squat, mirror and table searches, often accompanied by verbal abuse. An independent panel of inquiry into the treatment of men and women in Armagh and the Long Kesh/Maze H-Blocks from 1976 to 1981 found 'overwhelming evidence of torture, inhuman and degrading treatment, citing strip searching as a core element of this hostile and sectarian regime' (Coiste na nIarchimí 2020: 7). Within this context the function of strip searches was not primarily safety and security, but rather to break the will of protesting prisoners through pain and humiliation (Byrne 2022; Coiste na nIarchimí 2020).

Within any context other than the penal system the 'coerced removal of clothes would constitute sexual assault' (McCulloch and George 2009: 109). In the context of the Troubles, aspects of the strip searching process can be seen as constituting conflict-related sexual violence and abuse, defined by the United Nations as any form of sexual violence 'of comparable gravity' to rape and other forms of serious violence, 'directly or indirectly linked to a conflict' (Guterres 2020: 3). The strip searching of women in Armagh has been widely recognised as sexualised abuse (Aretxaga 2001; McCulloch and George 2009; Pickering 2002; Wahidin 2016). All of the women in Wahidin's study experienced searching as 'brutal, intimidatory, sexualised and degrading' (Wahidin 2016: 174). The history of strip searching of women in Northern Ireland represents different points on the continuum of sexual violence at the heart of the processes of incarceration (McCulloch and George 2009), ranging from extreme violence and bodily intrusion in the searching of politically motivated prisoners during the Conflict, with a legacy that persisted years beyond the peace process impacting also on 'ordinary prisoners', through to the ostensibly less intrusive 'gender-specific' methods adopted in women's prisons post-Corston (2007). Gender-specific practice is notionally based on ideals of 'sensitivity' and awareness of trauma, yet prisoners have little choice but to tolerate the touch of 'rub' or 'pat down' searches, in the knowledge that should they refuse to co-operate then force or conditions of isolation may be applied. Where there is 'intelligence' or 'reasonable suspicion', then nakedness may be demanded. Despite the modifications in policy and practice, being required to remove one's clothes for scrutiny by officers, continues to represent an imposition of gendered coercive power over women, many of whom have histories of experiencing abuse and violence. Yet, whereas politically motivated prisoners were likely to identify their treatment as violent and sexual abuse, at the same times as acknowledging the distress and shame involved, women imprisoned for 'ordinary' offences were more likely to say that officers were 'only doing their job' in implementing the rules, and that officers disliked the searches themselves.

While there has been a body of evidence on the gendered impact of strip searching on women in Northern Ireland, the harms caused by the strip searching of men has received less attention. The underreporting by men of sexual violence during conflict may be linked with 'destructive conceptions of gender, sex and (homo)sexuality' that create a particular stigma for male victims (Lewis 2009: 6). Some of Byrne's interviewees preferred not to identify what happened to them in the Maze as sexual abuse, although others were quite clear that their treatment had amounted to sectarian, sexual violence. For some men, realisation that the treatment they had received was sexual violence came only on reflection years afterwards. As Rolston and McKeown (2017: 283) note, 'most of our interviewees said that they did not think of the mirror searches at the time as sexual assault, they are convinced in retrospect that that was what was involved.' The scarcity of research on gender and male politically motivated prisoners in Northern Ireland, indicates a need to expand the knowledge base, and studies of masculinity can inform our understanding of the role of hegemonic masculinity in the intensely male environment of the prison, the strategies and tactics used by both the institution and individual prison officers, and the impact of strip searching and enforced nakedness for men in prison and their responses to this, including the creation of alternative expressions of masculinity (Bryne 2022).

More recently there has been increasing acknowledgement that the violent and intrusive strip searching experienced by the Blanketmen amounted to sexual assault (Byrne 2022; Coiste na nIarchimí 2020; O'Branksi 2014; O'Hearn 2009; Rolston and McKeown 2017). Describing a persistent 'climate of fear' in the Maze (Coiste na nIarchimí 2020: 7), the independent inquiry documented men's experiences of being beaten, having objects such as pens and pliers inserted into the anus, testicles squeezed and twisted, thrown against walls and tables, and dragged by the hair. The inquiry concluded that the 'frequency, violence and violation' of strip searching in the Maze and Armagh constituted 'institutionalised conduct that systemically breached prisoners' rights, inflicting cruel and inhuman treatment' (Coiste na nIarchimí 2020: 29).

While strip searching fundamentally represents the power of the state over the individual, there is a growing body of research on the role that a naked body has in relation to an individual or group's resistance (O' Keefe 2006; Sutton 2007; Tyler 2013). The implementation of an embodied protest through nakedness has been identified as a tool with the capacity to cause an impact on a macro level (Sutton 2007). As observed by Sykes (1958: 8), 'disturbances within the walls must often be viewed as highly dramatic efforts to communicate with the outside world' and sometimes have the power to 'capture the attention of the public'. Strip searching in Armagh attracted widespread protests within nationalist communities in Northern Ireland and beyond, attracting global media attention and condemnation from women's and human rights organisations.

There is a difference however to be observed between the collective will, strength and organisation of politically affiliated prisoners, and the situation for individual prisoners remanded and sentenced for 'ordinary offences', many of whom are physically vulnerable or face mental health issues and who are more isolated within the prison environment. Republican men and women strenuously resisted strip searching (sometimes physically and sometimes stoically enduring the process for strategic reasons), gaining strength from their political motivation, support through collective organisation and with prisoners helping each other to cope through homosocial relationships (Rolston and McKeown 2017; Byrne 2022). Shared political beliefs and living in such close quarters created strong solidarity, enhancing the ability to withstand the treatment being meted out by the institution:

> You have these outside forces trying to break you. So, through struggle a very close bond does develop. (Participant P in Byrne 2022)

Collective organisation rendered coercive strategies less effective, and when such tactics were too heavily depended on, rather than restoring order, coercion and hostility may encourage further resistance. For individuals imprisoned for ordinary offences it may be more difficult to offer open resistance, being atomised, stigmatised, anxious not to lose visits from family, especially children, and fearful of punishment for refusal to comply (Moore and Scraton 2014). Moreover, even though politically motivated prisoners did offer strong, collective, research and testimonies suggest that the traumatic 'pains of imprisonment' associated with strip searching have persisted for many former prisoners, living with them long after release.

References

Aretxaga, B. 2001. The Sexual Games of the Body Politic: Fantasy and State Violence in Northern Ireland. *Culture, Medicine and Psychiatry* 25: 1–27.

Ashe, F. 2012. Gendering War and Peace: Militarized Masculinities in Northern Ireland. *Men and Masculinities* 15 (3): 230–248.

Belfast (Good Friday) Agreement. 1998. Agreement Between the Government of the United Kingdom of Great Britain and Northern Ireland and the Government of Ireland. https://www.gov.uk/government/publications/the-belfast-agreement. Accessed 5 December 2022.

Brady, E., E. Patterson, K. McKinney, R. Hamill, and P. Jackson. 2011. *In the Footsteps of Anne: Stories of Republican Women Ex-Prisoners*. Belfast: Shanway Press.

Bryson, A., K. McEvoy and A. Albert. 2021. Political Prisoners and the Irish Conflict 100 years on. *The Howard Journal of Crime and Justice* 60 (S1): 79–91.

Byrne, C. 2022. *Political Prisoner Resistance and the Blanket Protest: A Case Study on Political Imprisonment, Power Relations and Performative Masculinity in Northern Ireland*. Unpublished PhD: Ulster University.

CAIN (Conflict Archive on the Internet). 2007. *Fact Sheet on the Conflict in and About Northern Ireland: Thurs 21 June 2007*. Derry: CAIN Ulster University. https://cain.ulster.ac.uk/victims/docs/group/htr/day_of_reflection/htr_0607c.pdf. Accessed 21 June 2022.

Calamati, S. 2002. *Women's Stories from the North of Ireland*. Belfast: Beyond the Pale publications.

Coiste na nIarchimí. 2020. *'I am Sir, You Are a Number': Report of the Independent Panel of Inquiry into the Circumstances of the H-Block and Armagh Prison Protests 1976–1981*. Béal Feirste/Belfast: Coiste na nIarchimí.

Campbell, B. 1994. *Nor Meekly Serve My Time: The H Block Struggle 1978–1981*. Belfast: Beyond the Pale Publications.

Connell, R.W. 1995. *Masculinities*. Cambridge: Polity Press.

Connolly, K. 2013. Thatcher's tenure shaped by Ireland, 8 April 2013 *BBC News*: https://www.bbc.co.uk/news/uk-northern-ireland-11598877. Accessed 26 June 2022.

Corcoran, M. 2006. *Out of Order: The Political Imprisonment of Women in Northern Ireland 1972–1998*. Cullompton: Willan.

Corston, J. 2007. *The Corston Report: A Report by Baroness Jean Corston of a Review of Women with Particular Vulnerabilities in the Criminal Justice System.* London: Home Office.

Criminal Justice Inspection Northern Ireland (CJINI). 2020. *Report on an Unannounced Inspection of Ash House Women's Prison Hydebank Wood June 2020, 23–24 October & 4–7 November 2019.* Belfast: CJINI.

Foucault, M. 1977. *Discipline and Punish: The Birth of the Prison.* New York: Pantheon Books.

Goffman, E. 1961. *Asylums: Essays on the social situation of mental patients and other inmates.* New York: Anchor Books.

Guterres, A. 2020, June 3. *Conflict-Related Sexual Violence. Report of the United Nations Secretary-General.* s/2020/487.

Her Majesty's Chief Inspector of Prisons (HMCIP). 2003. *Report of a full announced inspection of HM Prison Maghaberry, 13–17 May 2002.* London: The Stationary Office.

Hillsborough Agreement Castle. 2010, February 5. https://assets.publishing.service.gov.uk/government/uploads/system/uploads/attachment_data/file/136435/agreement_at_hillsborough_castle_5_february_2010.pdf. Accessed 5 December 2022.

Lewis, D. (2009). Unrecognized Victims: Sexual Violence Against Men in Conflict Settings Under International Law. *Wisconsin International Law Journal 27* (1).

Loughran, C. 1986. Armagh and Feminist Strategy: Campaigns around Republican Women Prisoners in Armagh Jail. *Feminist Review* 23: 59–79.

McCracken, N. 2014, March 3. Prison strip searching is being reduced – but is modernisation coming quickly enough? *The Detail.* https://www.thedetail.tv/articles/prison-strip-searching-is-being-reduced-but-is-modernisation-coming-quickly-enough. Accessed 1 July 2022.

McCulloch, J. and A. George. 2009. Naked Power: Strip Searching Women in Prison. In *The Violence of Incarceration*, ed. P. Scraton and J. McCulloch, 107–123. London: Routledge.

McEvoy, K. 2001. *Paramilitary Imprisonment in Northern Ireland.* Oxford: Oxford University Press.

McEvoy, K., K. McConnachie and R. Jamieson. 2007. Political imprisonment and the 'War on Terror.' In *Handbook on Prisons*, ed. Y. Jewkes, 293–323. Cullompton: Willan Publishing.

McLaughlin, C. 2020. Memory, Place and Gender - Armagh Stories: Voices from the Gaol. *Memory Studies* 13 (4): 677–690.

Moore, L. and P. Scraton. 2014. *The Incarceration of Women: Punishing Bodies, Breaking Spirits*. Basingstoke: Palgrave Macmillan.

Northern Ireland Prison Service (NIPS). 2010. *Ash House: Full Search Procedures for Women Prisoners: Policy and Guidance for Staff*. Belfast: NIPS.

O'Branski, M. 2014. 'The Savage Reduction of the Flesh': Violence, Gender and Bodily Weaponisation in the 1981 Irish Republican Hunger Strike Protest. *Critical Studies on Terrorism* 7 (1): 97–111.

O'Keefe, T. 2006. Menstrual Blood as a Weapon of Resistance. *International Feminist Journal of Politics* 8 (4): 535–556.

O'Hearn, D. 2009. Repression and Solidary Cultures of Resistance: Irish Political Prisoners on Protest. *American Journal of Sociology* 115 (2): 491–526.

Phoenix, E. 2007, December 29. Start of Blanket Protest Detailed in Cabinet Files: The Beginning of the 'Blanket Protest' and the Segregation of Paramilitary Prisoners in the Maze and Other Jails in the North. *Irish Times*. https://www.irishtimes.com/news/start-of-blanket-protest-detailed-in-cabinet-files-1.994928. Accessed 7 July 2022.

Pickering, S. 2002. *Women, Policing and Resistance in Northern Ireland*. Belfast: Beyond the Pale publications.

Prison Review Team. 2011a, February. *Review of the Northern Ireland Prison Service: Conditions, management and oversight of all prisons, Interim Report.* Belfast: PRT/Department of Justice NI.

Prison Review Team. 2011b, October. *Review of the Northern Ireland Prison Service: Conditions, management and oversight of all prisons*. Belfast: PRT/Department of Justice NI.

Rolston, B. and L. McKeown. 2017. Male Republican Prisoners in Northern Ireland. *State Crime* 6 (2): 265–295.

Safety Review Team. 2003, August 29. *Review of Safety at HMP Maghaberry*. The Steele Review.

Scraton, P. and L. Moore. 2005. *The Hurt Inside*. Belfast: Northern Ireland Human Rights Commission.

Scraton, P. and L. Moore. 2007. *The Prison Within: the imprisonment of girls and women at Hydebank Wood 2004–2006*. Belfast: Northern Ireland Human Rights Commission.

Sutton, B. 2007. Naked protest: Memories of Bodies and Resistance at the World Social Forum. *Journal of International Women's Studies* 8 (3): 139–148.

Sykes, G. (1958). *The society of captives: A study of a maximum security prison.* Princeton University Press.

Tyler, I. 2013. Naked Protest: The Maternal Politics of Citizenship and Revolt. *Citizenship Studies* 17 (2): 211–226.

Wahidin, A. 2016. *Ex-Combatants, Gender and Peace in Northern Ireland: Women, Political Protest and the Prison Experience*. London: Palgrave Macmillan.

"There's a Tech for That": Balancing Dignity and Security in Carceral Settings Through Alternative Technology Devices

Anaïs Tschanz

1 Introduction

Body searches are such a routine and widespread practice in prisons all over the world that they seem to be almost immutable and embedded in the very carceral logic. Yet they are continuously denounced, whether by imprisoned people, national or supranational authorities as well as by academics, as inherently degrading, humiliating and inhumane, inviting to the exploration of other means of guaranteeing the security and control of correctional facilities. Such is the proposed purpose of this chapter, which looks into technology as a potential alternative to the practice of body searches in prison.

A. Tschanz (✉)
National Correctional Administration Academy (ENAP), Agen, France
e-mail: anais.tschanz@justice.fr

T. Daems (ed.), *Body Searches and Imprisonment*,
Palgrave Studies in Prisons and Penology,
https://doi.org/10.1007/978-3-031-20451-7_11

Body searches intriguingly lack prominence in the criminology or prison sociology literature, often analysed as one of the many restrictive practices to which individuals are subject in prison. In his essay on the social condition of those cut off from the world in "total institutions", Erving Goffman (1961) analyses body searches as a mortification process, carried out as part of the admission ceremony to detainment, with the function of desecrating the personality of the individuals subject to it and stripping them of their identity. He maintains that "…it is the searcher as well as the search that penetrates the private reserve of the individual and violates the territories of his self" (Goffman 1961: 29). Body searches in prison, materialising a domination by the institution over incarcerated people, is said to be experienced by the latter as a loss of privacy that affects the self and results in a sense of contempt and humiliation (Fassin 2015; Frigon 2001; Welzer-Lang et al. 1997). Feminist and abolitionist movements have recently seized upon the matter, bringing to light the physical, emotional and psychological consequences which it can bring about, particularly among women survivors of childhood and adult sexual violence. Hutchison (2019a: 14), for instance, describes body searches as "…a form of state-inflicted sexual assault", emphasising the practice's violence. Discussing the quite widespread discretion around this practice, these studies identify body searches as a gendered discipline (Balfour 2017) and a discriminatory practice (Marcoux-Rouleau 2021), which prompts them to question the relevance of keeping in place a violent control tool that generates suffering, in particular in light of its effectiveness. Marcoux-Rouleau (2021: 324) effectively sums up this question: "is the potential danger to staff and detained people greater than the psychological, physical and structural harms caused by a strip search?" For if body searches are an inevitable component of prison management and life in prison experience, it is because they are claimed to be the most "efficient" way to meet the security imperative predominant in correctional facilities. The practice thus finds itself the node of a tension between dignity and security in prison, the challenge for prison administrations being to find a balance between maintaining security while safeguarding the human rights and dignity of the persons deprived of liberty.

In the face of the controversies raised by a security practice considered intrusive but necessary, Rule 52 of the UN's Standard Minimum Rules provides that "Prison administrations shall be encouraged to develop and use appropriate alternatives to intrusive searches", opening the way to the search for an alternative solution to the practice of body searches, capable of limiting its use or possibly even replacing it entirely. In Canada, the quest for a potentially less intrusive practice than body searches was triggered by a special report shown on a major television channel in 1994, revealing strip searches on women at the Kingston Prison, carried out by an intervention team composed solely of men. In the wake of that controversy, in 2001, the Correctional Service of Canada (CSC) set up a working group on strip searches, the recommendations of which led to the adoption of several measures to respect the privacy and dignity of persons subject to searches in correctional settings. It declared then: "We view this practice as necessary but degrading and humiliating. We support the adoption of new technologies that will reduce the need for such searches".[1] Canada is not the only country to see technology as a potential guarantor of the privacy of persons subject to search. In France, for example, the National Advisory Commission on Human Rights (CNCDH) advised in one of its recommendations issued in 2008 that "...modern means of detection guaranteeing respect for the dignity of the person and their physical and psychological integrity should replace full body searches". Could the miracle cure to body searches indeed lie in technology, as several institutional and political actors suggest? Within a broader move to modernise penal and carceral facilities through the increasing adoption of mechanisms that serve the managerial imperatives of productivity, efficiency and security (Hancock and Jewkes 2011; Kaminski 2013; Moran and Jewkes 2015), technology is indeed increasingly seen as a potential response to the two-fold requirement of transparency and normalisation of detention, provided conditions conducive to reconciling the imperative of securing correctional facilities on the one hand and protecting the privacy and dignity of the incarcerated persons on the other.

[1] Report of the Task Force on Security, Correctional Service Canada, 2001. https://www.csc-scc.gc.ca/text/pblct/security/toc-eng.shtml.

We are thus witnessing the convergence of a market (that of technology) and political and institutional actors around a problem (that of body searches) and a motion for a resolution: technology. The aim of this chapter is therefore to analyse how the significant tension between intimacy/dignity and security at the heart of the practice of body searching is "translated" in prisons, through the choice of a specific security technology, but also in the uses and appropriations thereof. Could it be that a detection technology serving security functions similar to those of body searches might replace this degrading practice, all the while limiting violations of the individuals' dignity and intimacy? In other words, could a technology guarantee the dignity, intimacy and security needed in this context? By setting my analysis in a socio-technical perspective inspired by actor-network theory (Callon et al. 2006), I propose to consider here the practice of body searches in correctional institutions as a problem common to multiple actors, human and non-human, brought together in a heterogeneous network that endeavours to solve it. At the heart of this problem lies the tension between dignity/privacy and security which is then "translated" by the actants within a security device. This approach, increasingly popular in analyses of the use of security technologies (Poirier 2021), goes beyond the so-called "black box" perspective, which considers them only from a functionalist and deterministic point of view. It does not stop at assessing the efficiency and productivity of neutral and inert technologies, but considers them as complex instruments and invites an understanding of their design and social and ideological integration through the political, scientific, strategic and practical debates that accompany them, as well as a grasp on their effects from the individual, societal, institutional, etc. standpoints. In so doing, it helps bring to light the interactions between users and technology, the policies regarding the development, implementation and use of these technologies and the differences between initial functions and uses.

2 Methodology

The analysis presented in this chapter draws on a multi-method research, applied to a Canadian field of investigation and enabling systematic questioning of the problem of body searches and the technological solution thereto, from the perspective of each actant identified (political and institutional actors, designers, providers and users of the technology, as well as the device itself).

The practice of body searching was explored through semi-directed interviews with forty-four people—twenty-nine men and fifteen women—incarcerated at five provincial prisons in Quebec and aged 20–65. These interviews were conducted as part of a doctoral thesis on the intimacy of incarcerated persons, drawing on a phenomenological approach, designed so that the individuals could establish the boundaries on their own. It was during this doctoral work that I became familiar with one specific technology: the BOSS. Intrigued by its design and potential effects, I explored this device through documentary analysis, which forms the second methodological section of this article. Specifically, three data sources, each shedding their own light on the issues raised by the BOSS, were selected.

1. The provider's websites: detailing the BOSS' technical specifications and functionalities, these websites can be used as a compilation of all the necessary information relevant to this study. The three following websites were viewed: that of RSD Security Scanners, which produces the BOSS; that of the company Xeku, the main provider of the BOSS in the United States; and that of I.T.S. Canada Inc., which is responsible for distribution in Canada.
2. Canadian Government documents: a debate and parliamentary report, as well as calls for tenders and contracts granted by the Government for the purchase of the BOSS chair, were analysed in order to identify the motives underpinning the roll-out of this detection technology in Canadian detention centres, the grounds for its implementation, and its costs.
3. Online journals and blog articles (mainly from the United States and the United Kingdom) that focussed on the BOSS: these were often

accounts from correctional officers or incarcerated people, an important source of information for further understanding the use of this device in prisons.

BOSS' technical characteristics

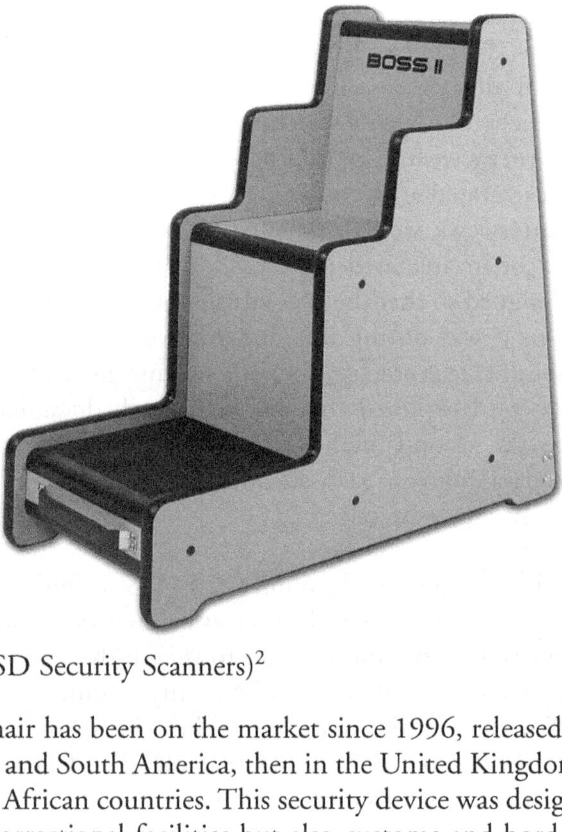

(*Source:* RSD Security Scanners)[2]

The BOSS chair has been on the market since 1996, released first in the United States and South America, then in the United Kingdom, Canada, Australia and African countries. This security device was designed for use not only in correctional facilities but also customs and border facilities, precious metal mines, etc. According to its developers, it guarantees a complete scan of the entire body. The BOSS II 5-Zone's dimensions (41 inches by 36 inches long and 22 inches wide) and its features (backrest, seat, armrests and footrest) are similar to those of a simple living room

[2] For a more thorough analysis of the BOSS' implementation in Canadian correctional facilities, see Tschanz (2016).

chair. Each side of the BOSS detection chair is capable of scanning the part of the body with which it is in contact. Before sitting down on the BOSS chair, the person undergoing the scan must place his chin on the tablet in order to detect any object that may have been inserted in his mouth, such as a razor blade. Under the supervision of a member of staff, the incarcerated individual then proceeds to sit on the BOSS, to undergo a scan of his remaining body cavities. The magnetic field sensors inside the chair and at the level of the oral cavity detector are activated in order to identify the presence of any metallic objects that may have been inserted into the person's body. If an object is detected, a loud alarm sounds. In addition, a red light, placed on a small board on the side of the chair indicates the location of the object.

3 Searched Bodies, (Dis)Respected Dignity

Although the framework governing the procedure differs from one country to another, three types of body searches are traditionally distinguished: a pat-down or technical search during which the individual remains clothed; a strip search, which requires the person being examined to disrobe and submit to a visual inspection, without physical contact; and lastly, an intimate search, which entails a physical examination of the bodily cavities. In Canada, the practice of body search is governed by Articles 46 to 67 of the Corrections and Conditional Release Act. Routine non-intrusive or frisk searches may be carried out without individualised suspicion, in certain prescribed circumstances justified by security concerns. A staff member may also conduct a strip search in situations in which the individual has been in a place where there was a likelihood of access to contraband or if they have reasonable grounds to believe that the person being examined is carrying a prohibited object that threatens the security of the facility. If it is suspected that the object is hidden in a body cavity, a medical practitioner may be authorised to perform an examination to detect or seize it, with the person's consent. The institutional head may also authorise the use of an X-ray machine to find the contraband, with the consent of the individual. In the event of non-consent, the person might be placed in isolation in a dry cell—i.e., with no running water—until the object is expelled.

Because of its intrusive nature, the use of body searches should, if not prohibited, be subject to strict requirements of necessity, proportionality and legality and be conducted in a manner that respects the dignity of the individual. Yet whatever the legal framework around searches, this practice is inherently violent and humiliating.

3.1 The Ritual of a Body Exposed

From the political and institutional perspective, body searches, along with the regulation and execution thereof, are problematic in that they open the door to controversies, complaints and even sanctions (Daems 2014; Schlanger 2008). For correctional institutions, there are multiple benefits to avoiding this practice. In addition to ensuring legal compliance and the protection of its "users" bodily integrity, finding an alternative solution to body searches could also limit the tensions associated with this practice, ultimately making it possible to meet a security imperative that remains prevalent, as we will discuss later. As the organisation Penal Reform International emphasised in its 2015 report "Balancing security and dignity in prisons": "Security and control are best ensured in environments that respect the inherent dignity of detainees". Lastly, it may also imply doing away with a task considered thankless by the correctional officers performing it.

Yet if we want to analyse the dehumanising dimension of the body search, it is the words of the incarcerated persons that speak with the greatest clarity, revealing particularly strong experiences, reactions, feelings and emotions. For instance, they describe the body search as a routine and standard-procedure practice, a true rite of entry and exit from the institution. Body searches can also be carried out at the end of certain activities in prison, in particular when incarcerated people are required to work with instruments that are considered dangerous, for example, in the kitchen, or, for instance, after time spent in the visitation rooms, especially when it involved contact with a visitor. Putting emphasis on how exposed their naked bodies were during the search, several of the persons interviewed described the ritualised process of this practice, sometimes miming the well-engrained choreography through which they must pass so that every nook and cranny of their body can undergo visual scrutiny by the one performing it:

> They take your underwear off, then it's 'lift your breasts with both your hands', then 'touch one foot, touch your other foot, bend over, spread your buttocks, do two squats'. The whole time, you're completely naked. You gotta imagine you're completely naked, then they go, 'run your fingers through your hair' or they do it themselves. Sometimes they add 'open your mouth, raise your tongue, lower your tongue'. (Laura, 31 years old)

This well-established ritual leaves the interviewees with a sense of humiliation, anger, embarrassment and assault on their modesty "...to have to show myself that way" (Annick, 37 years old), or having to expose their "private parts" (Sabrina, 20 years old). It is indeed the visibility of the body envelope combined with the constraining nature of this practice that particularly affects the intimacy of the searched persons. Louis-Philippe puts harsh words to describe his experience, attesting to the violence implicit in the procedure:

> It's a violation of your intimacy, you could say. They violate your intimacy. [...] Yeah, basically it's rape. It's psychological rape. Totally. It's just to get you off-kilter, it's to break you. (Louis-Philippe, 30 years old)

While the violence of body search is not gender discriminating, the feelings of humiliation seem to be heightened in the case of women. First of all, when they have suffered physical or sexual violence in their past and are forced to experience further intrusions into their bodily reserve. Secondly, when in addition to having to expose themselves, they are sometimes forced to reveal their intimate hygiene during their menstrual cycle, resulting in a double level of intrusion, as Sabrina explains:

> Body searches also, when you talk about intimacy... This is exactly the kind of thing that you don't want to be seen... I mean, when a girl is having her period, it's something private and it's embarrassing when you

> have to bend over and be searched but you're wearing a pad. (Sabrina, 20 years old)

The practice is degrading for the individual who undergoes it, and an ungrateful task for the correctional staff conducting it. Forced to enter the intimacy of the person being examined, prison guards see body searches as an unpleasant, humiliating and uncomfortable practice, albeit one essential to the security of the facility (Chantraine 2004; Welzer-Lang et al. 1997). Yet since body searches take place in the interaction between the person being examined and the person doing the examining, the feelings of incarcerated people regarding this practice are directly dependent on the behaviour of the agents during the process:

> It doesn't have to be the worst thing. When they're not the slobbery kind. Ha, definitely, when the correctional officer isn't all slobbery, it's OK, but when he is, then it can get more aggressive. [...] You have staff who are alright, courteous, and respectful. But then you've got others, it's like day and night. There are others still who have no notion of respect. Then, it's out of control. (Jerome, 30 years old)

In other words, while the invasive nature of the body search seems less prominent, albeit persistent, when the officer performing it takes a respectful attitude to the searched person, the sense that the bodily reserve has been violated is inversely reinforced when augmented by nudity and visual examination of private body parts and the sometimes-derogatory comments of certain officers:

> Strip search is tedious. It's very, very tedious. Like, when I leave here [the visitation room where we are meeting] I'm going to have to go through a strip search. Even though we're not passing each other anything at all. It's degrading, it's outright humiliating. Once, I had a strip search where 12 of them got together, making jokes, inappropriate jokes. (Étienne, 51 years old)

3.2 The Paradox of a Humanising Technology

Faced with the degree of dehumanisation which the body search entails, the promise of technology as a replacement for this procedure seems enticing. This is, in any case, the issue which the technology market endeavours to address, in particular by deploying a whole range of detection technologies for prisons, ranging from basic manual metal mass detectors to the most advanced scanners that produce sound and visual alarms. It is in this category of "security devices" that the BOSS fits.

Described by its suppliers as a non-intrusive, non-invasive search method that does not require contact, the BOSS does not create virtual images of the scanned body and thus neither produces nor stores data, in contrast to millimetre-wave detection scanners. Likened by some users to a simple metal detection scanner, the BOSS seems capable of solving the recurring problem of violation of incarcerated people intimacy resulting from body searches. Instead of having to go through the particularly humiliating ritual of being searched, the incarcerated person purportedly has only to sit on the detection chair, which then sweeps his body cavities without any physical intrusion by a third party and without having to completely undress. In this set-up, simply by sitting in the scanner chair, the scanned individual can bypass the entire search procedure customarily carried out in order to detect contraband objects. An article by the BBC News[3] dealing with the use of the detection chair in UK prisons describes the BOSS as follows:

> It's a highly sensitive metal detector which reduces the need for intimate and confrontational body cavity searches. Rubber gloves are being put away in favour of technology and a patient waiting game.

The purpose of a body search that provides information on the presence of an object hidden inside the person and carried out without human contact, without nudity and thus with respect for intimacy, seems within reach. However, several dimensions stemming from the use, structural

[3] D. Casciani, "Care to sit on the Boss chair?", *BBC News,* 20 December 2007.

choices and design of the BOSS raise questions concerning respect for human dignity:

1. The new ritual was instituted by the use of the BOSS. Though the incarcerated persons do not have to bare themselves in front of others, one can reasonably posit that the request that they sit on the BOSS to have the most intimate parts of their body scanned according to a well-established ritual and in front of witnesses could be experienced as degrading and humiliating. In an article on airport security scanners, Valkenburg and van der Ploeg (2015: 233), for instance, argue that "… it is recognized that bodily integrity can in fact be violated, or at least be felt to be violated, by something as seemingly non-invasive as a body scanner", depending in particular on the representations which individuals have of their own intimacy.
2. The name ascribed to the detector chair. As ingenious as the acronym is—the initials, when unfurled, reveal its primary purpose, i.e., Body Orifice Security Scanner—, it is hard to believe that the decision to call this security technology "BOSS" had only practical purposes. The word "boss" is used in English-speaking countries to refer to a leader, a person who heads a company. The Cambridge Dictionary lists the following definition: "person who is in charge of an organisation and who tells others what to do". The term boss therefore implies an idea of hierarchy and control. The play on words has not been lost on the media, which have unabashedly asked: "who's the boss"[4] in prisons, since these scanners were first rolled out.
3. The detector chair's cynically evocative design. While it could achieve "privacy by design" embedded in the device, likened by some to a shoe-shine kiosk, the BOSS is much more reminiscent of the distinctive design of the electric chair. Indeed, the image which this instrument gives off is that of a cold, metallic appearance, carrying particularly strong undertones in a prison environment still marked by the recent stigmas of the death penalty.

[4] The blog Engadget (24 December 2007) captioned "Body-scanning chair to show UK prisoners who's BOSS", while *The Guardian* (7 January 2016) announced that a "Metal-detecting chair at Goulburn Supermax shows prisoners who's Boss".

The structural and design choices for the BOSS make it difficult to see in it the humanist rationale purportedly underpinning the evolution of prisons, given that it contributes to reinforcing the divide between those in positions of power and those forced to comply with the institution's rules. Nonetheless, the device is seen by incarcerated persons as a significant compromise when it comes to the practice of body searches. In one column, the BBC News looks back at protest movements that took place between 2010 and 2012 at a prison in Northern Ireland. As one of their demands, the people incarcerated at this facility asked that strip searches be replaced by the installation of body scanners and, more specifically, BOSS detection chairs. Reading the demands of those incarcerated at the Irish prison, who insist that these detection devices, which they see as the solution, be implemented, one can see the policy of the "lesser evil" implicit in the use of such technologies: specifically, it is considered a "lesser evil" to have to submit to a screening of one's intimate parts than to be forced to undress before the inquisitive and intrusive eyes of prison officers. The same rhetoric also emerges from the comments of some of the people interviewed who, considering the sense of shame that swells up in them as the procedure is carried out, wonder about the possibility of finding an alternative to body searches, listing in particular the scanners used at airports:

> All they would have to do is put us through an X-ray or whatever, there are those things at the airport that zoom around you, then look inside. Why don't they have that here, instead of making us get naked! (Fabien, 37 years old)

Further emerging from these claims is a form of acceptance of the institutional detection policy, not questioning the security imperative used to substantiate it, but expressing the desire that the solution least harmful to individuals' intimacy and dignity be adopted: specifically, technology.

4 Securing the Settings, Monitoring the Bodies

Despite the numerous criticisms under which it comes, body searches are still regarded as a legitimate means of ensuring safety in prison. All the while emphasising the routine, humiliating and discriminatory nature of body searches, particularly in the case of strip searches, the organisation Penal Reform International (2015) maintains that "...searches of various kinds are a necessary and legitimate means of preventing prisoners from having access to dangerous or prohibited items or substances, which may constitute a threat to the safety and health of staff, other prisoners and visitors". This security rhetoric, advocating a zero-risk policy on the circulation of prohibited goods, justifies the use and continuation of body searches in prison. More than that, it legitimises its discretionary use.

4.1 The Body as Dangerous and an Agent of Contraband

From the perspective of the prison administration, although inconvenient, body searches are perceived as a necessary security procedure, best capable of preventing the entry of illegal items liable of disturbing the prison order. Body searches continue to be seen as the instrument of choice when it comes to securing institutions and their perimeter, as well as a safety guard, for society (in that they help prevent the risk of escape or the continuation of criminal activities within their walls), for prison staff and for detained persons. Concurrently, the issue of drug use in penitentiary environments is, in public policy, gaining magnitude. In Canada, a National Anti-Drug Strategy was instituted in 1998 by the CSC in order to curb the supply of illicit substances and reduce demand from imprisoned people (Roy 2001). Significant resources were made available to correctional facilities as part of the implementation of a zero-tolerance policy towards drugs, in which body searches were elevated to the status of full-fledged instrument for fighting trafficking in prison.[5]

The implementation of a security risk management policy prompted leads to soften the conditions governing body searches. While the present study cannot lay claim to an exhaustive comparative analysis, it emerges clearly that the criteria legitimising the use of body searches are generally quite broad or subject to interpretation, creating a particularly flexible discretion, dictated mainly by safety concerns. For example, Articles 47 and 48 of the Canadian Corrections and Conditional Release Act allow routine strip search to be carried out "without individualised suspicion" when an incarcerated individual enters or leaves a structured intervention unit, a family visit or a work area. In France, a recent law has helped facilitate the conduct of full body searches, while enshrining them as part of standard practice, through quite broad wording: "They may be carried out as a matter of standard procedure when so required by public order and the constraints of the public prison service" (my translation).[6] In an environment where everything (or almost everything) falls within the realm of public order, the use of body searches can thus easily be justified, as evidenced by their routine and everyday nature. Yet, as Marcoux-Rouleau (2021) discusses, this discretion extended for security reasons is not trivial, as it increases the potential for racially or sexually motivated discretionary practices.

Nonetheless, the construction of a rhetoric of the "common good" or "greater security for all" makes it possible, from an institutional point of view, to justify that the balance leans more towards security than to the dignity of individuals through the use of body searches. This same discourse can thus also be used to establish it as legitimate and ordinary with the people who are its main victims, a way of saying "you are hurt by it, but it's also for your own good". The fact that this rhetoric has been internalised by the incarcerated people is reflected in their words,

---

[5] Daems (2014: 82), mentions that during the same period, strip searches "…were perceived and justified as indispensable instruments in the fight against drug smuggling and drug use inside Belgian prisons".

[6] Paragraph 1, Article 57 of the Penitentiary Act, as amended by the Programming Law on Justice of 23 March 2019.

which sometimes attest to euphemisation of the violence inherent in body searches, seen as nothing but a task for the prison staff, who have no choice but to carry it out, in the name of "safety for all":

> The guards just want to see if you might be hiding something. Plus, it can't be pleasant for them either, to check your penis then to check your anus to see if you have … so that's what I'm saying … it's part of the law, it's not pleasant, but you get used to it, like anything else: after a while, you get used to it … . (Jean-François, 28 years old)

Annick's words in particular show a sense of ambivalence between her own experience and the rationalisation of the act carried out by the officers, which enables her to give meaning to the assault on her intimacy:

> Getting completely naked, then having to spread your buttocks, then ... it's just slightly uncomfortable... I feel like it's an abuse of power, but at the same time I tell myself it's their job because there are so many people who, yeah, maybe they're hiding drugs or whatever. Which means they have no choice but to do this to everyone. (Annick, 37 years old)

That being as it may, not all the imprisoned people's statements reflect an acceptance of the act for security reasons, instead tending to consider body searches as a procedure founded above all on a rationale of humiliation and body control:

> Sometimes, you get the feeling they're abusing the situation but... I can't 100% say they're abusing it, but definitely, they do more than they have to... like searching you or making you squat, like when you go to court, there's nothing you can bring with you. Plus, when you get to court you get searched too, anyway. You go through a detector. So, at worst, if you had something, the alarm would go off. Maybe it would make more sense on the way back, but on the way there, you can't bring anything, what are you supposed to bring there? Nothing! (Edwige, 33 years old)

The vulnerability that forced nudity implies is thus experienced by some as a basis for institutional domination and the power which agents can exercise over their bodies, over which they, under these circumstances, no longer have control. In this sense, and as Frigon (2001) in particular states, body searches of incarcerated persons appear to come in addition to measures aimed, with the help of humiliating techniques, at securing the enslavement and docility of the individuals subject to it. The real rationale behind body searches is said to be not the safety of the facility and its public, but the control of individuals through humiliation and fear, leading to the objectification of their bodies seen as "... vessels to transport drugs and other types of contraband" (Hutchison 2019b: 80). This is also evident from the demands put forth by incarcerated people, as reported in the BBC News article referred to earlier: for them, the use of technology rather than a body search would indeed allow the security imperative to prevail over the desire to subdue individuals.

4.2 Managing Risks Through Technology

While security devices may be perceived as a response to managerial needs or a requirement for transparency and standardisation of detainment or even protection of rights, their primary objective when put to use in prison is to satisfy the imperative for institutional security, aimed at protecting the infrastructure, staff and detained persons, as well as society. Securing prison settings through technology has also become a governmental strategy in many countries, to which significant financial resources are dedicated. In addition to physical security and movement control, these technologies may appear to be a solution to specific problems that extend across the prison environment, such as the fight against smuggling, reducing violence or managing risks of suicide.

The BOSS is described by its suppliers as a simple, effective, fast and safe technological tool, which guarantees the reduction of violence between incarcerated people and prison wardens. Its use is said to create a safe and secure environment, by enabling the detection of illegal and dangerous metal objects potentially usable as weapons, such as razor blades, knives, nails, tools or even ammunition for firearms. In addition to ensuring the safety of individuals by fighting the introduction of dangerous objects into detention, the BOSS is said to also help facilitate and make the work of correctional officers safer.

While the introduction of the BOSS detection chair could have been considered a response to the controversial procedure of body searching, it was in fact in the context of Canada's search for a technological solution to the problem of drug trafficking and consumption, then part of the political agenda, that the BOSS was considered a potentially beneficial technological solution. To wit, in 2012, the House of Commons of the Canadian Parliament recommended the use of three types of devices to deal with this what was considered a worrying phenomenon: ionic detectors, effective in detecting traces of cocaine on packages, incarcerated people, staff and visitors, but less so with marijuana; radar/infrared detection systems, which make it possible to identify at any time individuals approaching the facility's security perimeter; and the BOSS, which, by electronically scanning bodily orifices would, according to the Committee, "…help determine whether an individual has secreted packages containing drugs in a body cavity". This rationale for implementing the BOSS echoes the CSC Commissioner's 2011 speech, in which he stated that the BOSS had been introduced in Canadian prisons "…to combat the introduction of drugs concealed inside body cavities". The reference to the BOSS is surprising because, insofar as it is a metal detector, it is not designed to directly detect drugs inserted into the body cavities of those scanned. The company Xeku, incidentally makes this very clear, insisting that only the presence of metal objects can trigger the alarm. Emphasising how frequently this error is made, the company even goes so far as to draw up a list of targets that the BOSS is unable to detect, such as drug capsules or sachets, tobacco products or, for instance, plastic weapons.

That said, while the BOSS detection chair is not able to flag the presence of drugs, it can help combat trafficking thereof by targeting drug accessories. Its use has, in this spirit, shifted towards the detection of mobile phones, presumably used to keep up contact with dealers outside the walls and facilitate criminal activities inside (Burke and Owen 2010). It is, in fact, a technology capable of detecting mobile telephones and thus preventing dangerous actions related to drug trafficking that the BOSS is primarily described by online media. What one sees is thus a displacement in the functionality of the BOSS by the CSC. Presented by its suppliers as a tool for detecting dangerous weapons and perceived by several actors as having the potential to replace intrusive practices such as body searches, its use has been directed towards combating the trafficking of illegal substances, in order to respond to the government's anti-drug strategy deployed in recent years in Canada. This shift in the use of the BOSS makes it possible to underscore, in the words of Kaufmann (2016: 86) "…that the technical potential for action possessed by an object is only realised through its use". In this instance, whatever intentions were behind the design or marketing strategy for BOSS, these quickly faded into the background in the use made of it.

The use of the BOSS in prisons thus tends to show, as suggested by Hancock and Jewkes (2011), that the modernisation of the prison system, which takes place in particular through the acquisition of "new technologies", contributes to strengthening the institution's control. Several articles in fact testify to a BOSS technology that "at best" has been combined with other devices in addition to body searches: "While the machine is touted as a replacement to strip searches, a spokeswoman for Community Safety and Correctional Services Minister Yasir Naqvi said the machines won't mark the end of traditional metal detectors or strip searches. It will be used in conjunction with the more traditional search methods currently in use in provincial jails" (Seymour 2019). When it comes on top of the range of techniques already used to detect contraband objects, the use of the BOSS in prisons contributes to an accumulation of physical controls on imprisoned people and to the extension of institutional power.

5 Discussion

One question remains unresolved: despite its inability to alert to the presence of any non-metallic objects, such as drug sachets, could the BOSS be considered an alternative to body searches? Spoiler alert: it doesn't. Indeed, if the chair's alarm remains silent when an individual is seated on it, how can the authorities be sure that no other object has been inserted into the body cavities of the person scanned? Such "false negatives" bring about the risk of hazardous materials remaining unidentified (Kaufmann 2016). When the BOSS does signal an object concealed in the bodily cavities, this can constitute the necessary proof justifying the execution of a strip search. The *Washington Post* to wit states that "If an officer has evidence that there's been an insertion, he can ask medical personnel for a search. A BOSS hit can provide good reason to take that next step" (Morse 2009). Thus, as shown by MacKenzie (2019) in an article on the ion scanners used in Canadian prisons, the procedure and its outcome depend on the machine operator more than on the technology itself. While detection technologies can be perceived as "democratic machines" able to indicate the presence of the object outside, unconnected with any individual or discriminating consideration, the suspicion here is only displaced. As Kaufmann (2016) points out, it depends, firstly, on the discernment of the technology operator who chooses which person will be required to submit to the detection technology and on the context which determines whether the information produced is sufficient. In this instance, by producing information—the presence and location of a metal object—that is not sufficient in itself to detect the object, or on the contrary, by not producing any information at all—which does not guarantee the absence of inserted objects—the detection chair thus in reality doubly legitimises a practice which it was initially supposed to replace. Instead of acting as a technological compromise on an intrusive practice, the BOSS becomes the perfect accessory.

The BOSS seems to be an obsolete technology today, in particular, due to the emergence of a parallel technological market: "Beat the Boss" metal-free mini cell-phones, designed to outwit the BOSS, ironically revealing the implementation of technological resistance by the very people who initially suffered from (and pleaded for) it.[7] Since it cannot detect drugs or miniature mobile phone models of this kind, the BOSS does not, in the end, do any more than a simple metal detector. Nonetheless, it remains worthwhile to analyse it, as one can, in so doing, extend the scope to other detection and security technologies used in prisons. The analytical framework suggested in this chapter, aimed at moving

[7] See, for example, the article dated 19 April 2016 "Beat the Boss: UK prisons' mobile phone epidemic" by Allegra Straton, on the ITV website.

beyond a deterministic approach to technology in order to examine its interaction with institutions, actors and practices, is thus akin to analytics of devices, which, as proposed by Amicelle, Aradau and Jeandesboz (2015: 294) "...makes possible the examination of the configuration and reconfiguration of security practices by attending to the equipment or instrumentation that makes these practices possible and temporarily stabilises them". Specifically, this approach makes it possible to:

1. suggest that considering a technological alternative to the practice of searching cannot be done without considering the trajectories of the translation of a problem into a solution that can be influenced by different intentions, appropriations and uses, as the BOSS aptly illustrates. Indeed, by making it possible to justify the use of body searches—either by the detection of a metallic object or by the non-detection of possible drugs—this technology produces outcomes different from the stated objectives of non-intrusion by allowing, quite to the contrary, a use that legitimises invasive practices. Instead of acting as a technological compromise to a dehumanising practice, the BOSS becomes the perfect accessory and demonstrates a genuine autonomous force of action, its use going beyond the intention that underpins its design (Lyon 2001) in order to respond to both political and institutional risk management logics. In the end, it thus legitimises this use and consolidates the place of the search as an essential security practice in prison.
2. engage in a broader reflection on the phenomenon of technological solutionism which, in addition to spreading within society (Morozov 2013), has definitely made its way into the criminal and prison spheres. This mounting search for a way to solve the various problems which the criminal justice, probation and incarceration spheres raise is prompting device-makers to offer a proliferation of technological solutions. These include various types of electronic bracelets (electronically monitored placement, anti-seizure bracelets), the increasingly effective virtual reality, hand-held cameras worn by prison guards, etc. The result is a delegation of security, control and surveillance responsibilities to technologies (Kaufmann 2016), which combine with one another in a zero-tolerance perspective. Yet the use

of technologies is not bringing about any real change, hence the question, following from Devresse (2007), as to whether "… with such a tool, the aim is to do something new or to do the same thing differently?" [« avec un tel outil, s'agit-il de faire quelque chose de nouveau ou s'agit-il de faire la même chose autrement ?», my translation]. Ultimately, the introduction of new technologies in prisons contributes first and foremost to stepping up the security measures already implemented by the penitentiary institution, in addition to adding to the tasks of officers, without changing their practices. In this sense, technology can give the illusion of taking a problem into account, but by shifting it elsewhere, rather than doing away with it. For want of proposing real change, it helps reinforce the punitive logic of the carceral institution by creating new forms of suspicion, endorsing the malleability of bodies and reinforcing the control of individuals and the mechanisms of domination already at work.

References

Amicelle, A., C. Aradau, and J. Jeandesboz. 2015. Questioning Security Devices: Performativity, Resistance, Politics. *Security Dialogue* 46 (4): 293–306.

Balfour, G. 2017. Searching Prison Cells and Prisoner Bodies: Redacting Carceral Power and Glimpsing Gendered Resistance in Women's Prisons. *Criminology & Criminal Justice* 18 (2): 139–155.

Burke, T.W., and S.S. Owen. 2010. Cell Phones as Prison Contraband. *FBI Law Enforcement Bulletin* 79 (7): 10–15.

Callon, M., M. Akrich, and B. Latour. 2006. *Sociologie de la traduction. Textes fondateurs*. Paris: Presses des Mines.

Chantraine, G. 2004. Ordre, pouvoir et domination en détention: Les relations surveillants-détenus dans une maison d'arrêt en France. *Criminologie* 37 (2): 197–223.

Daems, T. 2014. 'Ceci n'est pas une fouille à corps': The Denial of Strip Searches in Belgian Prisons. In *Punishment and Incarceration: A Global Perspective*, ed. M. Deflem, 75–94. Bingley: Emerald Group Publishing.

Devresse, M.-S. 2007. Innovation pénale et surveillance électronique: quelques réflexions sur une base empirique, *Champ pénal/Penal field*, http://champpenal.revues.org/1641

Fassin, D. 2015. *L'ombre du monde: Une anthropologie de la condition carcérale*. Paris: Seuil.

Frigon, S. 2001. Femmes et emprisonnement: Le marquage du corps et l'automutilation. *Criminologie* 34 (2): 31–56.

Goffman, E. 1961. *Asylums. Essays on the Social Situation of Mental Patients and Other Inmates*. New York: Anchor Books.

Hancock, P., and Y. Jewkes. 2011. Architectures of Incarceration. *The Spatial Pains of Imprisonment, Punishment & Society* 13 (5): 611–629.

Huber, A., Bernath, B., Allen, R., and Delaplace, E. 2015. *Balancing security and dignity in prisons: a framework for preventive monitoring*. Penal Reform International and the Association for the Prevention of Torture. London and Geneva.

Hutchison, J. 2019a. "It's Sexual Assault. It's Barbaric": Strip Searching in Women's Prisons as State-Inflicted Sexual Assault, *Affilia* 35 (2): 160–176.

Hutchison, J. 2019b. "Bend Over and Spread Your Butt Cheeks": Access to Justice for Women Strip Searched in Prison. *Annual Review of Interdisciplinary Justice Research* 8: 65–90.

Kaminski, D. 2013. Que font faire les technologies à la justice pénale? *Déviance Et Société* 37 (3): 255–264.

Kaufmann, S. 2016. Security Through Technology? *Logic, Ambivalence and Paradoxes of Technologised Security, European Journal for Security Research* 1 (1): 77–95.

Lyon, D. 2001. *Surveillance Society: Monitoring Everyday Life*. Buckingham: Open University Press.

Mackenzie, K. 2019. "La seule constance ... c'est l'inconstance": Les répercussions des faux positifs des scanneurs à ions sur les familles des détenus canadiens. *Criminologie* 52 (1): 157–176.

Marcoux-Rouleau, A. 2021. Reform to Abolish: A Pragmatic Analysis of Prison Labor & Strip Searches in Quebec Correctional Law. *Lex Electronica* 26 (2): 302–332.

Moran, D., and Y. Jewkes. 2015. Linking the Carceral and the Punitive State: A Review of Research on Prison Architecture, Design, Technology and the

Lived Experience of Carceral Space. *Annales De Géographie* 702–703: 163–184.
Morozov, E. 2013. *To Save Everything, Click Here: The Folly of Technological Solutionism.* New York: Public Affairs.
Morse, D. 2009. Maryland Using Body Scanner to Find Contraband in Prisons, *The Washington Post*, November 5.
Poirier, B. 2021. Comprendre le succès et l'échec de l'innovation policière: Une analyse du déploiement de caméras portatives dans un service policier. *Criminologie* 54 (1): 69–96.
Roy, M. 2001. La Stratégie nationale antidrogue du Service Correctionnel du Canada, *Forum—Recherche sur l'actualité correctionnelle* 13 (3): 5–6.
Schlanger, M. 2008. Jail Strip-Search Cases: Patterns and Participants. *Law and Contemporary Problems* 71 (2): 65–88.
Seymour, A. 2019. High Tech Body Scanner for Ottawa Jail 'Reveals Everything', *Ottawa Citizen*, May 9.
Tschanz, A. 2016. Le nouveau BOSS en prison: Une alternative technologique à la pratique de la fouille? *Déviance & Société* 40 (4): 457–475.
Valkenburg, G., and I. van der Ploeg. 2015. Materialities Between Security and Privacy: A Constructivist Account of Airport Security Scanners. *Security Dialogue* 46 (4): 326–344.
Welzer-Lang, D., L. Mathieu, and M. Faure. 1997. Effets de l'incarcération sur le corps et l'estime de soi. *Quasimodo* 2: 21–25.

What Future for Body Searches in Prisons?

Tom Daems

On 14 October 2021 the British Ministry of Justice issued a press release with as title: "Over 10,000 attempts to smuggle contraband thwarted by X-ray body scanners".[1] The scanners are part of a wider package of investments in security in UK prisons. They are described as a "game-changing technology". In recent years, such scanners increasingly pop up in prisons across the globe. This often happens in the context of the fight against drugs and other contraband. Just like scanners in airports, scanners in prisons increase visibility. For that reason they also act as a source of deterrence, so the argument goes. But the scanners are also

[1] https://www.gov.uk/government/news/over-10-000-attempts-to-smuggle-contraband-thwarted-by-x-ray-body-scanners.

T. Daems (✉)
Faculty of Law and Criminology, KU Leuven, Leuven, Belgium
e-mail: tom.daems@kuleuven.be

T. Daems (ed.), *Body Searches and Imprisonment*, Palgrave Studies in Prisons and Penology, https://doi.org/10.1007/978-3-031-20451-7_12

advocated and sold as an alternative to strip searches. Scanners in prison therefore seem to be a "win–win" option: they increase prison security and they are better at respecting the dignity of the prisoner.

Is that true? Can scanning technology offer an alternative? As Anaïs Tschanz demonstrates in her chapter on the introduction of the BOSS in Canada, technological innovation seldomly offers an easy, quick-fix solution. Moreover, as we know from other penal innovations, such as electronic monitoring, there is no guarantee that the dreams of reformers, or the promises of manufacturers or salesmen, come true. Indeed, ankle bracelets did not make prisons obsolete nor did they reduce prison overcrowding (Devresse 2007; Daems 2020).

For the time being evaluation research is lacking. What is certain, however, is that the British scanners are *not* an alternative to strip searches. Indeed, at this moment they are not even meant to be such an alternative: "…an X-ray body scan must not be used as an alternative to a full or rub down search", so we can read in the instructions of HM Prison and Probation Service (2020: 5). And, indeed, as Barbara Bernath discusses in her chapter, also monitoring bodies in the UK have observed that scanning technology is not being used as an alternative for strip searches. The British scanners are therefore not a fully-fledged alternative to strip searches; they are rather an addition to the existing toolbox of security instruments.

But what if the scanners were intended to replace strip searches? What if the technology could help to reduce the use of strip searches? More research seems to be necessary: at this moment we know too little about the effects and side-effects of the scanners. However, we do know that strip searches are inherently problematic and controversial. Indeed, several chapters in this book detail and problematize the impact of body searches on prisoners and are critical about the lack of respect for international human rights standards and national laws that aim to restrict and regulate body searches.

Moreover, in recent years we have seen various calls to explore alternatives for body searches. Rule 20 of the 2010 "Rules for the Treatment of Women Prisoners and Non-custodial Measures for Women Offenders" (the Bangkok Rules) states the following about this: "Alternative screening methods, such as scans, shall be developed to replace strip searches and invasive body searches, in order to avoid the harmful psychological and possible physical impact of invasive body searches". Rule 52 of "The United Nations Standard Minimum Rules for the Treatment of Prisoners" (the Mandela Rules) encourages prison administrations to develop appropriate alternatives to "intrusive searches". The UN checklist lists "scans" as an example of such an alternative (UNODC 2017: 42). The Association for the Prevention of Torture (APT) and Penal Reform International (PRI) also seem to expect a lot from technological innovation: "Alternatives, such as electronic scanning devices, should be developed and used wherever possible and when body searches are unavoidable, the least invasive method should be applied" (APT and PRI 2015: 1).

There seems to be a willingness amongst at least some human rights bodies and NGO's to embrace technological progress in order to reduce strip search practices. Moreover, in view of the increasing use of monitoring and scanning technologies in the outside world, one can only expect that such technologies will also increasingly enter the closed world of the prison. There is an important role, then, for prison scholars here: when the introduction of scanning technology can be done safely and if the technology is being used as a true substitute for strip searches, then it might be worthwhile to further explore how this can be done in the best conditions. However, if scanners fail to replace strip searches, then such technology will rather become an add-on and contribute to strengthening the security focus of penal institutions.

Throughout this book it has repeatedly been argued that striking a balance between security and dignity is of vital importance: what role will technology play in the future for body searches in prisons?

References

APT and PRI. 2015. *Body Searches. Addressing Risk Factors to Prevent Torture and Ill-Treatment.* London: Penal Reform International.

Daems, T. 2020. *Electronic Monitoring. Tagging Offenders in a Culture of Surveillance.* London: Palgrave Macmillan.

Devresse, M.-S. 2007. Innovation pénale et surveillance électronique: Quelques réflexions sur une base empirique. *Champ Pénal*. https://doi.org/10.4000/champpenal.1641.

HM Prison and Probation Service. 2020. *Use of X-Ray Body Scanners (Adult Male Prisons)*, 18 May. https://assets.publishing.service.gov.uk/government/uploads/system/uploads/attachment_data/file/886000/x-ray-body-scanners-use-pf.pdf

UNODC. 2017. *Assessing Compliance with the Nelson Mandela Rules. A Checklist for Internal Inspection Mechanisms*. New York: United Nations.

Correction to: Stripping the Self Away: Security, Control, and Punishment in the Practice of Strip Searches in Spanish Prisons

Cristina Güerri

Correction to:
Chapter 9 in: T. Daems (ed.), ***Body Searches and Imprisonment*****, Palgrave Studies in Prisons and Penology,**
https://doi.org/10.1007/978-3-031-20451-7_9

The original version of this book was inadvertently published with inappropriate abstract on online version in Chapter 9, which has now been corrected. The correction to the chapter has been updated with the changes.

The updated original version of this chapter can be found at
https://doi.org/10.1007/978-3-031-20451-7_9

T. Daems (ed.), *Body Searches and Imprisonment*,
Palgrave Studies in Prisons and Penology,
https://doi.org/10.1007/978-3-031-20451-7_13

Index

T. Daems (ed.), *Body Searches and Imprisonment*, Palgrave Studies in Prisons and Penology, https://doi.org/10.1007/978-3-031-20451-7

S

T

The manufacturer's authorised representative in the EU is Springer Nature Customer Service Centre GmbH, Europaplatz 3, 69115 Heidelberg, Germany. If you have any concerns regarding our products, please contact ProductSafety@springernature.com

Printed and bound by CPI Group (UK) Ltd, Croydon, CR0 4YY
28/09/2026
02224072-0008